Sources of
World Societies

Volume 1: To 1600

Third Edition

THE COMPANION READER FOR
A HISTORY OF WORLD SOCIETIES

ELEVENTH EDITION

Merry E. Wiesner-Hanks
Patricia Buckley Ebrey
Roger B. Beck
Jerry Dávila
Clare Haru Crowston
John P. McKay

 bedford/st.martin's
Macmillan Learning

Boston | New York

For Bedford/St. Martin's

Vice President, Editorial, Macmillan Learning Humanities: Edwin Hill
Program Director for History: Michael Rosenberg
Senior Program Manager for History: William J. Lombardo
History Marketing Manager: Melissa Rodriguez
Director of Content Development: Jane Knetzger
Developmental Editor: Tess Fletcher
Senior Content Project Manager: Christina M. Horn
Senior Workflow Manager: Jennifer Wetzel
Production Assistant: Brianna Lester
Senior Media Project Manager: Michelle Camisa
Editorial Services: Lumina Datamatics Inc.
Composition: Lumina Datamatics Inc.
Photo Editor: Christine Buese
Cover Design: William Boardman
Cover Art: China: Detail of a warrior, Head and Chest, from the terra-cotta army guarding the tomb of Qin Shi Huang, first emperor of a unified China (r. 246–221 B.C.E.), Xi'an/Pictures from History/Bridgeman Images
Printing and Binding: LSC Communications

Manufactured in the United States of America.

2   1   0
f   e   d

For information, write: Bedford/St. Martin's, 75 Arlington Street, Boston, MA 02116

ISBN 978-1-319-07038-0

Acknowledgments

Acknowledgments and copyrights appear on the same page as the text and art selections they cover; these acknowledgments and copyrights constitute an extension of the copyright page.

PREFACE

The primary sources contained in *Sources of World Societies* span prehistory to the present, capturing the voices of individuals within the context of their times and ways of life, while enriching the cross-cultural fabric of history as a whole. Now with more visual sources and an emphasis on developing historical thinking skills, *Sources* draws from the records of rulers and subjects alike — from men and women, philosophers, revolutionaries, economists, laborers, and artists, among others, to present a textured view of the past. With a parallel chapter structure and documents handpicked to extend the textbook, this reader is designed to complement *A History of World Societies*, Eleventh Edition. *Sources of World Societies* animates the past for students, providing resonant accounts of the people and events that changed the face of world history, from myths of creation to accounts of hardship and conflict, from a local to a global scale.

With input from the textbook authors, as well as from current instructors of the world history survey course, we have compiled these documents with one goal foremost in mind: to make history's most classic and compelling voices accessible to students, from the most well-known thinkers and documentarians of their times to the galvanized or introspective commoner. While students have access to formative documents of each era, lesser-heard voices reveal life as the great majority of people lived it. In Chapter 30, for example, students can juxtapose President Truman's press release on the bombing of Hiroshima with the firsthand account of a Japanese survivor of the atomic bomb drop.

We have stepped back from drawing conclusions and instead provide just enough background to enable students' own analysis of the sources at hand. Chapter-opening paragraphs briefly review the major events of the time and place relevant to the documents that follow, within the framework of the corresponding textbook chapter. A concise headnote for each document provides context about the author and the circumstances surrounding the document's creation, while gloss notes supply clarification to aid comprehension of unfamiliar terms and references. Each document is followed by Reading and Discussion Questions that spur student analysis of the material, while chapter-concluding Comparative Questions encourage students to contemplate the relationships among the sources within and, when called for, between the chapters. All of the questions in *Sources* aim to form a dynamic connection for students that bridges the events of the past with their own evolving understandings of power and its abuses, of the ripple effects of human agency, and of the material conditions of life. The excerpts range in length to allow for a variety of class assignments.

CONTENTS

The Earliest Human Societies

to 2500 B.C.E.

Chapter 1 of your textbook explores the beginnings of human society and culture, so it is appropriate that this source book begins by looking at origin stories, the answers human societies have offered to the basic question of how the world began. The three origin stories included here were written down long after the period covered in this chapter, but the questions they raise are as old as human society itself. Evidence that this is the case is provided by the chapter's final two primary sources, photographs of a Paleolithic grave site and an example of Paleolithic cave art. Humans communicated their thoughts, desires, anxieties, and stories for thousands of years before the invention of writing, and these artifacts offer clues about the beliefs and values of the people who created them. The sources included in this chapter strongly suggest that early human societies were concerned with more than mere survival; they were also built around ideas, religious beliefs, and aesthetic values.

VIEWPOINTS

Origin Stories

All societies have origin stories, accounts of creation that address fundamental questions about the beginnings of the universe, of nature, and of human beings. Each story is rooted in the values and beliefs of the society that created it, telling as much about how its authors saw their own world as it does about how they viewed the distant past. In a sense, the first chapter of this textbook is an origin story. Building on core ideas about biological, social, and cultural change, it offers an explanation of how human history began. As you read the three origin stories included in this chapter, ask yourself what they reveal about the societies that created them. What do they tell you about their authors' central beliefs about human beings, nature, and the divine?

1-1 | An Indian View of Creation

From the Rig Veda: *"The Creation Hymn"* (ca. 600 b.c.e.)

The *Rig Veda* is the oldest and most important Indian scripture. Originally composed and transmitted in oral form between 1500 and 1000 b.c.e., it was written down in Sanskrit around 800 to 500 b.c.e. The *Rig Veda* includes compositions by many different authors and contains several different types of texts, including hymns to gods, creation stories, and instructions for religious rituals. The hymn included here asks as many questions as it answers about the creation of the universe. As you read it, pay particular attention to the way it treats apparent opposites, such as light and dark, existence and nonexistence, and knowing and not knowing. What point was its author trying to make about the essential nature of the universe?

1. Then was not non-existent nor existent: there was no realm of air, no sky beyond it.
   What covered in, and where and what gave shelter? Was water there, unfathomed depth of water?
2. Death was not then, nor was there aught immortal: no sign was there, the day's and night's divider.
   That One Thing, breathless, breathed by its own nature: apart from it was nothing whatsoever.
3. Darkness there was: at first concealed in darkness this All was indiscriminated chaos.
   All that existed then was void and formless: by the great power of Warmth was born that Unit.
4. Thereafter rose Desire in the beginning—Desire, the primal seed and germ of Spirit.
   Sages who searched with their heart's thought discovered the existent's kinship in the non-existent.
5. Transversely was their severing line extended: what was above it then, and what below it?
   There were begetters, there were mighty forces, free action here and energy up yonder.
6. Who verily knows and who can here declare it, whence it was born and whence comes this creation?
   The Gods are later than this world's production. Who knows then whence it first came into being?

Charles F. Horne, ed., *The Sacred Books and Early Literature of the East*, vol. 9: *India and Brahmanism* (New York: Parke, Austin, and Lipscomb, 1917), 48.

7. He, the first origin of this creation, whether he formed it all or did not form it, Whose eye controls this world in highest heaven, he verily knows it, or perhaps he knows not.

READING AND DISCUSSION QUESTIONS

1. How does this hymn characterize the period before the creation of the universe? What essential ingredient of reality was missing?

2. What importance do you attach to the hymn's insistence that "the Gods are later than this world's production"? If the gods did not create the world, then who or what did?

3. Do you agree with the hymn's claim that certain questions about the origins of the universe are unanswerable? Why or why not?

1-2 | The Yuchi People Explain Their Origins

YUCHI TRIBE OF NORTH AMERICA, *In the Beginning*

When Spanish explorer Hernando de Soto came upon the Yuchi ca. 1550, the tribe was living in eastern Tennessee. De Soto described several settlements in the region that consisted of small, fortified villages dominated by constructed mounds, which may have functioned as tombs for elite members of society. The Yuchi language is unrelated to any other known language and currently has fewer than a dozen speakers. After European encroachment on their territory, the Yuchi first moved south into Georgia and Florida before being forced into Oklahoma by the U.S. government in the early 1800s. There, they related this story to their Creek Indian neighbors about how they came to be.

In the beginning there was only water. And Someone said, "Who will make the land?"

"I will make the land," said Crawfish. And he dived down to the bottom of that great sea and stirred up the mud with his eight legs and his tail. And he took the mud in his fingers and made a little pile.

The owners of the mud down there said, "Who is stirring up the mud?" And they watched to see. But Crawfish kept stirring up the mud with his tail so that they could not see.

Every day Crawfish dived into the deep water and got a little more mud and put it on the pile. Day by day he piled it up. At last one day as he piled the mud on top of the pile, his hands came out of the water into the air! At last the land appeared above the water.

It was very soft, for it was mud.

Maria Leach, *The Beginning: Creation Myths Around the World* (New York: Funk & Wagnalls, 1956), 88–89. Reprinted by permission of Macdonald H. Leach.

Someone said, "Who will stretch out the land? Who will make it hard? Who will make it dry?"

Buzzard stretched out the earth and dried it. He spread his long wings and stretched it. He sailed over the earth; he spread it wide and dried it. Then, tiring, he had to flap his wings and this made the mountains and valleys.

Someone said, "Who will make the light?"

Star said, "I will make light." But it was not enough.

It was said, "Who will make more light?"

"I will make light," said Moon. But it was still night.

Someone said, "More light."

Sun said, "I will make light. I am the mother."

So Sun moved over into the east, and all at once a great beautiful light spread over the world. And then as Sun moved from east to west, a drop of her blood fell and sank into the earth. From this blood and this earth came forth the first people, the Yuchi Indians. They called themselves *Tsohaya*, People of the Sun, and every man who took this name had a picture of the sun on his door.

READING AND DISCUSSION QUESTIONS

1. According to the Yuchi, what was the role of animals in the creation of the world?

2. Where did the Yuchi believe they came from? What did they feel was their place in the world? What was their relationship to the sun?

1-3 | A Greek Description of the Elemental Forces

HESIOD, From *Theogony* (ca. 700 B.C.E.)

Hesiod was one of the earliest Greek authors, along with Homer (see Document 5-1). His most famous work, *The Works and Days*, describes contemporary Greek society and recounts how his brother unlawfully took his family's inheritance. The creation story included here appears in his other major work, *Theogony*, which means "the birth of the gods." In this passage, we learn of Chaos, the personification of the empty void that preceded creation, and of Gaia, the personification of the earth. We also learn of the children who resulted from Gaia's union with Ouranos, the personification of the sky. These children, known as the Titans, would one day do battle with the Olympian gods for mastery of the universe.

First of all there came Chaos,
    and after him came
Gaia[1] of the broad breast,
    to be the unshakable foundation
of all the immortals who keep the crests
    of snowy Olympos,[2]

[1] **Gaia:** The earth.
[2] **Olympos:** In Greek mythology, the mountain where the gods lived.

and Tartaros[3] the foggy in the pit
    of the wide-wayed earth,
and Eros, who is love, handsomest among all
    the immortals,
who breaks the limbs' strength,
    who in all gods, in all human beings
overpowers the intelligence in the breast,
    and all their shrewd planning.
From Chaos was born Erebos, the dark,
    and black Night,
and from Night again Aither and Hemera,
    the day, were begotten,
for she lay in love with Erebos
    and conceived and bore these two.
But Gaia's first born was one
    who matched her every dimension,
Ouranos, the starry sky,
    to cover her all over,
to be an unshakable standing-place
    for the blessed immortals.
Then she brought forth the tall Hills,
    those wild haunts that are beloved
by the goddess Nymphs who live on the hills
    and in their forests.
Without any sweet act of love
    she produced the barren
sea, Pontos, seething in his fury of waves,
    and after this
she lay with Ouranos, and bore him
    deep-swirling Okeanos
the ocean-stream; and Koios, Krios,
    Hyperion, Iapetos,
and Theia too and Rheia, and Themis,
    and Mnemosyne,
Phoibe of the wreath of gold,
    and Tethys the lovely.[4]
After these her youngest-born
    was devious-devising Kronos,
most terrible of her children;
    and he hated his strong father.

---

   [3] **Tartaros:** The prison beneath the Underworld.
   [4] **Koios . . . Tethys the lovely:** Those named were all Titans who were overthrown by the Olympian gods.

READING AND DISCUSSION QUESTIONS

1. According to Hesiod, where does the world come from?

2. How does Hesiod describe the primordial gods? In what ways are they like humans? In what ways are they like natural forces?

VIEWPOINTS COMPARATIVE QUESTIONS

1. How are natural forces described in each of the three origin stories? What does this tell you about how their authors viewed nature?

2. What does each story suggest about the spiritual life of the society that created it? How do the stories differ, and what might explain these differences?

1-4 | Clues About Early Human History in a Neolithic Grave
Double Burial from Mantua, Italy (ca. 6000–5000 B.C.E.)

When studying the period before written documents, scholars have to turn to other methods of discovering the past, such as archaeology. Occasionally, modern construction uncovers archaeological remains, like the burial shown here from Mantua, Italy. The teeth of these individuals are only slightly worn, suggesting that they died relatively young. Their grave included several flint stone tools (one lying on the individual on the right). Near this burial site were a number of other burials, all of single individuals, and a small Neolithic village.

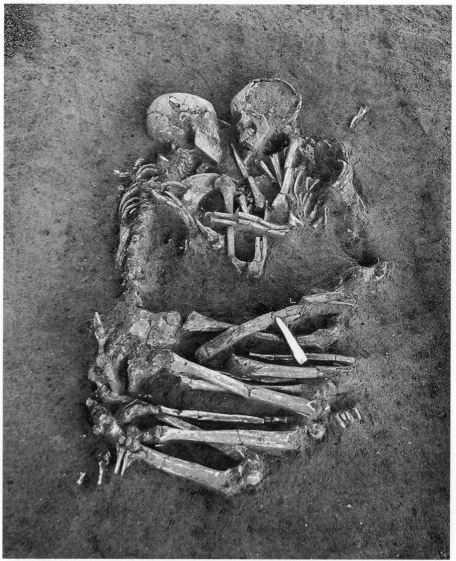

2430/Getty Images.

READING AND DISCUSSION QUESTIONS

1. What can this burial tell us about the relationships among humans at this time? Why do you think the individuals were buried in such an intimate fashion?

2. How can we use grave goods, such as the flint tool seen here, but also pottery and jewelry, to understand more about human life in the past? What if an individual was buried without grave goods? What might grave goods indicate about the formation of social hierarchies?

3. Why do you think these individuals were buried with useful items?

1-5 | Artistic Expression in the Paleolithic Era
Cave Painting of a Male and Female Deer
(ca. 13,000 B.C.E.)

Even though writing was not invented until the late fourth millennium B.C.E., humans had been expressing themselves for thousands of years through artwork. Archaeologists think the earliest surviving paintings in caves date to 30,000 years ago, but body art may have been practiced even earlier. This cave painting of a large male deer and a smaller female deer was discovered in southwestern France in 1901. The subject suggests the importance of animals in Paleolithic society and culture, at the same time that it reveals something of Paleolithic social norms. As you examine it, think about what it tells you about the artist's views on gender roles. What qualities did the artist see as essentially male? What qualities did the artist see as essentially female?

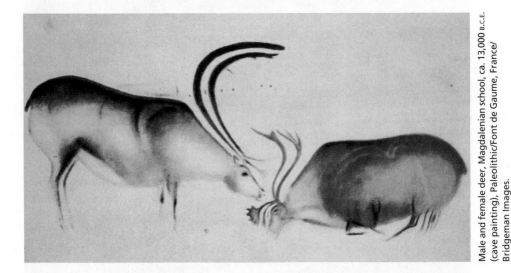

Male and female deer, Magdalenian school, ca. 13,000 B.C.E. (cave painting), Paleolithic/Font de Gaume, France/ Bridgeman Images.

READING AND DISCUSSION QUESTIONS

1. How did the artist see the relationship between the male and female deer? How did the composition of the painting help express that relationship?

2. What does the painting tell us about the society in which it was created?

▪ COMPARATIVE QUESTIONS ▪

1. Do the origin stories share similar themes? If so, what specifically is similar? What is different?

2. Taken together, what do the burial site and the image of the male and female deer tell you about early human societies?

3. What connections can you make between the Yuchi origin story and the image of the male and female deer? How did each society use animals as a vehicle of cultural expression?

Complex Societies in Southwest Asia and the Nile Valley

3800–500 B.C.E.

With the development of agriculture and animal husbandry in the Neo-lithic period (ca. 7000–3000 B.C.E.), humans began to construct more complex societies that required systems of organization and communication. Around 3000 B.C.E., the Sumerians in Mesopotamia invented writing for administrative purposes. Early writing was cumbersome and limited to a select group of scribes, but as writing became less complex, more people learned to read and write. Although literacy was still restricted to the priests and elite members of society, this larger audience prompted the recording of cultural, political, and religious documents such as myths, laws, scriptures, imperial propaganda, poems, and personal letters. Ancient Egyptians developed writing soon after the Sumerians, possibly after seeing how it was used in Mesopotamia. All successive civilizations in the Near East, such as the Hebrews, Assyrians, and Phoenicians, followed with written forms of their own languages.

2-1 | A Mesopotamian Quest for Immortality
From *The Epic of Gilgamesh* (ca. 2700–2500 B.C.E.)

The exact composition date of *The Epic of Gilgamesh* is unknown, but the legendary king Gilgamesh probably ruled the city of Uruk around 2700 B.C.E. While the core of the poem had been written by 2000 B.C.E., each successive culture in Mesopotamia added to or altered elements

---

of the story to incorporate its own myths. The epic recounts the friendship of Gilgamesh and the warrior Enkidu and their various adventures in Mesopotamia and the Near East. A fire in the seventh century B.C.E. destroyed the library of Nineveh in ancient Assyria, but clay tablets bearing the standard text of the epic survived, and they were later excavated from the library's ruins.

As Enkidu slept alone in his sickness, in bitterness of spirit he poured out his heart to his friend. "It was I who cut down the cedar,[1] I who leveled the forest, I who slew Humbaba[2] and now see what has become of me. Listen, my friend, this is the dream I dreamed last night. The heavens roared, and earth rumbled back an answer; between them stood I before an awful being, the somber-faced man-bird; he had directed on me his purpose. His was a vampire face, his foot was a lion's foot, his hand was an eagle's talon. He fell on me and his claws were in my hair, he held me fast and I was smothered; then he transformed me so that my arms became wings covered with feathers. He turned his stare towards me, and he led me away to the palace of Irkalla, the Queen of Darkness [Goddess of the underworld], to the house from which none who enters ever returns, down the road from which there is no coming back.

"There is the house whose people sit in darkness; dust is their food and clay their meat. They are clothed like birds with wings for covering, they see no light, they sit in darkness. I entered the house of dust and I saw the kings of the earth, their crowns put away forever; rulers and princes, all those who once wore kingly crowns and ruled the world in the days of old. They who had stood in the place of the gods like Anu [King of the gods] and Enlil,[3] stood now like servants to fetch baked meats in the house of dust, to carry cooked meat and cold water from the waterskin. In the house of dust which I entered were high priests and acolytes, priests of the incantation and of ecstasy; there were servers of the temple, and there was Etana, that king of Kish[4] whom the eagle carried to Heaven in the days of old. There was Ereshkigal the Queen of the Underworld; and Belit-Sheri squatted in front of her, she who is recorder of the gods and keeps the book of death. She held a tablet from which she read. She raised her head, she saw me and spoke: 'Who has brought this one here?' Then I awoke like a man drained of blood who wanders alone in a waste of rushes; like one whom the bailiff has seized and his heart pounds with terror."

[After Enkidu dies Gilgamesh realizes that fame is no substitute for life. Facing his own imminent death, he begins a desperate search for immortality. He travels to the end of the Earth where he meets Siduri, a female tavern keeper, who offers the following advice:]

"Gilgamesh, where are you hurrying to? You will never find that life for which you are looking. When the gods created man they allotted to him death, but life they

---

[1] **cedar:** He refers to a journey to Lebanon during which Gilgamesh and Enkidu cut down the cedar forest that Humbaba was appointed to guard.

[2] **Humbaba:** A giant from Lebanon whom Gilgamesh and Enkidu killed.

[3] **Enlil:** God of the sky who guided human affairs.

[4] **Kish:** A Sumerian city. Etana wanted to obtain a magical plant from heaven that would allow him to father a son.

retained in their own keeping. As for you, Gilgamesh, fill your belly with good things; day and night, night and day, dance and be merry, feast and rejoice. Let your clothes be fresh, bathe yourself in water, cherish the little child that holds your hand, and make your wife happy in your embrace; for this too is the lot of man."

[Gilgamesh refuses to be deterred. After many harrowing experiences he finally reaches Utnapishtim, a former mortal whom the gods had sent to eternal paradise, and addresses him.]

"Oh, father Utnapishtim, you who have entered the assembly of the gods, I wish to question you concerning the living and the dead, how shall I find the life for which I am searching?"

Utnapishtim said, "There is no permanence. Do we build a house to stand forever, do we seal a contract to hold for all time? Do brothers divide an inheritance to keep forever, does the flood-time of rivers endure? It is only the nymph of the dragon-fly who sheds her larva and sees the sun in his glory. From the days of old there is no permanence. The sleeping and the dead, how alike they are, they are like a painted death. What is there between the master and the servant when both have fulfilled their doom? When the Anunnaki [gods], the judges, come together, and Mammetun, the mother of destinies, together they decree the fates of men. Life and death they allot but the day of death they do not disclose."

Then Gilgamesh said to Utnapishtim the Faraway, "I look at you now, Utnapishtim, and your appearance is no different from mine; there is nothing strange in your features. I thought I should find you like a hero prepared for battle, but you lie here taking your ease on your back. Tell me truly, how was it that you came to enter the company of the gods and to possess everlasting life?" Utnapishtim said to Gilgamesh, "I will reveal to you a mystery, I will tell you a secret of the gods."

"You know the city Shurrupak [a Sumerian city] it stands on the banks of Euphrates? That city grew old and the gods that were in it were old. There was Anu, lord of the firmament, their father, and warrior Enlil their counselor, Ninurta the helper, and Ennugi watcher over canals; and with them also was Ea [God of water]. In those days the world teemed, the people multiplied, the world bellowed like a wild bull, and the great god was aroused by the clamor. Enlil heard the clamor and he said to the gods in council, 'The uproar of mankind is intolerable and sleep is no longer possible by reason of the babel.' So the gods agreed to exterminate mankind. Enlil did this, but Ea because of his oath [to protect mankind] warned me in a dream. He whispered their words to my house of reeds, 'Reed-house, reed-house! Wall, O wall, hearken reed-house, wall reflect; O man of Shurrupak, son of Ubara-Tutu; tear down your house and build a boat, abandon possessions and look for life, despise worldly goods and save your soul alive. Tear down your house, I say, and build a boat. . . . Then take up into the boat the seed of all living creatures.'

"When I had understood I said to my lord, 'Behold, what you have commanded I will honor and perform, but how shall I answer the people, the city, the elders?' Then Ea opened his mouth and said to me, his servant, 'Tell them this: I have learnt that Enlil is wrathful against me, I dare no longer walk in his land nor live in his city; I will go down to the Gulf to dwell with Ea my lord. But on you he will rain down abundance, rare fish and shy wildfowl, a rich harvest-tide. In the evening the rider of the storm will bring you wheat in torrents.' . . .

"On the seventh day the boat was complete. . . .

"I loaded into her all that I had of gold and of living things, my family, my kin, the beast of the field both wild and tame, and all the craftsmen. I sent them on board. . . . The time was fulfilled, the evening came, the rider of the storm sent down the rain. I looked out at the weather and it was terrible, so I too boarded the boat and battened her down. . . .

"For six days and six nights the winds blew, torrent and tempest and flood overwhelmed the world, tempest and flood raged together like warring hosts. When the seventh day dawned the storm from the south subsided, the sea grew calm, the flood was stilled; I looked at the face of the world and there was silence, all mankind was turned to clay. The surface of the sea stretched as flat as a roof-top; I opened a hatch and the light fell on my face. Then I bowed low, I sat down and I wept, the tears streamed down my face, for on every side was the waste of water. I looked for land in vain, but fourteen leagues distant there appeared a mountain, and there the boat grounded; on the mountain of Nisir the boat held fast, she held fast and did not budge. . . . When the seventh day dawned I loosed a dove and let her go. She flew away, but finding no resting-place she returned. Then I loosed a swallow, and she flew away but finding no resting-place she returned. I loosed a raven, she saw that the waters had retreated, she ate, she flew around, she cawed, and she did not come back. Then I threw everything open to the four winds, I made a sacrifice and poured out a libation [liquid offering] on the mountain top. Seven and again seven cauldrons I set up on their stands, I heaped up wood and cane and cedar and myrtle. When the gods smelled the sweet savor, they gathered like flies over the sacrifice.[5] Then, at last, Ishtar [Goddess of love and war] also came, she lifted her necklace with the jewels of Heaven [rainbow] that once Anu had made to please her. 'O you gods here present, by the lapis lazuli[6] round my neck I shall remember these days as I remember the jewels of my throat; these last days I shall not forget. Let all the gods gather round the sacrifice, except Enlil. He shall not approach this offering, for without reflection he brought the flood; he consigned my people to destruction.'

"When Enlil had come, when he saw the boat, he was wrath and swelled with anger at the gods, the host of Heaven, 'Has any of these mortals escaped? Not one was to have survived the destruction.' Then the god of the wells and canals Ninurta opened his mouth and said to the warrior Enlil, 'Who is there of the gods that can devise without Ea? It is Ea alone who knows all things.' Then Ea opened his mouth and spoke to warrior Enlil, 'Wisest of gods, hero Enlil, how could you so senselessly bring down the flood? . . . It was not that I revealed the

---

[5] **like flies over the sacrifice:** The gods were thought to consume the smoke of incense and animal offerings.

[6] **lapis lazuli:** A gemstone with a deep blue color often used in Egyptian jewelry.

secret of the gods; the wise man learned it in a dream. Now take your counsel what shall be done with him.'

"Then Enlil went up into the boat, he took me by the hand and my wife and made us enter the boat and kneel down on either side, he standing between us. He touched our foreheads to bless us saying, 'In time past Utnapishtim was a mortal man; henceforth he and his wife shall live in the distance at the mouth of the rivers.' Thus it was that the gods took me and placed me here to live in the distance, at the mouth of the rivers."

Utnapishtim said, "As for you, Gilgamesh, who will assemble the gods for your sake, so that you may find that life for which you are searching?"

[After telling his story, Utnapishtim challenges Gilgamesh to resist sleep for six days and seven nights. When Gilgamesh fails the test, Utnapishtim points out how preposterous it is to search for immortality when one cannot even resist sleep. Out of kindness, Utnapishtim does tell Gilgamesh where he can find a submarine plant that will at least rejuvenate him. Consequently, the hero dives to the bottom of the sea and plucks it. However, humanity is to be denied even the blessing of forestalling old age and decrepitude, because the plant is stolen from Gilgamesh by a serpent. His mission a failure, Gilgamesh returns to Uruk.]

The destiny was fulfilled which the father of the gods, Enlil of the mountain, had decreed for Gilgamesh: "In nether-earth the darkness will show him a light: of mankind, all that are known, none will leave a monument for generations to come to compare with his. The heroes, the wise men, like the new moon have their waxing and waning. Men will say, 'Who has ever ruled with might and with power like him?' As in the dark month, the month of shadows, so without him there is no light. O Gilgamesh, this was the meaning of your dream. You were given the kingship, such was your destiny, everlasting life was not your destiny. Because of this do not be sad at heart, do not be grieved or oppressed; he has given you power to bind and to loose, to be the darkness and the light of mankind. He has given unexampled supremacy over the people, victory in battle from which no fugitive returns, in forays and assaults from which there is no going back. But do not abuse this power, deal justly with your servants in the palace, deal justly before the face of the Sun." . . .

Gilgamesh, the son of Ninsun, lies in the tomb. At the place of offerings he weighed the bread-offering, at the place of libation he poured out the wine. In those days the lord Gilgamesh departed, the son of Ninsun, the king, peerless, without an equal among men, who did not neglect Enlil his master. O Gilgamesh, lord of Kullab [in Uruk], great is thy praise.

READING AND DISCUSSION QUESTIONS

1. How does this passage describe the afterlife?

2. How are the gods characterized in this passage? What role do they play in the lives of individual human beings?

3. Would you describe *The Epic of Gilgamesh* as pessimistic or optimistic? Why?

2-2 | Law and Order in Ancient Babylonia

HAMMURABI, *Hammurabi's Code: Laws on Society and Family Life* (ca. 1800 B.C.E.)

Among Hammurabi of Babylon's many accomplishments were the unification of Mesopotamia under Babylonian rule, the establishment of the supremacy of the Babylonian god Marduk, and the composition of a law code. Although Hammurabi's code is not the first known law code, it is the earliest one to survive largely intact. The code deals with the family, commercial activities, and agricultural life, providing valuable insight into Babylonian society. The following selections are typical of the laws in the code and exemplify the brutal nature of Babylonian justice, often characterized by the phrase "an eye for an eye."

The Prologue

When lofty Anum, king of the Anunnaki,[7]
(and) Enlil, lord of heaven and earth,
the determiner of the destinies of the land,
determined for Marduk, the first-born of Enki,[8]
the Enlil functions over all mankind,
he made him great among the Igigi,[9]
called Babylon by its exalted name,
made it supreme in the world,
established for him in its midst an enduring kingship,
whose foundations are as firm as heaven and earth—
at that time Anum and Enlil named me
to promote the welfare of the people,
me, Hammurabi, the devout, god-fearing prince,
to cause justice to prevail in the land,
to destroy the wicked and the evil,
that the strong might not oppress the weak,
to rise like the sun over the black-headed (people),
and to light up the land. . . .

Code of Laws

128. If a seignior[10] acquired a wife, but did not draw up the contracts for her, that woman is no wife.

James B. Pritchard, ed., *Ancient Near Eastern Texts Relating to the Old Testament*, 3d ed. with supplement. © 1950, 1955, 1969, renewed 1978 Princeton University Press. Reprinted by permission of Princeton University Press.

[7] **Anunnaki:** Divine servants of Anu.
[8] **Enki:** God of the Earth and springs, father of Marduk.
[9] **Igigi:** Divine servants of Enlil.
[10] **seignior:** A free man (not a slave). A seignior could be a member of the upper class.

129.   If the wife of a seignior has been caught while lying with another man, they shall bind them and throw them into the water. If the husband of the woman wishes to spare his wife, then the king in turn may spare his subject.

130.   If a seignior bound the (betrothed) wife of a(nother) seignior, who had had no intercourse with a male and was still living in her father's house, and he has lain in her bosom and they have caught him, that seignior shall be put to death, while that woman shall go free.

131.   If a seignior's wife was accused by her husband, but she was not caught while lying with another man, she shall make affirmation by god and return to her house.

132.   If the finger was pointed at the wife of a seignior because of another man, but she has not been caught while lying with the other man, she shall throw herself into the river for the sake of her husband.

133.   If a seignior was taken captive, but there was sufficient to live on in his house, his wife [shall not leave her house, but she shall take care of her person by not] entering [the house of another].

133a.   If that woman did not take care of her person, but has entered the house of another, they shall prove it against that woman and throw her into the water.

134.   If the seignior was taken captive and there was not sufficient to live on in his house, his wife may enter the house of another, with that woman incurring no blame at all.

135.   If, when a seignior was taken captive and there was not sufficient to live on in his house, his wife has then entered the house of another before his (return) and has borne children, (and) later her husband has returned and has reached his city, that woman shall return to her first husband, while the children shall go with their father.

136.   If when a seignior deserted his city and then ran away, his wife has entered the house of another after his (departure), if that seignior has returned and wishes to take back his wife, the wife of the fugitive shall not return to her husband because he scorned his city and ran away.

137.   If a seignior has made up his mind to divorce a lay priestess, who bore him children, or a hierodule[11] who provided him with children, they shall return her dowry to that woman and also give her half of the field, orchard and goods in order that she may rear her children; after she has brought up her children, from whatever was given to her children they shall give her a portion corresponding to (that of) an individual heir in order that the man of her choice may marry her.

138.   If a seignior wishes to divorce his wife who did not bear him children, he shall give her money to the full amount of her marriage-price and he shall also make good to her the dowry which she brought from her father's house and then he may divorce her.

---

[11] **hierodule:** A female slave of the temple.

139. If there was no marriage-price, he shall give her one mina[12] of silver as the divorce-settlement.

140. If he is a peasant, he shall give her one-third mina of silver.

141. If a seignior's wife, who was living in the house of the seignior, has made up her mind to leave in order that she may engage in business, thus neglecting her house (and) humiliating her husband, they shall prove it against her; and if her husband has then decided on her divorce, he may divorce her, with nothing to be given her as her divorce-settlement upon her departure. If her husband has not decided on her divorce, her husband may marry another woman, with the former woman living in the house of her husband like a maidservant.

142. If a woman so hated her husband that she has declared, "You may not have me," her record shall be investigated at her city council, and if she was careful and was not at fault, even though her husband has been going out and disparaging her greatly, that woman, without incurring any blame at all, may take her dowry and go off to her father's house.

143. If she was not careful, but was a gadabout, thus neglecting her house (and) humiliating her husband, they shall throw that woman into the water.

144. When a seignior married a hierodule and that hierodule gave a female slave to her husband and she has then produced children, if that seignior has made up his mind to marry a lay priestess, they may not allow that seignior, since he may not marry the lay priestess.

145. If a seignior married a hierodule and she did not provide him with children and he has made up his mind to marry a lay priestess, that seignior may marry the lay priestess, thus bringing her into his house, (but) with that lay priestess ranking in no way with the hierodule.

146. When a seignior married a hierodule and she gave a female slave to her husband and she has then borne children, if later that female slave has claimed equality with her mistress because she bore children, her mistress may not sell her; she may mark her with the slave-mark and count her among the slaves.

147. If she did not bear children, her mistress may sell her.

148. When a seignior married a woman and a fever has then seized her, if he has made up his mind to marry another, he may marry (her), without divorcing his wife whom the fever seized; she shall live in the house which he built and he shall continue to support her as long as she lives.

149. If that woman has refused to live in her husband's house, he shall make good her dowry to her which she brought from her father's house and then she may leave.

150. If a seignior, upon presenting a field, orchard, house, or goods to his wife, left a sealed document with her, her children may not enter a claim against her after (the death of) her husband, since the mother may give her inheritance to that son of hers whom she likes, (but) she may not give (it) to an outsider. . . .

---

[12] **mina:** A weight equal to just over one pound.

153. If a seignior's wife has brought about the death of her husband because of another man, they shall impale that woman on stakes.

154. If a seignior has had intercourse with his daughter, they shall make that seignior leave the city.

155. If a seignior chose a bride for his son and his son had intercourse with her, but later he himself has lain in her bosom and they have caught him, they shall bind that seignior and throw him into the water.

156. If a seignior chose a bride for his son and his son did not have intercourse with her, but he himself has lain in her bosom, he shall pay to her one-half mina of silver and he shall also make good to her whatever she brought from her father's house in order that the man of her choice may marry her.

157. If a seignior has lain in the bosom of his mother after (the death of) his father, they shall burn both of them. . . .

195. If a son has struck his father, they shall cut off his hand.

196. If a seignior has destroyed the eye of a member of the aristocracy, they shall destroy his eye.

197. If he has broken a(nother) seignior's bone, they shall break his bone.

198. If he has destroyed the eye of a commoner or broken the bone of a commoner, he shall pay one mina of silver.

199. If he has destroyed the eye of a seignior's slave or broken the bone of a seignior's slave, he shall pay one-half his value.

200. If a seignior has knocked out a tooth of a seignior of his own rank, they shall knock out his tooth.

201. If he has knocked out a commoner's tooth, he shall pay one-third mina of silver.

202. If a seignior has struck the cheek of a seignior who is superior to him, he shall be beaten sixty (times) with an oxtail whip in the assembly.

203. If a member of the aristocracy has struck the cheek of a(nother) member of the aristocracy who is of the same rank as himself, he shall pay one mina of silver.

204. If a commoner has struck the cheek of a(nother) commoner, he shall pay ten shekels [coins] of silver.

205. If a seignior's slave has struck the cheek of a member of the aristocracy, they shall cut off his ear.

206. If a seignior has struck a(nother) seignior in a brawl and has inflicted an injury on him, that seignior shall swear, "I did not strike him deliberately"; and he shall also pay for the physician.

207. If he has died because of his blow, he shall swear (as before), and if it was a member of the aristocracy, he shall pay one-half mina of silver.

208. If it was a member of the commonalty, he shall pay one-third mina of silver.

209. If a seignior struck a(nother) seignior's daughter and has caused her to have a miscarriage, he shall pay ten shekels of silver for her fetus.

210. If that woman has died, they shall put his daughter to death.

211. If by a blow he has caused a commoner's daughter to have a miscarriage, he shall pay five shekels of silver.

212. If that woman has died, he shall pay one-half mina of silver.

213. If he struck a seignior's female slave and has caused her to have a miscarriage, he shall pay two shekels of silver.

214. If that female slave has died, he shall pay one-third mina of silver.

215. If a physician performed a major operation on a freeman with a bronze lancet and has saved the freeman's life, or he opened up the eye-socket of a freeman with a bronze lancet and has saved the freeman's eye, he shall receive ten shekels of silver.

216. If it was a commoner, he shall receive five shekels of silver.

217. If it was a freeman's slave, the owner of the slave shall give two shekels of silver to the physician.

218. If a physician performed a major operation on a freeman with a bronze lancet and has caused the freeman's death, or he opened up the eye-socket of a freeman and has destroyed the freeman's eye, they shall cut off his hand.

219. If a physician performed a major operation on a commoner's slave with a bronze lancet and has caused his death, he shall make good slave for slave.

220. If he opened up [the slave's] eye-socket with a bronze lancet and has destroyed his eye, he shall pay half his value in silver.

READING AND DISCUSSION QUESTIONS

1. Why did Hammurabi produce this code of laws? Where does he claim his authority and kingship come from?

2. What distinctions does the code make on the basis of social status? Are all of Hammurabi's subjects bound by the same rules?

3. In what ways do these selections attempt to regulate familial relationships? What practices are banned? Why?

2-3 | Moses Leads the Hebrews from Egypt
Book of Exodus (ca. 950–450 B.C.E.)

The book of Exodus, the second book of the Hebrew Torah and the Christian Old Testament, recounts the escape of the Hebrew people (Israelites) from captivity in Egypt and their forty-year journey through the desert to the "promised land," modern-day Israel and Palestine. Although Moses, who led the Hebrew people, is traditionally thought to have written the Torah, modern scholars argue that the work was composed over many centuries. The

Exodus, from the *American Standard Version of the Bible*, 1901.

following passage recounts the climactic events of the Exodus, when the Hebrew people fled Egypt and later when Moses received the Covenant from God. It establishes monotheism, the worship of only one God, as a tenet of the Hebrew religion.

[14:5–16]

And it was told the king of Egypt that the people were fled: and the heart of Pharaoh and of his servants was changed towards the people, and they said, What is this we have done, that we have let Israel go from serving us? And he made ready his chariot, and took his people with him: and he took six hundred chosen chariots, and all the chariots of Egypt, and captains over all of them. And Jehovah hardened the heart of Pharaoh king of Egypt, and he pursued after the children of Israel: for the children of Israel went out with a high hand. And the Egyptians pursued after them, all the horses and chariots of Pharaoh, and his horsemen, and his army, and overtook them encamping by the sea, beside Pi-hahiroth, before Baal-zephon.

And when Pharaoh drew nigh, the children of Israel lifted up their eyes, and, behold, the Egyptians were marching after them; and they were sore afraid: and the children of Israel cried out unto Jehovah. And they said unto Moses, Because there were no graves in Egypt, hast thou taken us away to die in the wilderness? wherefore hast thou dealt thus with us, to bring us forth out of Egypt? Is not this the word that we spake unto thee in Egypt, saying, Let us alone, that we may serve the Egyptians? For it were better for us to serve the Egyptians, than that we should die in the wilderness. And Moses said unto the people, Fear ye not, stand still, and see the salvation of Jehovah, which he will work for you to-day: for the Egyptians whom ye have seen to-day, ye shall see them again no more for ever. Jehovah will fight for you, and ye shall hold your peace.

And Jehovah said unto Moses, Wherefore criest thou unto me? speak unto the children of Israel, that they go forward. And lift thou up thy rod, and stretch out thy hand over the sea, and divide it: and the children of Israel shall go into the midst of the sea on dry ground. . . .

[14:21–31]

And Moses stretched out his hand over the sea; and Jehovah caused the sea to go back by a strong east wind all the night, and made the sea dry land, and the waters were divided. And the children of Israel went into the midst of the sea upon the dry ground: and the waters were a wall unto them on their right hand, and on their left. And the Egyptians pursued, and went in after them into the midst of the sea, all Pharaoh's horses, his chariots, and his horsemen. And it came to pass in the morning watch, that Jehovah looked forth upon the host of the Egyptians through the pillar of fire and of cloud, and discomfited the host of the Egyptians. And he took off their chariot wheels, and they drove them heavily; so that the Egyptians said, Let us flee from the face of Israel; for Jehovah fighteth for them against the Egyptians.

And Jehovah said unto Moses, Stretch out thy hand over the sea, that the waters may come again upon the Egyptians, upon their chariots, and upon their horsemen. And Moses stretched forth his hand over the sea, and the sea returned to its strength when the morning appeared; and the Egyptians fled against it; and Jehovah overthrew the Egyptians in the midst of the sea. And the waters returned, and covered the chariots, and the horsemen, even all the host of Pharaoh that went in after them into the sea; there remained not so much as one of them. But the children of Israel walked upon dry land in the midst of the sea; and the waters were a wall unto them on their right hand, and on their left. Thus Jehovah saved Israel that day out of the hand of the Egyptians; and Israel saw the Egyptians dead upon the sea-shore. And Israel saw the great work which Jehovah did upon the Egyptians, and the people feared Jehovah: and they believed in Jehovah, and in his servant Moses. . . .

[19:16–25]

And it came to pass on the third day, when it was morning, that there were thunders and lightnings, and a thick cloud upon the mount, and the voice of a trumpet exceeding loud; and all the people that were in the camp trembled. And Moses brought forth the people out of the camp to meet God; and they stood at the nether part of the mount. And mount Sinai, the whole of it, smoked, because Jehovah descended upon it in fire; and the smoke thereof ascended as the smoke of a furnace, and the whole mount quaked greatly. And when the voice of the trumpet waxed louder and louder, Moses spake, and God answered him by a voice. And Jehovah came down upon mount Sinai, to the top of the mount: and Jehovah called Moses to the top of the mount; and Moses went up. And Jehovah said unto Moses, Go down, charge the people, lest they break through unto Jehovah to gaze, and many of them perish. And let the priests also, that come near to Jehovah, sanctify themselves, lest Jehovah break forth upon them. And Moses said unto Jehovah, The people cannot come up to mount Sinai: for thou didst charge us, saying, Set bounds about the mount, and sanctify it. And Jehovah said unto him, Go, get thee down; and thou shalt come up, thou, and Aaron with thee: but let not the priests and the people break through to come up unto Jehovah, lest he break forth upon them. So Moses went down unto the people, and told them.

[20:1–26]

And God spake all these words, saying, I am Jehovah thy God, who brought thee out of the land of Egypt, out of the house of bondage. Thou shalt have no other gods before me.

Thou shalt not make unto thee a graven image, nor any likeness of any thing that is in heaven above, or that is in the earth beneath, or that is in the water under the earth: thou shalt not bow down thyself unto them, nor serve them; for I Jehovah thy God am a jealous God, visiting the iniquity of the fathers upon the children, upon the third and upon the fourth generation of them that hate me, and showing lovingkindness unto thousands of them that love me and keep my commandments.

Thou shalt not take the name of Jehovah thy God in vain; for Jehovah will not hold him guiltless that taketh his name in vain.

Remember the sabbath day, to keep it holy. Six days shalt thou labor, and do all thy work; but the seventh day is a sabbath unto Jehovah thy God: in it thou shalt not do any work, thou, nor thy son, nor thy daughter, thy man-servant, nor thy maid-servant, nor thy cattle, nor thy stranger that is within thy gates: for in six days Jehovah made heaven and earth, the sea, and all that in them is, and rested the seventh day: wherefore Jehovah blessed the sabbath day, and hallowed it.

Honor thy father and thy mother, that thy days may be long in the land which Jehovah thy God giveth thee.

Thou shalt not kill.

Thou shalt not commit adultery.

Thou shalt not steal.

Thou shalt not bear false witness against thy neighbor.

Thou shalt not covet thy neighbor's house, thou shalt not covet thy neighbor's wife, nor his man-servant, nor his maid-servant, nor his ox, nor his ass, nor anything that is thy neighbor's.

And all the people perceived the thunderings, and the lightnings, and the voice of the trumpet, and the mountain smoking: and when the people saw it, they trembled, and stood afar off. And they said unto Moses, Speak thou with us, and we will hear; but let not God speak with us, lest we die. And Moses said unto the people, Fear not: for God is come to prove you, and that his fear may be before you, that ye sin not. And the people stood afar off, and Moses drew near unto the thick darkness where God was.

And Jehovah said unto Moses, Thus thou shalt say unto the children of Israel, Ye yourselves have seen that I have talked with you from heaven. Ye shall not make other gods with me; gods of silver, or gods of gold, ye shall not make unto you. An altar of earth thou shalt make unto me, and shalt sacrifice thereon thy burnt-offerings, and thy peace-offerings, thy sheep, and thine oxen: in every place where I record my name I will come unto thee and I will bless thee. And if thou make me an altar of stone, thou shalt not build it of hewn stones; for if thou lift up thy tool upon it, thou hast polluted it. Neither shalt thou go up by steps unto mine altar, that thy nakedness be not uncovered thereon.

[21:1–36]

Now these are the ordinances which thou shalt set before them.

If thou buy a Hebrew servant, six years he shall serve: and in the seventh he shall go out free for nothing. If he come in by himself, he shall go out by himself: if he be married, then his wife shall go out with him. If his master give him a wife, and she bear him sons or daughters; the wife and her children shall be her master's, and he shall go out by himself. But if the servant shall plainly say, I love my master, my wife, and my children; I will not go out free: then his master shall bring him unto God, and shall bring him to the door, or unto the door-post; and his master shall bore his ear through with an awl; and he shall serve him for ever.

And if a man sell his daughter to be a maid-servant, she shall not go out as the men-servants do. If she please not her master, who hath espoused her to himself, then shall he let her be redeemed: to sell her unto a foreign people he shall have no power, seeing he hath dealt deceitfully with her. And if he espouse her unto his son, he shall deal with her after the manner of daughters. If he take him another wife; her food, her raiment, and her duty of marriage, shall he not diminish. And if he do not these three things unto her, then shall she go out for nothing, without money.

He that smiteth a man, so that he dieth, shall surely be put to death. And if a man lie not in wait, but God deliver him into his hand; then I will appoint thee a place whither he shall flee. And if a man come presumptuously upon his neighbor, to slay him with guile; thou shalt take him from mine altar, that he may die.

And he that smiteth his father, or his mother, shall be surely put to death.

And he that stealeth a man, and selleth him, or if he be found in his hand, he shall surely be put to death.

And he that curseth his father or his mother, shall surely be put to death.

And if men contend, and one smite the other with a stone, or with his fist, and he die not, but keep his bed; if he rise again, and walk abroad upon his staff, then shall he that smote him be quit: only he shall pay for the loss of his time, and shall cause him to be thoroughly healed.

And if a man smite his servant, or his maid, with a rod, and he die under his hand; he shall surely be punished. Notwithstanding, if he continue a day or two, he shall not be punished: for he is his money.

And if men strive together, and hurt a woman with child, so that her fruit depart, and yet no harm follow; he shall be surely fined, according as the woman's husband shall lay upon him; and he shall pay as the judges determine. But if any harm follow, then thou shalt give life for life, eye for eye, tooth for tooth, hand for hand, foot for foot, burning for burning, wound for wound, stripe for stripe.

And if a man smite the eye of his servant, or the eye of his maid, and destroy it; he shall let him go free for his eye's sake. And if he smite out his man-servant's tooth, or his maid-servant's tooth; he shall let him go free for his tooth's sake.

And if an ox gore a man or a woman to death, the ox shall be surely stoned, and its flesh shall not be eaten; but the owner of the ox shall be quit. But if the ox was wont to gore in time past, and it hath been testified to its owner, and he hath not kept it in, but it hath killed a man or a woman; the ox shall be stoned, and its owner also shall be put to death. If there be laid on him a ransom, then he shall give for the redemption of his life whatsoever is laid upon him. Whether it have gored a son, or have gored a daughter, according to this judgment shall it be done unto him. If the ox gore a man-servant or a maid-servant, there shall be given unto their master thirty shekels of silver, and the ox shall be stoned.

And if a man shall open a pit, or if a man shall dig a pit and not cover it, and an ox or an ass fall therein, the owner of the pit shall make it good; he shall give money unto the owner thereof, and the dead beast shall be his.

And if one man's ox hurt another's, so that it dieth, then they shall sell the live ox, and divide the price of it; and the dead also they shall divide. Or if it be known that the ox was wont to gore in time past, and its owner hath not kept it in; he shall surely pay ox for ox, and the dead beast shall be his own.

READING AND DISCUSSION QUESTIONS

1. What role does the Hebrew God play for his people? How does Moses act as an intermediary between God and the people?

2. How does the Hebrew God differ from other Near Eastern deities?

3. What do these passages reveal about Hebrew society? What, if any, evidence of different social classes can you find?

Imperial Propaganda in the Ancient Near East

In theory, a Near Eastern emperor was an absolute ruler whose will was not to be questioned and whose every command was to be obeyed. In reality, the emperor who wanted to hold his empire together, and keep himself securely on the throne, did not take his position or his subjects' belief in his merits for granted. Instead, he used every opportunity to articulate the connection between his deeds and his fitness to rule. The two Near Eastern rulers featured here, Ashur-Nasir-Pal II of Assyria and Cyrus the Great of Persia, understood the importance of imperial propaganda. Their approaches to this task, however, could not have been more different. As you read their accounts of their achievements, note the aspects of their rule on which they chose to focus. What light do these documents shed on Assyrian and Persian ideas about what made a good ruler?

2-4 | An Assyrian Emperor's Résumé

ASHUR-NASIR-PAL II, *Inscription* (ca. 875 B.C.E.)

Ashur-Nasir-Pal II (r. 883–859 B.C.E.) was responsible for expanding the emerging Neo-Assyrian Empire west from northern Mesopotamia to the Mediterranean. His description of his military

D. D. Luckenbill, ed., *Ancient Records of Assyria and Babylonia* (Chicago: University of Chicago Press, 1926), 1:151–154. Reprinted by permission of The Oriental Institute of the University of Chicago.

campaigns in Mesopotamia is typical of such accounts produced by Assyrian kings. It empha-
sized three points: that the emperor was acting at the behest of Assyria's gods, that he and his
army were an unstoppable force, and that the price of resisting the Assyrians was utter annihi-
lation. As you read his account, ask yourself how different audiences were meant to react to
it. What lessons were Assyria's neighbors expected to take from it? What message was it
intended to send to Ashur-Nasir-Pal II's fellow Assyrian elites?

Year 4: A Third Campaign Against Zamua

In the eponymy of Limutti-adur,[13] while I was staying in Nineveh, men brought
me word that Ameka and Arashtua [Mesopotamian cities] had withheld the
tribute and forced labor due unto Assur,[14] my lord. At the word of Assur,
the great lord, my lord, and of Nergal [God of war and the sun], my leader, on
the first day of the month of *Simanu*[15] I ordered a call to arms for the third time
against the land of Zamua. I did not wait for my chariots and hosts; I departed
from the city of Kakzi, the Lower Zab I crossed. I entered the pass of Babite,
I crossed the Radanu, drawing nearer every day to the foot of Mount Simaki.
Cattle, sheep and wine, the tribute of the land of Dagara, I received. The chariots
and picked cavalry (men) I took with me, and all the night, until the dawn,
I marched from (along) the foot of the mountain of Simaki. I crossed the Turnat,
and with all haste to the city of Ammali, the stronghold of Arashtua, I drew
near. With battle and assault I stormed the city, I took (it). 800 of their fighting
men I struck down with the sword, with their corpses I filled the streets of their
city, with their blood I dyed their houses. Many men I captured alive with my
hand, and I carried off great spoil from them; the city I destroyed, I devastated,
I burned with fire.

The city of Hudun and twenty cities of its neighborhood I captured; I slew
the inhabitants thereof, their spoil, their cattle, and their sheep I carried off; their
cities I destroyed, I devastated, I burned with fire; their young men and their
maidens I burned in the flames. The city of Kisirtu, their stronghold, ruled by
Sabini, together with ten cities of its neighborhood, I captured, I slew their inhabitants, their spoil I carried away. The cities of the Bareans, which were ruled by
Kirtiara, and those of the men of Dera and of Bunisa, as far as the pass of
Hashmar, I destroyed, I devastated, I burned with fire, I turned them into
mounds and ruins. I departed from the cities of Arashtua, I entered the pass
between the steep mountains of Lara and Bidirgi, which for the passage of chariots and hosts was not suited to Zamri, the royal city of Ameka of the land of
Zamua, I drew near.

Ameka became afraid before my mighty weapons and my fierce battle array,
and occupied a steep mountain. The goods of his palace and his chariot I carried

---

[13] **eponymy of Limutti-adur:** In the Assyrian calendar, the names of an elected official
called "limmu" were used to name the year. The name Limutti-adur does not survive in any of
the Assyrian lists, but this year probably corresponds to 879 B.C.E.

[14] **Assur:** Chief god of the Assyrians.

[15] *Simanu:* May or June in the modern calendar.

away; from the city of Zamri I departed. I crossed the Lalle and marched to Mount Etini, a difficult region, which was not suited for the passage of chariots and armies, and unto which none among the kings, my fathers, had come nigh. The king, together with his armies, climbed up into Mount Etini. His goods and his possessions, many copper utensils, a copper wild-ox, vessels of copper, bowls of copper, cups of copper, the wealth of his palace, his heaped-up treasures, I carried out of the mountain, returned to my camp and spent the night. With the help of Assur and Shamash [God of justice], the gods, my helpers, I departed from that camp, and I set out after him. I crossed the Edir River and in the midst of the mighty mountains of Su and Elaniu I slew multitudes of them. His goods and his possessions, a copper wild-ox, vessels of copper, bowls of copper, dishes of copper; many copper utensils, tables which were overlaid with gold, their cattle and their flocks, their possessions, their heavy spoil, from the foot of Mount Elaniu I carried off. I took his horse from him. Ameka, to save his life, climbed up into Mount Sabua.

The cities of Zamru, Arasitku, Ammaru, Parsindu, Iritu, and Suritu, his strongholds, together with 150 cities which lay round about, I destroyed, I devastated, I burned with fire, into mounds and ruin heaps I turned them. While I was staying before the city of Parsindi, I placed in reserve the cavalry and pioneers.[16] Fifty of Ameka's warriors I slew in the field, I cut off their heads and bound them to the tree trunks within his palace court. Twenty men I captured alive and I immured them in the wall of his palace. From the city of Zamri I took with me the cavalry and pioneers, and marched against the cities of Ata, of Arzizu, unto which none among the kings my fathers had come nigh. The cities of Arzizu and Arsindu, his strongholds, together with ten cities which lay round about on the steep mountain of Nispi, I captured. I slew the inhabitants thereof; the cities I destroyed, I devastated, I burned with fire, and returned to my camp.

At that time I received copper, *tabbili* of copper, and rings of copper, and many *shariate* from the land of Sipirmena who(se inhabitants) speak like women.

From the city of Zamri I departed and into the difficult mountain of Lara, which was not suited for the passage of chariots and armies, with hatchets of iron I cut and with axes of bronze I hewed (a way), and I brought over the chariots and troops and came down to the city of Tukulti-Assur-asbat, which the men of the land of Lullu call Arakdi. All the kings of the land of Zamua were affrighted before the fury of my arms and the terror of my dominion, and embraced my feet. Tribute and tax,—silver, gold, lead, copper, vessels of copper, garments of brightly colored wool, horses, cattle, sheep, and wine I laid upon them (in greater measure) than before and used their forced laborers in the city of Calah. While I was staying in the land of Zamua, the men of the cities Huduni, Hartishi, Hubushkia and Gilzani were overwhelmed with the terrifying splendors of Assur, my lord, and they brought me tribute and tax,—silver, gold, horses,

---

[16] **pioneers:** Soldiers trained in siege warfare.

garments of brightly colored wool, cattle, flocks, and wine. The people, such as had fled from before my arms, climbed up into the mountains. I pursued them. Between the mountains of Aziru and Simaki they had settled themselves, and had made the city of Mesu their stronghold. Mount Aziru I destroyed, I devastated, and from the midst of Mount Simaki as far as the river Turnat I strewed their corpses. 500 of their warriors I slew and carried off their heavy spoil, the cities I burned with fire.

At that time, in the land of Zamua, the city of Atlila, which for the scepter of the king of Karduniash they had seized, had decayed and had become a mound and ruin heap. Assur-Nasir-Pal restored it. I surrounded it with a wall, and I erected therein a palace for my royal dwelling, I adorned it and made it glorious and greater than it was before. Grain and straw from the whole land I heaped up within it, and I called its name Der-Assur.

READING AND DISCUSSION QUESTIONS

1. How does Ashur-Nasir-Pal II describe his victories? What aspects of the story might he have exaggerated to make them seem more impressive?

2. Why would Ashur-Nasir-Pal II want to publicize his conquests? What connection did he implicitly make between his military prowess and his legitimacy as a ruler?

2-5 | A Persian Emperor Proclaims His Righteousness

CYRUS OF PERSIA, *Righteous Rule* (ca. 530 B.C.E.)

An important aspect of Cyrus the Great's imperial strategy, and one that would be continued by his successors, was the effort to present Persian kings as righteous rulers. Cyrus depicted himself as a champion of right order, restoring traditions and bringing prosperity to the regions he conquered. As he described them, his wars were not against other peoples, but against their leaders, men who, through their own misdeeds, had betrayed their people and forfeited the right to rule. As you read the royal inscription included below, compare it to Ashur-Nasir-Pal II's account of his accomplishments (Document 2-4). How do they differ? What do the differences you note tell you about the governing strategies of the two emperors?

I am Cyrus, king of the world, great king, legitimate king, king of Babylon, king of Sumer and Akkad, king of the four rims [of the earth], son of Cambyses, great king, king of Anshan, grandson of Cyrus, great king, king of Anshan, descendant of Teispes, great king, king of Anshan, of a family [that] always [exercised]

James B. Pritchard, ed., *Ancient Near Eastern Texts Relating to the Old Testament*, 3d edition with Supplement. © 1950, 1955, 1969, renewed 1978 by Princeton University Press.

kingship; whose rule Bel and Nabu[17] love, whom they want as king to please their hearts.

When I entered Babylon as a friend and [when] I established the seat of government in the palace of the ruler under jubilation and rejoicing, Marduk,[18] the great lord (induced) the magnanimous inhabitants of Babylon (to love me), and I was daily endeavoring to worship him. My numerous troops walked around in Babylon in peace, I did not allow anybody to terrorize [any place] of the [country of Sumer] and Akkad. I strove for peace in Babylon, [I abolished] the [labor tribute] which was against their [social] standing. I brought relief to their dilapidated housings, putting an end to their complaints. Marduk, the great Lord, was well pleased with my deeds and sent friendly blessings to myself, Cyrus, the king who worships him, to Cambyses, my son, the offspring of my loins, as well as to all my troops, and we all [praised] his great [godhead] joyously, standing before him in peace.

All the kings of the entire world from the Upper to the Lower Sea, those who are seated in throne rooms, [those who] live in other [types of buildings as well as] all the kings of the West land living in tents, brought their heavy tributes and kissed my feet in Babylon. [As to the region] from . . . as far as Ashur and Susa, Agade, Eshnuna, the towns of Zamban, Me-Turnu, Der, as well as the region of the Gutium, I returned to [these] sacred cities on the other sides of the Tigris, the sanctuaries of which have been ruins for a long time, the images which [used] to live therein and established for them permanent sanctuaries. I [also] gathered all their [former] inhabitants and returned [to them] their habitations. Furthermore, I resettled upon the command of Marduk, the great lord, all the gods of Sumer and Akkad who Nabonidus[19] has brought into Babylon to the anger of the lord of the gods, unharmed, in the [former] chapels, the places which make them happy.

May all the gods whom I have resettled in their sacred cities ask daily Bel and Nabu for a long life for me and may they recommend me [to him]; to Marduk, my lord, they may say this: "Cyrus, the king who worships you, and Cambyses, his son, . . . all of them I settled in a peaceful place . . . ducks and doves . . . I endeavored to repair their dwelling places."

READING AND DISCUSSION QUESTIONS

1. What does Cyrus mean when he claims that he entered Babylon as a friend? To whom was he a friend?

2. What reforms and improvements did Cyrus bring to Babylon? What motives might he have had for his actions?

3. Why might it have been important to Cyrus to be seen as a good king?

---

[17] **Bel and Nabu:** Babylonian gods.
[18] **Marduk:** The Mesopotamian god who created humans.
[19] **Nabonidus:** The last king of the Neo-Babylonian empire, whom Cyrus overthrew.

VIEWPOINTS COMPARATIVE QUESTIONS

1. What qualities did the Assyrians look for in an emperor? What about the Persians? What characteristics, if any, did both societies associate with a successful ruler?

2. How do these documents help explain the fact that the Persian Empire was both larger and more enduring than that of the Assyrians?

▪ COMPARATIVE QUESTIONS ▪

1. How are the laws in Hammurabi's code similar to or different from those in the Hebrew book of Exodus?

2. What do the sources in the chapter tell you about the different ways in which the peoples of the ancient world saw the relationship between the individual and the divine? What do they tell you about the relationship between the state or ruler and the divine?

3. How do the depictions of kings differ in Hammurabi's code, Ashur-Nasir-Pal II's résumé, and Cyrus the Great's inscription?

The Foundation of Indian Society

to 300 C.E.

The earliest society in South Asia was the Harappan civilization (ca. 2500–2000 B.C.E.) based in the Indus River Valley. They left written records, but their script remains undeciphered. With the Harappans' decline, a group who called themselves Aryans came to dominate North India. Around 1500 B.C.E., the Aryans began to compose oral poetry in Sanskrit, an Indo-European language closely related to ancient Persian and Hittite. According to the *Rig Veda* (see Document 1-1), the earliest record of this sacred poetry, the Aryan religion initially focused on ritual sacrifices conducted by the priestly caste (Brahmins), who sought material benefits. Later religious movements in India, such as Buddhism, instead sought to fill spiritual needs and ignored the Aryans' strict caste system. In reaction to Buddhism, the Brahmins rejected ritual sacrifices and helped spread the worship of gods, such as Krishna, to all levels of society.

3-1 | Harappan Urban Planning

A Residential Street in Mohenjo-daro
(ca. 2500–2000 B.C.E.)

The Harappan civilization had a system of writing, but no one has been able to decipher it. Consequently, our understanding of Harappan society and culture depends largely on archaeological evidence. Instead of reading Harappan records, we must study the physical artifacts of Harappan civilization and draw inferences about the people who created them. This photograph of a residential street in the great city of Mohenjo-daro contains no written symbols, no sculptures, no depictions of any kind of Harappan life. Nonetheless it has much to tell us about Harappan society. As you examine it, think about what it reveals about the people who built Mohenjo-daro. What does it tell you about the resources they controlled, the organization of their society, and the power and authority of their leaders?

WERNER FORMAN ARCHIVE/Bridgeman Images.

READING AND DISCUSSION QUESTIONS

1. What adjectives would you use to describe this street? What does the street suggest about the values of Mohenjo-daro's residents?

2. What must have been required to build a city with streets like this? What kind of society could marshal the necessary labor, resources, and planning?

VIEWPOINTS

The Path to Enlightenment

Buddhism offered a direct challenge to the Brahmanic religion, rejecting both animal sacrifice and the caste system. In so doing, it attacked the privileged role of Brahmins in religious life. No longer would contact with the divine require priestly mediation. Instead, the road to spiritual advancement and enlightenment would be open to everyone. In response to Buddhism, Brahmanism evolved into Hinduism, a religion that retained the caste system but created more space for non-Brahmins to participate in unmediated and personal religious experiences. The documents included in this feature provide an opportunity to compare and contrast the answers of Buddhism and Hinduism to a question that was at the heart of both religions: how does one achieve enlightenment? As you read the documents, be sure to look for similarities as well as differences. Are there important spiritual issues on which the two religions agree? On what essential points do they diverge?

3-2 | Suffering and Enlightenment
THE BUDDHA, *The Buddha Obtains Enlightenment* (ca. 530–29 B.C.E.)

The Buddha was born into a *kshatriya* (warrior caste) family near the Himalayas around 563 B.C.E. At the age of twenty-nine, he had four visions that made him question the value of his sheltered and comfortable life. He envisioned an old man, a sick person, a dead person, and a monk. Following in the path of the monk, he experimented with extreme forms of asceticism before developing the "Middle Path." Through meditation he obtained enlightenment, or the freedom from reincarnation and desire that results from understanding the reality of life, which the Buddha taught was based on suffering. He spent the rest of his life promoting his ideas throughout the Ganges Valley.

The following passage includes two selections from the "Pali Canon." Theravada Buddhists believe that the "Pali Canon" contains the words of the Buddha, but the current text was not written down until 29 B.C.E., after having circulated orally for five centuries.

And the Future Buddha, thinking, "I will carry austerity to the uttermost," tried various plans, such as living on one sesamum seed or on one grain of rice a day, and even ceased taking nourishment altogether, and moreover rebuffed the gods

---

Henry C. Warrant, ed. and trans., *Buddhism in Translation* (Cambridge, Mass.: Harvard University Press, 1909), 70–81.

when they came and attempted to infuse nourishment through the pores of his skin. By this lack of nourishment his body became emaciated to the last degree, and lost its golden color, and became black, and his thirty-two physical characteristics as a great being became obscured. Now, one day, as he was deep in a trance of suppressed breathing, he was attacked by violent pains, and fell senseless to the ground, at one end of his walking-place. . . .

Now the six years which the Great Being thus spent in austerities were like time spent in endeavoring to tie the air into knots. And coming to the decision, "These austerities are not the way to enlightenment," he went begging through villages and market-towns for ordinary material food, and lived upon it. And his thirty-two physical characteristics as a great being again appeared, and the color of his body became like unto gold. . . .

Then the Great Being, saying to himself, "This is the immovable spot on which all The Buddhas have planted themselves! This is the place for destroying passion's net!" took hold of his handful of grass by one end, and shook it out there. And straightway the blades of grass formed themselves into a seat fourteen cubits long, of such symmetry of shape as not even the most skillful painter or carver could have designed.

Then the Future Buddha turned his back to the trunk of the Bo-tree and faced the east. And making the mighty resolution, "Let my skin, and sinews, and bones become dry, and welcome! and let all the flesh and blood in my body dry up! but never from this seat will I stir, until I have attained the supreme and absolute wisdom!" he sat himself down cross-legged in an unconquerable position, from which not even the descent of a hundred thunder-bolts at once could have dislodged him.

At this point the god Māra,[1] exclaiming, "Prince Siddhattha is desirous of passing beyond my control, but I will never allow it!" went and announced the news to his army, and sounding the Māra war-cry, drew out for battle. Now Māra's army extended in front of him for twelve leagues, and to the right and to the left for twelve leagues, and in the rear as far as to the confines of the world, and it was nine leagues high. And when it shouted, it made an earthquake-like roaring and rumbling over a space of a thousand leagues. And the god Māra, mounting his elephant, which was a hundred and fifty leagues high, and had the name "Girded-with-mountains," caused a thousand arms to appear on his body, and with these he grasped a variety of weapons. Also in the remainder of that army, no two persons carried the same weapon; and diverse also in their appearances and countenances, the host swept on like a flood to overwhelm the Great Being.

. . . [Buddha is attacked many times by the armies of Māra, but he resists them.]

And the followers of Māra fled away in all directions. No two went the same way, but leaving their head-ornaments and their cloaks behind, they fled straight before them.

---

[1] **Māra:** Here, ignorance of the true nature of reality is represented as a demon.

Then the hosts of the gods, when they saw the army of Māra flee, cried out, "Māra is defeated! Prince Siddhattha has conquered! Let us go celebrate the victory!" And the snakes egging on the snakes, the birds the birds, the deities the deities, and the Brahma-angels the Brahma-angels, they came with perfumes, garlands, and other offerings in their hands to the Great Being on the throne of wisdom. And as they came—

274. "The victory now hath this illustrious Buddha won!
    The Wicked One, the Slayer, hath defeated been!"
    Thus round the throne of wisdom shouted joyously
    The bands of snakes their songs of victory for the Sage; . . .

When thus he had attained to omniscience, and was the center of such unparalleled glory and homage, and so many prodigies were happening about him, he breathed forth that solemn utterance which has never been omitted by any of The Buddhas:—

278. "Through birth and rebirth's endless round,
    Seeking in vain, I hastened on,
    To find who framed this edifice.
    What misery!—birth incessantly!

279. "O builder! I've discovered thee!
    This fabric thou shalt ne'er rebuild!
    Thy rafters all are broken now,
    And pointed roof demolished lies!
    This mind has demolition reached,
    And seen the last of all desire!"

At that time The Buddha, The Blessed One, was dwelling at Uruvelā at the foot of the Bo-tree on the banks of the river Nerañjarā, having just attained the Buddhaship. Then The Blessed One sat cross-legged for seven days together at the foot of the Bo-tree experiencing the bliss of emancipation.

Then The Blessed One, during the first watch of the night, thought over Dependent Origination both forward and back:—

On ignorance depends karma;
On karma depends consciousness;
On consciousness depend name and form;
On name and form depend the six organs of sense;
On the six organs of sense depends contact;
On contact depends sensation;
On sensation depends desire;
On desire depends attachment;
On attachment depends existence;
On existence depends birth;
On birth depend old age and death, sorrow, lamentation, misery, grief, and
    despair.

Thus does this entire aggregation of misery arise. But on the complete fading out and cessation of ignorance ceases karma; on the cessation of karma ceases consciousness; on the cessation of consciousness cease name and form; on the cessation of name and form cease the six organs of sense; on the cessation of the six organs of sense ceases contact; on the cessation of contact ceases sensation; on the cessation of sensation ceases desire; on the cessation of desire ceases attachment; on the cessation of attachment ceases existence; on the cessation of existence ceases birth; on the cessation of birth cease old age and death, sorrow, lamentation, misery, grief, and despair. Thus does this entire aggregation of misery cease.

READING AND DISCUSSION QUESTIONS

1. How does the Buddha begin his quest for enlightenment? Is he successful?
2. What does the Buddha try in his second attempt? What opposes him?
3. In this passage, Māra (Ignorance) is personified. Why?
4. What knowledge does enlightenment bring? How is enlightenment described?

3-3 | The Search for Enlightenment in the *Upanishads*

From the Upanishads: *On the Nature of the Soul*
(ca. 450 B.C.E.)

The development of Buddhism, which stressed spiritual, rather than material, concerns, led to reform within the priestly caste in India. Although the Vedas were still revered, the Vedic sacrifices and rituals became less important than a metaphysical understanding of the world and humankind's place within it. This movement is represented in the texts called the *Upanishads*, which are considered the end of the Vedas (*vedanta*). Composed by many different writers with many different philosophical viewpoints, the *Upanishads* stress that each individual soul (*atman*) is a part of the spiritual substance of the universe (*Brahman*).

The Need for a Competent Teacher of the Soul

7. He who by many is not obtainable even to hear of,
   He whom many, even when hearing, know not—
   Wonderful is the declarer, proficient the obtainer of Him!
   Wonderful the knower, proficiently taught!
8. Not, when proclaimed by an inferior man, is He
   To be well understood, [though] being manifoldly considered.
   Unless declared by another, there is no going thither;
   For He is inconceivably more subtle than what is of subtle measure.

Robert Ernest Hume, *The Thirteen Principal Upanishads* (London: Oxford University Press, 1921), 347–352.

36 Chapter 3 The Foundation of Indian Society, to 300 C.E.

VIEWPOINTS

9. Not by reasoning is this thought to be attained.
    Proclaimed by another, indeed, it is for easy understanding, dearest
        friend!—
    This which thou hast attained! Ah, thou art of true steadfastness!
    May there be for us a questioner the like of thee, O Naciketas!

Steadfast Renunciation and Self-Meditation Required

Naciketas:[2]

10. I know that what is known as treasure is something inconstant.
    For truly, that which is steadfast is not obtained by those who are
        unsteadfast.
    Therefore the Naciketas-fire has been built up by me,
    And with means which are inconstant I have obtained that which is
        constant.

Death:

11. The obtainment of desire, the foundation of the world,
    The endlessness of will, the safe shore of fearlessness,
    The greatness of praise, the wide extent, the foundation (having seen),
    Thou, O Naciketas, a wise one, hast with steadfastness let [these] go!
12. Him who is hard to see, entered into the hidden,
    Set in the secret place [of the heart], dwelling in the depth, primeval—
    By considering him as God, through the Yoga-study of what pertains to self,
    The wise man leaves joy and sorrow behind.

The Absolutely Unqualified Soul

13. When a mortal has heard this and fully comprehended,
    Has torn off what is concerned with the right, and has taken Him as the
        subtle,
    Then he rejoices, for indeed he has obtained what is to be rejoiced in.
    I regard Naciketas a dwelling open [for Ātman].
14. Apart from the right and apart from the unright,
    Apart from both what has been done and what has not been done here,
    Apart from what has been and what is to be—
    What thou seest as that, speak that!

[Naciketas being unable to mention that absolutely unqualified object, Death
continues to explain:]

---

[2] **Naciketas:** The seeker of knowledge.

The Mystic Syllable "Om" as an Aid

15. The word which all the Vedas rehearse,
    And which all austerities proclaim,
    Desiring which men live the life of religious studentship—
    That word to thee I briefly declare.
    That is *Om*!
16. That syllable, truly, indeed, is Brahma!
    That syllable indeed is the supreme!
    Knowing that syllable, truly, indeed,
    Whatever one desires is his!
17. That is the best support.
    That is the supreme support.
    Knowing that support,
    One becomes happy in the Brahma-world.

The Eternal Indestructible Soul

18. The wise one [i.e., the soul, the self] is not born, nor dies.
    This one has not come from anywhere, has not become anyone.
    Unborn, constant, eternal, primeval, this one
    Is not slain when the body is slain.
19. If the slayer think to slay,
    If the slain think himself slain,
    Both these understand not.
    This one slays not, nor is slain. . . .

[From the Third Valli]
Parable of the Individual Soul in a Chariot

3. Know thou the soul as riding in a chariot,
   The body as the chariot.
   Know thou the intellect as the chariot-driver,
   And the mind as the reins.
4. The senses, they say, are the horses;
   The objects of sense, what they range over.
   The self combined with senses and mind
   Wise men call "the enjoyer."
5. He who has not understanding,
   Whose mind is not constantly held firm—
   His senses are uncontrolled,
   Like the vicious horses of a chariot-driver.
6. He, however, who has understanding,
   Whose mind is constantly held firm—
   His senses are under control,
   Like the good horses of a chariot driver.

Intelligent Control of the Soul's Chariot Needed to Arrive Beyond Transmigration

7. He, however, who has not understanding,
   Who is unmindful and ever impure,
   Reaches not the goal,
   But goes on to transmigration.[3]
8. He, however, who has understanding,
   Who is mindful and ever pure,
   Reaches the goal
   From which he is born no more.
9. He, however, who has the understanding of a chariot-driver,
   A man who reins in his mind—
   He reaches the end of his journey,
   That highest place of Vishnu.[4]

READING AND DISCUSSION QUESTIONS

1. According to the text, why does a student need a teacher to understand the *Upanishads*? How should one go about seeking the nature of the soul? What ways of seeking ultimate reality are discouraged by this text?

2. What is the nature of the soul? What is the body?

3. How are the body and mind like a chariot and driver?

4. What is the consequence of not obtaining knowledge of the soul and the universe? What happens to a person who dies knowing about the soul?

VIEWPOINTS COMPARATIVE QUESTIONS

1. In Buddhism, what is the most important obstacle to achieving enlightenment, and how can that obstacle be overcome? What is the most important obstacle in Hinduism? How can it be overcome?

2. How does each religion characterize the relationship between the mind and the body? What importance is assigned to each?

---

[3] **transmigration:** In Hinduism, the soul is thought to live in many bodies through many cycles of reincarnation.

[4] **Vishnu:** This normally refers to the Hindu god of restoration, but here has a more metaphorical connotation of heavenly understanding.

3-4 | Social Mores in Ancient India
From *The Laws of Manu* (ca. 100 B.C.E.–200 C.E.)

The Laws of Manu were likely compiled by more than one person and later edited and expanded by others. In Indian mythology, Manu was the sole survivor of a flood, much like Utnapishtim from *The Epic of Gilgamesh* (Document 2-1). In many ways, *The Laws of Manu* are less a legal code than an instruction manual, explaining how different social classes by birth (*varna*) and occupation (*jati*) should fulfill their duty (*dharma*). Ascribing the laws to Manu suggests that they were given divine sanction and had universal meaning.

Varna[5]

The Brahmin, the Kshatriya, and the Vaisya castes are the twice-born ones,[6] but the fourth, the Sudra, has one birth only; there is no fifth caste.[7] . . .

To Brahmins he [Brahman, the creator god] assigned teaching and studying the Vedas, sacrificing for their own benefit and for others, giving and accepting of alms.

The Kshatriya he commanded to protect the people, to bestow gifts, to offer sacrifices, to study the Vedas, and to abstain from attaching himself to sensual pleasures.

The Vaisya to tend cattle, to bestow gifts, to offer sacrifices, to study the Vedas, to trade, to lend money, and to cultivate land.

One occupation only the lord prescribed to the Sudra, to serve meekly . . . these other three castes.

Jatis[8]

From a male Sudra are born an Ayogava, a Kshattri, and a Kandala, the lowest of men, by Vaisya, Kshatriya, and Brahmin females respectively, sons who owe their origin to a confusion of the castes.[9] . . .

Killing fish to Nishadas; carpenters' work to the Ayogava; to Medas, Andhras, Kunkus, and Madgus, the slaughter of wild animals. . . .

B. Guehler, trans., *The Laws of Manu*, in F. Max Mueller, ed., *The Sacred Books of the East*, 50 vols. (Oxford: Clarendon Press, 1879–1910), 25:24, 69, 84–85, 195–197, 260–263, 329–330, 343–344, 370–371, 402–404, 413–416, 420, 423.

[5] **varna:** The technical term for the castes, originally meaning "color." Some scholars believe that the caste system was originally based on skin color, with the lighter-skinned Aryans supplanting the darker-skinned Dasas.

[6] **the twice-born ones:** Those castes whose members could read the Vedas. They participated in a ceremony known as Upanayana in which they learned about the nature of the universe and so became born again.

[7] **fifth caste:** The untouchables would later rank below the Sudra.

[8] **jatis:** Occupations or subcastes.

[9] **sons . . . confusion of the castes:** These jatis were occupied by children whose parents belonged to different castes; the child of a male Sudra and female Brahmin occupied the lowest jati.

But the dwellings of Kandalas . . . shall be outside the village. . . .

Their dress shall be the garments of the dead, they shall eat their food from broken dishes, black iron shall be their ornaments, and they must always wander from place to place.

A man who fulfills a religious duty, shall not seek intercourse with them; their [Kandala] transactions shall be among themselves, and their marriages with their equals. . . .

At night they shall not walk about in villages and in towns.

By day they may go about for the purpose of their work, distinguished by marks at the king's command, and they shall carry out the corpses of persons who have no relatives; that is a settled rule.

By the king's order they shall always execute the criminals, in accordance with the law, and they shall take for themselves the clothes, the beds, and the ornaments of such criminals.

Dharma[10]

A king who knows the sacred law must inquire into the laws of castes [jatis], of districts, of guilds, and of families, and settle the peculiar law of each. . . .

Among the several occupations the most commendable are teaching the Vedas for a Brahmin, protecting the people for a Kshatriya, and trade for a Vaisya.

But a Brahmin, unable to subsist by his peculiar occupations just mentioned, may live according to the law applicable to Kshatriyas; for the latter is next to him in rank. . . .

A man of low caste [varna] who through covetousness lives by the occupations of a higher one, the king shall deprive of his property and banish.

It is better to discharge one's own duty incompletely than to perform completely that of another; for he who lives according to the law of another caste is instantly excluded from his own.

A Vaisya who is unable to subsist by his own duties, may even maintain himself by a Sudra's mode of life, avoiding however acts forbidden to him, and he should give it up, when he is able to do so. . . .

Abstention from injuring creatures, veracity, abstention from unlawfully appropriating the goods of others, purity, and control of the organs,[11] Manu has declared to be the summary of the law for the four castes.

The Nature of Women

It is the nature of women to seduce men in this world; for that reason the wise are never unguarded in the company of females. . . .

---

[10] **dharma:** The duties of each caste.
[11] **control of the organs:** Especially sexual organs.

For women no rite is performed with sacred texts, thus the law is settled; women who are destitute of strength and destitute of the knowledge of Vedic texts are as impure as falsehood itself; that is a fixed rule.

Honoring Women

Where women are honored, there the gods are pleased; but where they are not honored, no sacred rite yields rewards.

Where the female relations live in grief, the family soon wholly perishes; but that family where they are not unhappy ever prospers.

Female Property Rights

A wife, a son, and a slave, these three are declared to have no property; the wealth which they earn is acquired for him to whom they belong. . . .

What was given before the nuptial fire, what was given on the bridal procession, what was given in token of love, and what was received from her brother, mother, or father, that is called the six-fold property of a woman.

Such property, as well as a gift subsequent and what was given to her by her affectionate husband, shall go to her offspring, even if she dies in the lifetime of her husband. . . .

But when the mother has died, all the uterine [biological] brothers and the uterine sisters shall equally divide the mother's estate.

A Woman's Dependence

In childhood a female must be subject to her father, in youth to her husband, when her lord is dead to her sons; a woman must never be independent.

She must not seek to separate herself from her father, husband, or sons; by leaving them she would make both her own and her husband's families contemptible. . . .

Him to whom her father may give her, or her brother with the father's permission, she shall obey as long as he lives, and when he is dead, she must not insult his memory.

Betrothal

No father who knows the law must take even the smallest gratuity for his daughter; for a man who, through avarice, takes a gratuity, is a seller of his offspring. . . .

Three years let a damsel wait, though she be marriageable,[12] but after that time let her choose for herself a bridegroom of equal caste and rank. If, being not

---

[12] **marriageable:** Girls were often married beginning at age twelve.

given in marriage, she herself seeks a husband, she incurs no guilt, nor does he whom she weds.

Marriage and Its Duties

To be mothers were women created, and to be fathers men; religious rites, therefore, are ordained in the Vedas to be performed by the husband together with the wife. . . .

No sacrifice, no vow, no fast must be performed by women apart from their husbands; if a wife obeys her husband, she will for that reason alone be exalted in heaven. . . .

By violating her duty towards her husband, a wife is disgraced in this world, after death she enters the womb of a jackal, and is tormented by diseases as punishment for her sin. . . .

Let the husband employ his wife in the collection and expenditure of his wealth, in keeping everything clean, in the fulfillment of religious duties, in the preparation of his food, and in looking after the household utensils. . . .

Drinking spirituous liquor, associating with wicked people, separation from the husband, rambling abroad, sleeping at unreasonable hours, and dwelling in other men's houses, are the six causes of the ruin of women. . . .

Offspring, religious rites, faithful service, highest conjugal happiness and heavenly bliss for the ancestors and oneself, depend on one's wife alone. . . .

"Let mutual fidelity continue until death" . . . may be considered as the summary of the highest law for husband and wife.

Let man and woman, united in marriage, constantly exert themselves, that they may not be disunited and may not violate their mutual fidelity.

Divorce

For one year let a husband bear with a wife who hates him; but after a year let him deprive her of her property and cease to cohabit with her. . . .

But she who shows aversion towards a mad or outcaste[13] husband, a eunuch,[14] one destitute of manly strength, or one afflicted with such diseases as punish crimes,[15] shall neither be cast off nor be deprived of her property. . . .

A barren wife may be superseded [replaced] in the eighth year, she whose children all die in the tenth, she who bears only daughters in the eleventh, but she who is quarrelsome without delay.

But a sick wife who is kind to her husband and virtuous in her conduct, may be superseded only with her own consent and must never be disgraced.

---

[13] **outcaste:** Someone literally removed from their caste.
[14] **eunuch:** A castrated male. Here, *eunuch* may mean an impotent man.
[15] **such diseases as punish crimes:** Illness caused by evil karmic actions.

READING AND DISCUSSION QUESTIONS

1. According to the laws, how is society organized? What are the rights and obligations of each group within society?

2. What do the laws suggest about the status and role of women in Indian society?

3-5 | Ashoka Makes His Will Known

ASHOKA, From *Thirteenth Rock Edict* (256 B.C.E.)

Ashoka was the third king of the Mauryan Dynasty of India. Having embarked on a series of conquests culminating at the Battle of Kalinga, Ashoka converted to Buddhism. He began reforming the rule of his empire, and to publicize his actions, he set up fifty-foot-tall rock pillars in at least thirty locations. These pillars were rediscovered and translated in the early nineteenth century. They seem to reflect the speaking style of Ashoka himself and are not written in a highly polished style. In the following edict, Ashoka describes the reasons for his conversion to Buddhism.

When the king, Beloved of the Gods and of Gracious Mien, had been consecrated eight years Kalinga was conquered, 150,000 people were deported, 100,000 were killed, and many times that number died. But after the conquest of Kalinga, the Beloved of the Gods began to follow Righteousness (Dharma), to love Righteousness, and to give instruction in Righteousness. Now the Beloved of the Gods regrets the conquest of Kalinga, for when an independent country is conquered people are killed, they die, or are deported, and that the Beloved of the Gods finds very painful and grievous. And this he finds even more grievous—that all the inhabitants—bra-hmans, ascetics, and other sectarians, and householders who are obedient to superiors, parents, and elders, who treat friends, acquaintances, companions, relatives, slaves, and servants with respect, and are firm in their faith—all suffer violence, murder, and separation from their loved ones. Even those who are fortunate enough not to have lost those near and dear to them are afflicted at the misfortunes of friends, acquaintances, companions, and relatives. The participation of all men in common suffering is grievous to the Beloved of the Gods. Moreover there is no land, except that of the Greeks,[16] where groups of bra-hmans and ascetics are not found, or where men are not members of one sect or another. So now, even if the number of those killed and captured in the conquest of Kalinga had been a hundred or a thousand times less, it would be grievous to the Beloved of the Gods. The Beloved of the Gods will forgive as far as he can, and he even conciliates the forest tribes of his dominions;

[16] **Greeks:** Areas conquered by Alexander but by this time split up into many different realms, known as the Hellenistic kingdoms.

but he warns them that there is power even in the remorse of the Beloved of the Gods, and he tells them to reform, lest they be killed.

For all beings the Beloved of the Gods desires security, self-control, calm of mind, and gentleness. The Beloved of the Gods considers that the greatest victory is the victory of Righteousness; and this he has won here (in India) and even five hundred leagues beyond his frontiers in the realm of the Greek king Antiochus, and beyond Antiochus among the four kings Ptolemy, Antigonus, Magas, and Alexander.[17] Even where the envoys of the Beloved of the Gods have not been sent hear of the way in which he follows and teaches Righteousness, and they too follow it and will follow it. Thus he achieves a universal conquest, and conquest always gives a feeling of pleasure; yet it is but a slight pleasure, for the Beloved of the Gods only looks on that which concerns the next life as of great importance.

I have had this inscription of Righteousness engraved that all my sons and grandsons may not seek to gain new victories, that in whatever victories they may gain they may prefer forgiveness and light punishment, that they may consider the only [valid] victory the victory of Righteousness, which is of value both in this world and the next, and that all their pleasure may be in Righteousness.

READING AND DISCUSSION QUESTIONS

1. Why did Ashoka convert to Buddhism? What does this edict reveal about Buddhist ideas about war?

2. According to Ashoka, what is a Buddhist conquest? How should a Buddhist king rule?

▪ COMPARATIVE QUESTIONS ▪

1. Compare and contrast the *Upanishads* and *The Laws of Manu*. What aspects of Hinduism did each stress? How would you explain their differences in tone and emphasis?

2. Compare and contrast Buddhist and Hindu views on the quest for enlightenment. What similarities and differences do you note?

3. Compare Ashoka's edict in this chapter with Hammurabi's code (Document 2-2) and Ashur-Nasir-Pal II's résumé (Document 2-4) in Chapter 2. Are there more similarities or more differences between Indian styles of rule and those in Mesopotamia?

4. What are the differences between ancient Indian religion and the religions practiced in the ancient Near East? (See Chapter 2.)

---

[17] **Antiochus . . . Alexander:** Antiochus was the king of Seleucid Asia, which shared a border with Ashoka in Central Asia; Ptolemy was king of Hellenistic Egypt; Antigonus of Hellenistic Macedon; Magas of Cyrene (modern-day Libya); and Alexander of the island of Epirus on the west coast of Greece.

4

China's Classical Age
to 221 B.C.E.

The Shang Dynasty (ca. 1500–1050 B.C.E.) was the first Chinese dynasty to leave behind evidence of its culture, including written texts and bronze weapons. Following its collapse, China shifted between periods of unified empire and civil war, which often ushered in new dynasties. The Zhou Dynasty (ca. 1050–256 B.C.E.) helped establish this pattern by ascribing the fall of the Shang to the Mandate of Heaven, which argued that dynasties lose Heaven's blessing when they become corrupt and can at that point be legitimately overthrown. After a long period of rule, even the Zhou Dynasty lost control of China, leading to a period of civil war known as the Warring States Period (403–221 B.C.E.). The political chaos of this time inspired a series of important political philosophies, such as Confucianism, Daoism, and Legalism, on which later Chinese culture would be built.

4-1 | Art and Culture in Shang China
Detail of Ritual Vase Known as the Tigress
(ca. 1200 B.C.E.)

This ritual vase, known as the Tigress, provides a good example of the high quality and enigmatic nature of Shang bronze work. It is beautifully crafted, visually interesting, and bursting with animal motifs. Lizards crawl up the tigress's legs, animal heads attach the sides of the handle to the vase, snakes are etched into the tigress's face, and a deer is perched atop the tigress's head. The vase also includes a figure of a human child whose head is at least partially inside the tigress's mouth (see detail). As your textbook makes clear, there is no scholarly consensus on how to interpret pieces such as this. As you examine the vase, think about what it suggests to you about Shang China. If you had to speculate, what meanings would you attach to the form and decoration of the Tigress?

DE AGOSTINI EDITORE/Bridgeman Images.

READING AND DISCUSSION QUESTIONS

1. In your opinion, is the child clinging to the tigress for protection, or is the child about to be devoured?

2. What connections can you make between this object and what you know about Shang society and religion from your textbook?

3. What light does the vase shed on the artistic and aesthetic preferences of Shang elites?

4-2 | Confucius Offers Advice on Kingship
From *Book of Documents* (ca. 900–100 B.C.E.)

The *Book of Documents* is one of the five texts traditionally ascribed to Confucius (551–479 B.C.E.) and studied as the basis of Confucianism. It was compiled in its original form by 300 B.C.E.; however, it had to be reconstructed by Chinese scholars after the Qin Dynasty (221–206 B.C.E.) attempted to destroy all Confucian texts. The *Book of Documents* claims to draw from the most ancient periods of Chinese history, but many of the texts are forgeries or fakes. The following advice given to the heir of Zheng Tang, the first Shang king, by Zheng Tang's chief minister supposedly dates to the early Shang Dynasty (1500–1050 B.C.E.), but its references to the Mandate of Heaven suggest it was written during the Zhou period (1050–256 B.C.E.) to provide a precedent for revolt against the Shang Dynasty.

In the twelfth month of the first year . . . Yi Yin sacrificed to the former king [Zheng Tang], and presented the heir-king reverently before the shrine of his grandfather. All the princes from the domain of the nobles and the royal domain were present; all the officers also, each continuing to discharge his particular duties, were there to receive the orders of the chief minister. Yi Yin then clearly described the complete virtue of the Meritorious Ancestor [Zheng Tang] for the instruction of the young king.

He said, "Oh! of old the former kings of Xia[1] cultivated earnestly their virtue, and then there were no calamities from Heaven.[2] The spirits of the hills and rivers likewise were all in tranquility; and the birds and beasts, the fishes and tortoises, all enjoyed their existence according to their nature. But their descendant did not follow their example, and great Heaven sent down calamities, employing the agency of our ruler [Zheng Tang] who was in possession of its favoring appointment. The attack on Xia may be traced to the orgies in Ming Tiao [where Jie, the last Xia ruler, was defeated]. . . . Our king of Shang brilliantly displayed his sagely prowess; for oppression he substituted his generous gentleness; and the millions of the people gave him their hearts. Now your Majesty is entering on the inheritance of his virtue;—all depends on how you commence your reign. To set up love, it is for you to love your relations; to set up respect, it is for you to respect your elders. The commencement is in the family and the state. . . .

"Oh! the former king began with careful attention to the bonds that hold men together. He listened to expostulation, and did not seek to resist it; he conformed to the wisdom of the ancients; occupying the highest position, he displayed intelligence; occupying an inferior position, he displayed his loyalty; he

---

James Legge, trans., *The Sacred Books of China: The Texts of Confucianism*, in F. Max Mueller, ed., *The Sacred Books of the East*, 50 vols. (Oxford: Clarendon Press, 1879–1910), 3:92–95.

[1] **Xia:** Traditionally defined as the first dynasty in China.

[2] **no calamities from Heaven:** This seems to refer to the later concept of the Mandate of Heaven developed by the Zhou Dynasty and used to justify the overthrow of the Shang.

allowed the good qualities of the men whom he employed and did not seek that they should have every talent. . . .

"He extensively sought out wise men, who should be helpful to you, his descendant and heir. He laid down the punishments for officers, and warned those who were in authority, saying, 'If you dare to have constant dancing in your palaces, and drunken singing in your chambers,—that is called the fashion of sorcerers; if you dare to set your hearts on wealth and women, and abandon yourselves to wandering about or to the chase,—that is called the fashion of extravagance; if you dare to despise sage words, to resist the loyal and upright, to put far from you the aged and virtuous, and to seek the company of . . . youths,—that is called the fashion of disorder. Now if a high noble or officer be addicted to one of these three fashions with their ten evil ways, his family will surely come to ruin; if the prince of a country be so addicted, his state will surely come to ruin. The minister who does not try to correct such vices in the sovereign shall be punished with branding.' . . .

"Oh! do you, who now succeed to the throne, revere these warnings in your person. Think of them!—sacred counsels of vast importance, admirable words forcibly set forth! The ways of Heaven are not invariable:—on the good-doer it sends down all blessings, and on the evil-doer it sends down all miseries. Do you but be virtuous, be it in small things or in large, and the myriad regions will have cause for rejoicing. If you not be virtuous, be it in large things or in small, it will bring the ruin of your ancestral temple."

READING AND DISCUSSION QUESTIONS

1. How does Yi Yin tell his son how he should rule? What are the qualities of a good ruler?

2. What actions are evil, according to Zheng Tang? What are the consequences of living an evil life?

3. What connection does the document make between the stability of the state and the moral character of its ruler? Can immoral actions strengthen the state? Can moral actions weaken it?

Philosophical Responses to Social and Political Disorder

It is not a coincidence that the golden age of Chinese philosophy took place during a period of social and political upheaval. In the absence of a strong centralized government, and with the old aristocratic social order in disarray, scholars and thinkers had greater freedom to explore new ideas and to develop new answers to fundamental social and political questions. Responding to the chaos, misery, and destruction of the Warring States Period, Chinese philosophers engaged in a lively debate about the best solution to China's problems. Of the Hundred Schools of Thought that emerged in this period, three proved the most important and enduring: Confucianism, Daoism, and Legalism. As you read the documents included in this feature, ask yourself how proponents of each of these three schools defined good government. What qualities did each associate with ideal rulers and ideal states?

4-3 | Confucian Maxims and Sayings

CONFUCIUS, From *Analects* (ca. 500 B.C.E.–50 C.E.)

Like the *Book of Documents*, the *Analects* were ordered burned by Qin Shihuangdi (First Emperor). The surviving text was compiled and edited more than three hundred years after the death of Confucius. Confucius did not write down the *Analects*; rather, the sayings in the *Analects* were recorded after his death by his students. The actual text contains hundreds of sayings, completely out of context, and is traditionally read with later commentaries to aid in understanding. The readings in this passage are representative of the topics contained in the *Analects* and are presented without commentaries.

[Book I]

V. The Master said, "To rule a country of a thousand chariots, there must be reverent attention to business, and sincerity; economy in expenditure, and love for the people; and the employment of them at the proper seasons."

VI. The Master said, "A youth, when at home, should be filial, and, abroad, respectful to his elders. He should be earnest and truthful. He should overflow in love to all, and cultivate the friendship of the good. When he has time and opportunity, after the performance of these things, he should employ them in polite studies."

VII. Tsze-hea said, "If a man withdraws his mind from the love of beauty, and applies it as sincerely to the love of the virtuous; if, in serving his parents, he can exert his utmost strength; if, in serving his prince, he can devote his life; if, in his intercourse with his friends, his words are sincere: — although men say that he has not learned, I will certainly say that he has." . . .

James Legge, ed., *The Life and Teachings of Confucius* (London: N. Trübner & Co., 1872), 118, 122–123, 125–126, 134–137.

[Book II]

III. 1. The Master said, "If the people be led by laws, and uniformity sought to be given them by punishments, they will try to avoid *the punishment*, but have no sense of shame.

2. "If they be led by virtue, and uniformity sought to be given them by the rules of propriety, they will have the sense of shame, and moreover will become good.". . .

V. 1. Măng E asked what filial piety was. The Master said, "It is not being disobedient."

2. *Soon after*, as Fan Ch'e was driving him, the Master told him, saying, "Măng-sun asked me what filial piety was, and I answered him — 'Not being disobedient.'"

3. Fan Ch'e said, "What did you mean?" The Master replied, "That parents, when alive, should be served according to propriety; that when dead, they should be buried according to propriety; and that they should be sacrificed to according to propriety."

VI. Măng Woo asked what filial piety was. The Master said, "Parents are anxious lest their children should be sick."

VII. Tsze-yew asked what filial piety was. The Master said, "The filial piety of now-a-days means the support of one's parents. But dogs and horses likewise are able to do something in the way of support; — without reverence, what is there to distinguish the one support given from the other?"

VIII. Tsze-hea asked what filial piety was. The Master said, "The difficulty is with the countenance. If, when *their elders* have any *troublesome* affairs, the young take the toil of them, and if, when *the young* have wine and food, they set them before their elders, is THIS to be considered filial piety?". . .

XIX. The Duke Gae asked, saying, "What should be done in order to secure the submission of the people?" Confucius replied, "Advance the upright and set aside the crooked, then the people will submit. Advance the crooked and set aside the upright, then the people will not submit."

XX. Ke K'ang asked how to cause the people to reverence *their ruler*, to be faithful to him, and to urge themselves to virtue. The Master said, "Let him preside over them with gravity; — then they will reverence him. Let him be filial and kind to all; — then they will be faithful to him. Let him advance the good and teach the incompetent; — then they will eagerly seek to be virtuous." . . .

[Book IV]

II. The Master said, "Those who are without virtue cannot abide long either in a condition of poverty and hardship, or in a condition of enjoyment. The virtuous rest in virtue; the wise desire virtue."

III. The Master said, "It is only the truly virtuous man who can love, or who can hate, others."

IV. The Master said, "If the will be set on virtue, there will be no practice of wickedness."

V. 1. The Master said, "Riches and honors are what men desire. If it cannot be obtained in the proper way, they should not be held. Poverty and meanness are what men dislike. If it cannot be obtained in the proper way, they should not be avoided.

2. "If a superior man abandon virtue, how can he fulfill the requirements of that name?

3. "The superior man does not, even for the space of a single meal, act contrary to virtue. In moments of haste, he cleaves to it. In seasons of danger, he cleaves to it."

VI. 1. The Master said, "I have not seen a person who loved virtue, or one who hated what was not virtuous. He who loved virtue would esteem nothing above it. He who hated what is not virtuous, would practice virtue in such a way that he would not allow anything that is not virtuous to approach his person.

2. "Is any one able for one day to apply his strength to virtue? I have not seen the case in which his strength would be insufficient.

3. "Should there possibly be any such case, I have not seen it."

VII. The Master said, "The faults of men are characteristic of the class to which they belong. By observing a man's faults, it may be known that he is virtuous." . . .

X. The Master said, "The superior man, in the world, does not set his mind either for anything, or against anything; what is right he will follow."

XI. The Master said, "The superior man thinks of virtue; the small man thinks of comfort. The superior man thinks of the sanctions of law; the small man thinks of favors *which he may receive.*"

XII. The Master said, "He who acts with a constant view to his own advantage will be much murmured against."

XIII. The Master said, "If *a prince* is able to govern his kingdom with the complaisance proper to the rules of propriety, what difficulty will he have? If he cannot govern it with that complaisance, what has he to do with the rules of propriety?" . . .

XVI. The Master said, "The mind of the superior man is conversant with righteousness; the mind of the mean man is conversant with gain."

XVII. The Master said, "When we see men of worth, we should think of equaling them; when we see men of contrary character, we should turn inwards and examine ourselves."

READING AND DISCUSSION QUESTIONS

1. How, according to the *Analects*, should a son interact with his parents? What is filial piety?

2. How should a ruler govern his people?

3. What are the duties of a "superior man"? What is virtue?

4-4 | Laozi Offers Advice on Following the Way

LAOZI, From *Dao De Jing: Administering the Empire* (ca. 500–400 B.C.E.)

According to tradition, the *Dao De Jing* (*The Book of the Way*) was written by the sage Laozi, an official of the Zhou court. It was eventually adopted as the basis of the Chinese philosophy of Daoism, which teaches that action should be spontaneous, not purposeful, and that the universe works through the dual forces of yin and yang. The text of the *Dao De Jing* contains many short passages: some are speculative, some philosophical, and some, such as those printed here, give advice to the rulers of China. As you read this document, think about how different Laozi's advice is compared to that offered by Confucius (Document 4-3).

LXII

The way is the refuge for the myriad creatures.
It is that by which the good man protects,
And that by which the bad is protected.
Beautiful words when offered will win high rank in return;
Beautiful deeds can raise a man above others.
Even if a man is not good, why should he be abandoned?
Hence when the emperor is set up and the three ducal ministers [highest-
    ranking advisers] are appointed, he who makes a present of the way
    without stirring from his seat is preferable to one who offers presents of jade
    disks followed by a team of four horses. Why was this way valued of old?
    Was it not said that by means of it one got what one wanted and escaped the
    consequences when one transgressed?
Therefore it is valued by the empire.

LXIII

Do that which consists in taking no action; pursue that which is not
    meddlesome; savor that which has no flavor.
Make the small big and few many; do good to him who has done you an injury.
Lay plans for the accomplishment of the difficult before it becomes difficult;
    make something big by starting with it when small.
Difficult things in the world must needs have their beginnings in the easy; big
    things must needs have their beginnings in the small.
Therefore it is because the sage never attempts to be great that he succeeds in
    becoming great.
One who makes promises rashly rarely keeps good faith; one who is in the habit
    of considering things easy meets with frequent difficulties.

Therefore even the sage treats some things as difficult. That is why in the end no
   difficulties can get the better of him.

LXIV

It is easy to maintain a situation while it is still secure;
It is easy to deal with a situation before symptoms develop;
It is easy to break a thing when it is yet brittle;
It is easy to dissolve a thing when it is yet minute.
Deal with a thing while it is still nothing;
Keep a thing in order before disorder sets in.
A tree that can fill the span of a man's arms
Grows from a downy tip;
A terrace nine stories high
Rises from hodfuls of earth;
A journey of a thousand miles
Starts from beneath one's feet.
Whoever does anything to it will ruin it; whoever lays hold of it will lose it.
Therefore the sage, because he does nothing never ruins anything; and, because
   he does not lay hold of anything, loses nothing.
In their enterprises the people
Always ruin them when on the verge of success.
Be as careful at the end as at the beginning
And there will be no ruined enterprises.
Therefore the sage desires not to desire
And does not value goods which are hard to come by;
Learns to be without learning
And makes good the mistakes of the multitude
In order to help the myriad creatures to be natural and to refrain from daring
   to act.

LXV

Of old those excelled in the pursuit of the way did not use it to enlighten the
   people but to hoodwink them. The reason why the people are difficult to
   govern is that they are too clever.
Hence to rule a state by cleverness
Will be to the detriment of the state;
Not to rule a state by cleverness
Will be a boon to the state.
These two are models.
Always to know the models
Is known as mysterious virtue.
Mysterious virtue is profound and far-reaching,
But when things turn back it turns back with them.
Only then is complete conformity [to the way] realized.

READING AND DISCUSSION QUESTIONS

1. What advice does Laozi give to the rulers of China? Is this advice practical? Could an empire be run using Laozi's suggestions?

2. What role do opposites play in these verses?

3. Do these passages depict humans as good or evil? How do they depict government?

4-5 | Han Fei Lays Out the Legalist View of Good Government

HAN FEI, *The Five Vermin* (ca. 250–25 B.C.E.)

Han Fei (ca. 280–233 B.C.E.) is the best-known proponent of the Chinese philosophy called Legalism, created by combining elements of Confucianism, Daoism, and Han Fei's own ideas. Han Fei studied under a Confucian master, Xunzi, and wrote a commentary on the *Dao De Jing* (Document 4-4). He served as a minister of the Qin Dynasty until a rival forced him to commit suicide. Legalism is renowned for its emphasis on harsh punishments and penalties for petty crimes. In Legalism, power should be concentrated in the hands of the ruler.

Past and present have different customs; new and old adopt different measures. To try to use the ways of a generous and lenient government to rule the people of a critical age is like trying to drive a runaway horse without using reins or whip. This is the misfortune that ignorance invites.

   Now the Confucians and the Mohists[3] all praise the ancient kings for their universal love of the world, saying that they looked after the people as parents look after a beloved child. And how do they prove this contention? They say, "Whenever the minister of justice administered some punishment, the ruler would purposely cancel all musical performances; and whenever the ruler learned that the death sentence had been passed on someone, he would shed tears." For this reason they praise the ancient kings.

   Now if ruler and subject must become like father and son before there can be order, then we must suppose that there is no such thing as an unruly father or son. Among human affections none takes priority over the love of parents for their children. But though all parents may show love for their children, the children are not always well behaved. . . . And if such love cannot prevent children from becoming unruly, then how can it bring the people to order? . . .

   Now here is a young man of bad character. His parents rail at him, but he does not reform; the neighbors scold, but he is unmoved; his teachers instruct him, but he refuses to change his ways. Thus, although three fine influences are

---

William Theodore de Bary, ed., *Sources of East Asian Tradition*, vol. 1: *Premodern Asia* (New York: Columbia University Press, 2008), 112–114. Copyright © 2008 by Columbia University Press. Reprinted with permission of the publisher.

   [3] **Mohists:** A fourth school of thought in China that advocated moral values and rejected violence.

brought to bear on him—the love of his parents, the efforts of the neighbors, the wisdom of his teachers—yet he remains unmoved and refuses to change so much as a hair on his shin. But let the district magistrate send out the government soldiers to enforce the law and search for evildoers, and then he is filled with terror, reforms his conduct, and changes his ways. . . .

The best rewards are those that are generous and predictable, so that the people may profit by them. The best penalties are those that are severe and inescapable, so that the people will fear them. The best laws are those that are uniform and inflexible, so that the people can understand them. . . .

Hardly ten men of true integrity and good faith can be found today, and yet the offices of the state number in the hundreds. If they must be filled by men of integrity and good faith, then there will never be enough men to go around; and if the offices are left unfilled, then those whose business it is to govern will dwindle in numbers while disorderly men increase. Therefore the way of the enlightened ruler is to unify the laws instead of seeking for wise men, to lay down firm policies instead of longing for men of good faith. Hence his laws never fail him, and there is no felony or deceit among his officials. . . .

Farming requires a lot of hard work, but people will do it because they say, "This way we can get rich." War is a dangerous undertaking, but people will take part in it because they say, "This way we can become eminent." Now if men who devote themselves to literature or study the art of persuasive speaking are able to get the fruits of wealth without the hard work of the farmer and can gain the advantages of eminence without the danger of battle, then who will not take up such pursuits? . . .

Therefore, in the state of an enlightened ruler there are no books written on bamboo slips; law supplies the only instruction. There are no sermons on the former kings; the officials serve as the only teachers. There are no fierce feuds of private swordsmen; cutting off the heads of the enemy is the only deed of valor. Hence, when the people of such a state make a speech, they say nothing that is in contradiction to the law; when they act, it is in some way that will bring useful results; and when they do brave deeds, they do them in the army. Therefore, in times of peace the state is rich, and in times of trouble its armies are strong. . . .

These are the customs of a disordered state: Its scholars praise the ways of the former kings and imitate their humaneness and rightness, put on a fair appearance and speak in elegant phrases, thus casting doubt upon the laws of the time and causing the ruler to be of two minds. Its speechmakers propound false schemes and borrow influence from abroad, furthering their private interests and forgetting the welfare of the state's altars of the soil and grain. Its swordsmen gather bands of followers about them and perform deeds of honor, making a fine name for themselves and violating the prohibitions of the five government bureaus. Those of its people who are worried about military service flock to the gates of private individuals and pour out their wealth in bribes to influential men who will plead for them, in this way escaping the hardship of battle. Its merchants and artisans spend their time making articles of no practical use and gathering stores of luxury goods, accumulating riches, waiting for the best time to sell, and exploiting the farmers.

These five groups are the vermin of the state. If the rulers do not wipe out such vermin, and in their place encourage men of integrity and public spirit, then they should not be surprised, when they look about the area within the four seas, to see states perish and ruling houses wane and die.

READING AND DISCUSSION QUESTIONS

1. According to Han Fei, how should a ruler exercise power?

2. What kinds of laws does Han Fei advocate? Why?

3. Why does Han Fei consider education to be a problem for China? What should be done to scholars?

VIEWPOINTS COMPARATIVE QUESTIONS

1. According to each document, what policies and programs lead to social and political stability? What qualities do effective rulers possess?

2. What arguments did the Legalists make against the Confucian view of good government? How might a Confucian have countered the Legalist position?

3. How might proponents of each school have characterized the problems of the Warring States Period? What might each have seen as the root causes of disorder?

▪ COMPARATIVE QUESTIONS ▪

1. Compare the advice given to rulers in the *Book of Documents*, the *Analects*, and the *Dao De Jing*. What do these sources suggest about the similarities and differences between Confucianism and Daoism?

2. In what ways does Legalism, illustrated in the reading by Han Fei, directly attack Confucianism, as portrayed in the *Analects*?

3. What connections can you make between the conditions in China during the Warring States Period and the philosophical works included in this chapter? How did conditions during the period shape the development of Chinese philosophy?

The Greek Experience

3500–30 B.C.E.

Greek civilization supplied Rome and much of Europe with a cultural foundation in art, literature, architecture, and philosophy. The fundamentals of Greek life and religious beliefs were laid out in poetry, the earliest form of Greek literature, during the Archaic age (800–500 B.C.E.) by authors such as Homer, Hesiod, and Sappho, while philosophy took root under the Pre-Socratics. During the classical period (500–338 B.C.E.), authors including Herodotus, Thucydides, Sophocles, and Euripides created new genres such as history and drama, while philosophers such as Socrates, Plato, and Aristotle established the course of Western philosophy. Art focused on explorations of human perfection. After Alexander (d. 323 B.C.E.), Greek culture spread throughout Egypt and the Middle East. In this age, referred to as the Hellenistic period (336–100 B.C.E.), innovations in science and philosophy continued, but developments in the arts remain the best-known contribution of this period, as artists began to depict people in less idealized forms.

5-1 | Honor, Pride, and Anger in Ancient Greece

HOMER, *From the* Iliad: *Achilles's Anger and Its Consequences* (ca. 750 B.C.E.)

Homer (ca. 800–700 B.C.E.) is the traditional name of the blind, possibly illiterate, author of the two most important epics in Greek literature, the *Iliad* and the *Odyssey*. The *Iliad* takes place in the final year of the Trojan War (ca. 1250 B.C.E.), a Greek assault against the Trojans waged to avenge Paris of Troy's kidnapping of Helen from her husband, Menelaos, the king of the Greek city-state of Sparta. In this passage, Achilles (Achilleus in the translation below) becomes angry when the Achaian (Greek) king Agamemnon moves to take away a female slave whom Achilles had won in a previous battle. The passage begins with Achilles arguing with Agamemnon.

Then looking darkly at him Achilleus of the swift feet spoke:
"O wrapped in shamelessness, with your mind forever on profit,
how shall any one of the Achaians readily obey you
either to go on a journey or to fight men strongly in battle?
I for my part did not come here for the sake of the Trojan
spearmen to fight against them, since to me they have done nothing.
Never yet have they driven away my cattle or my horses,
never in Phthia where the soil is rich and men grow great did they
spoil my harvest, since indeed there is much that lies between us,
the shadowy mountains and the echoing sea; but for your sake,
o great shamelessness, we followed, to do you favor,
you with the dog's eyes, to win your honor and Menelaos'
from the Trojans. You forget all this or else you care nothing.
And now my prize you threaten in person to strip from me,
for whom I labored much, the gift of the sons of the Achaians.
Never, when the Achaians sack some well-founded citadel
of the Trojans, do I have a prize that is equal to your prize.
Always the greater part of the painful fighting is the work of
my hands; but when the time comes to distribute the booty
yours is far the greater reward, and I with some small thing
yet dear to me go back to my ships when I am weary with fighting.
Now I am returning to Phthia, since it is much better
to go home again with my curved ships, and I am minded no longer
to stay here dishonored and pile up your wealth and your luxury."
    Then answered him in turn the lord of men Agamemnon:
"Run away by all means if your heart drives you. I will not
entreat you to stay here for my sake. There are others with me
who will do me honor, and above all Zeus of the counsels.
To me you are the most hateful of all the kings whom the gods love." . . .
    Meanwhile Patroklos[1] came to the shepherd of the people, Achilleus,
and stood by him and wept warm tears, like a spring dark-running
that down the face of a rock impassable drips its dim water;
and swift-footed brilliant Achilleus looked on him in pity,
and spoke to him aloud and addressed him in winged words: "Why then
are you crying like some poor little girl, Patroklos,
who runs after her mother and begs to be picked up and carried,
and clings to her dress, and holds her back when she tries to hurry,
and gazes tearfully into her face, until she is picked up?

---

[1] **Patroklos:** Achilles's best friend.

You are like such a one, Patroklos, dropping these soft tears.
Could you have some news to tell, for me or the Myrmidons?"[2] . . .
	Then groaning heavily, Patroklos the rider, you answered:
"Son of Peleus, far greatest of the Achaians, Achilleus,
do not be angry; such grief has fallen upon the Achaians.
For all those who were before the bravest in battle
are lying up among the ships with arrow or spear wounds. . . .
	"Give me your armor to wear on my shoulders into the fighting;
so perhaps the Trojans might think I am you, and give way
from their attack, and the fighting sons of the Achaians get wind
again after hard work. There is little breathing space in the fighting.
We unwearied might with a mere cry pile men wearied
back upon their city, and away from the ships and the shelters."
	So he spoke supplicating in his great innocence; this was
his own death and evil destruction he was entreating.
But now, deeply troubled, swift-footed Achilleus answered him:
"Ah, Patroklos, illustrious, what is this you are saying?
I have not any prophecy in mind that I know of;
there is no word from Zeus my honored mother has told me,
but this thought comes as a bitter sorrow to my heart and my spirit
when a man tries to foul one who is his equal, to take back
a prize of honor, because he goes in greater authority.
This is a bitter thought to me; my desire has been dealt with
roughly. The girl the sons of the Achaians chose out for my honor,
and I won her with my own spear, and stormed a strong-fenced city,
is taken back out of my hands by powerful Agamemnon,
the son of Atreus, as if I were some dishonored vagabond.
Still, we will let all this be a thing of the past; and it was not
in my heart to be angry forever; and yet I have said
I would not give over my anger until that time came
when the fighting with all its clamor came up to my own ships.
So do you draw my glorious armor about your shoulders;
lead the Myrmidons whose delight is battle into the fighting,
if truly the black cloud of the Trojans has taken position
strongly about our ships, and the others, the Argives,[3] are bent back
against the beach of the sea, holding only a narrow division
of land, and the whole city of the Trojans has descended upon them
boldly; because they do not see the face of my helmet
glaring close; or else they would run and cram full of dead men
the water-courses; if powerful Agememnon treated me kindly. . . .
But even so, Patroklos, beat the bane aside from our ships; fall

---

[2] **Myrmidons:** Achilles's followers.
[3] **Argives:** Greeks from the city-state of Argos.

upon them with all your strength; let them not with fire's blazing
inflame our ships, and take away our desired homecoming.
But obey to the end this word I put upon your attention
so that you can win, for me, great honor and glory
in the sight of all the Danaans,[4] so they will bring back to me
the lovely girl, and give me shining gifts in addition.
When you have driven them from the ships, come back; although later
the thunderous lord of Hera might grant you the winning of glory,
you must not set your mind on fighting the Trojans, whose delight
is in battle, without me. So you will diminish my honor." . . .

He spoke, and Patroklos was helming himself in bronze that glittered.
First he placed along his legs the beautiful greaves, linked
with silver fastenings to hold the greaves at the ankles.
Afterwards he girt on about his chest the corselet
starry and elaborate of swift-footed Aiakides.
Across his shoulders he slung the sword with the nails of silver,
a bronze sword, and above it the great shield, huge and heavy. . . .

And Patroklos charged with evil intention in on the Trojans.
Three times he charged in with the force of the running war god,
screaming a terrible cry, and three times he cut down nine men;
but as for the fourth time he swept in, like something greater
than human, there, Patroklos, the end of your life was shown forth,
since Phoibus [Apollo] came against you there in the strong encounter
dangerously, nor did Patroklos see him as he moved through
the battle, and shrouded in a deep mist came in against him
and stood behind him, and struck his back and his broad shoulders
with a flat stroke of the hand so that his eyes spun. Phoibos
Apollo now struck away from his head the helmet
four-horned and hollow-eyed, and under the feet of the horses
it rolled clattering, and the plumes above it were defiled
by blood and dust. Before this time it had not been permitted
to defile in the dust this great helmet crested in horse-hair;
rather it guarded the head and the gracious brow of a godlike
man, Achilleus; but now Zeus gave it over to Hektor[5]
to wear on his head, Hektor whose own death was close to him.
And in his hands was splintered all the huge, great, heavy,
iron-shod, far-shadowing spear, and away from his shoulders
dropped to the ground the shield with its shield sling and its tassels.
The lord Apollo, son of Zeus, broke the corselet upon him.
Disaster caught his wits, and his shining body went nerveless.
He stood stupidly, and from close behind his back a Dardanian

---

[4] **Danaans:** Another word for Greeks.
[5] **Hektor:** Troy's best warrior and Achilles's fiercest enemy.

man hit him between the shoulders with a sharp javelin:
Euphorbos, son of Panthoös, who surpassed all men of his own age
with the throwing spear, and in horsemanship and the speed of his feet. He
had already brought down twenty men from their horses
since first coming, with his chariot and his learning in warfare.
He first hit you with a thrown spear, o rider Patroklos,
nor broke you, but ran away again, snatching out the ash spear
from your body, and lost himself in the crowd, not enduring
to face Patroklos, naked as he was, in close combat.
    Now Patroklos, broken by the spear and the god's blow, tried
to shun death and shrink back into the swarm of his own companions.
But Hektor, when he saw high-hearted Patroklos trying
to get away, saw how he was wounded with the sharp javelin,
came close against him across the ranks, and with the spear stabbed him
in the depth of the belly and drove the bronze clean through. He fell,
thunderously, to the horror of all the Achaian people. . . .
    Meanwhile the son of stately Nestor was drawing near him
and wept warm tears, and gave Achilleus his sorrowful message:
"Ah me, son of valiant Peleus; you must hear from me
the ghastly message of a thing I wish never had happened.
Patroklos has fallen, and now they are fighting over his body
which is naked. Hektor of the shining helm has taken his armor."
    He spoke, and the black cloud of sorrow closed on Achilleus.
In both hands he caught up the grimy dust, and poured it
over his head and face, and fouled his handsome countenance,
and the black ashes were scattered over his immortal tunic. . . .
[Angered because of the death of his friend, Achilles decides once again to fight
on the Greek side, and he confronts the Trojan champion Hektor.]
    Pulling out the sharp sword that was slung
at the hollow of his side, huge and heavy, and gathering
himself together, he made his swoop, like a high-flown eagle
who launches himself out of the murk of the clouds on the flat land
to catch away a tender lamb or a shivering hare; so
Hektor made his swoop, swinging his sharp sword, and Achilleus
charged, the heart within him loaded with savage fury.
In front of his chest the beautiful elaborate great shield
covered him, and with the glittering helm with four horns
he nodded; the lovely golden fringes were shaken about it
which Hephaistos[6] had driven close along the horn of the helmet.
And as a star moves among stars in the night's darkening,
Hesper, who is the fairest star who stands in the sky, such
was the shining from the pointed spear Achilleus was shaking

---

[6] **Hephaistos:** Greek god of fire and blacksmithing.

in his right hand with evil intention toward brilliant Hektor.
He was eyeing Hektor's splendid body, to see where it might best
give way, but all the rest of the skin was held in the armor,
brazen and splendid, he stripped when he cut down the strength of
        Patroklos;
yet showed where the collar-bones hold the neck from the shoulders,
the throat, where death of the soul comes most swiftly; in this place
brilliant Achilleus drove the spear as he came on in fury,
and clean through the soft part of the neck the spearpoint was driven.
Yet the ash spear heavy with bronze did not sever the windpipe,
so that Hektor could still make exchange of words spoken.
But he dropped in the dust, and brilliant Achilleus vaunted above him:
"Hektor, surely you thought as you killed Patroklos you would be
safe, and since I was far away you thought nothing of me,
o fool, for an avenger was left, far greater than he was,
behind him and away by the hollow ships. And it was I;
and I have broken your strength; on you the dogs and the vultures
shall feed and foully rip you; the Achaians will bury Patroklos." . . .
"We have won ourselves enormous fame; we have killed the great Hektor
whom the Trojans glorified as if he were a god in their city."
        He spoke, and now thought of shameful treatment for glorious Hektor.
In both of his feet at the back he made holes by the tendons
in the space between ankle and heel, and drew thongs of ox-hide through
        them,
and fastened them to the chariot so as to let the head drag,
and mounted the chariot, and lifted the glorious armor inside it,
then whipped the horses to a run, and they winged their way unreluctant.
A cloud of dust rose where Hektor was dragged, his dark hair was falling
about him, and all that head that was once so handsome was tumbled
in the dust; since by this time Zeus had given him over
to his enemies, to be defiled in the land of his fathers.
        So all his head was dragged in the dust; and now his mother
tore out her hair, and threw the shining veil far from her
and raised a great wail as she looked upon her son; and his father
beloved groaned pitifully, and all his people about him
were taken with wailing and lamentation all through the city.

READING AND DISCUSSION QUESTIONS

1. According to Achilles, why did the Greeks go to war? What connection does he
    make between the causes of the war and his unhappiness with his treatment?

2. How would you characterize the relationship between Achilles and Agamem-
    non? What is the basis of Agamemnon's authority over Achilles? What duties
    and obligations does Achilles have to Agamemnon?

3. What is the relationship between Achilles and Patroklos? How does it embody
    Greek ideas about male friendships?

5-2 | Socrates Defends Himself Against Criminal Charges
PLATO, From *Apologia* (ca. 399 B.C.E.)

Plato (427–347 B.C.E.), a classical Greek philosopher and founder of the Academy, was a pupil of the philosopher Socrates (ca. 470–399 B.C.E.) and sought to preserve his mentor's contributions to Athenian life. As Socrates recorded nothing, we must rely on Plato's documentation of his teachings. In the following speech, Socrates presents his defense in an Athenian court against the charges that he was impious and corrupted the youth. It is unclear to what extent the *Apologia* represents his actual words or merely Plato's reimagining of them. Although the exact date of the *Apologia* is unknown, Plato recorded this speech after Socrates's conviction and execution.

Men of Athens, do not interrupt me with noise, even if I seem to you to be boasting; for the word that I speak is not mine, but the speaker to whom I shall refer it is a person of weight. For of my wisdom—if it is wisdom at all—and of its nature, I will offer you the god of Delphi[7] as a witness. You know Chaerephon, I fancy. He was my comrade from a youth and the comrade of your democratic party.[8] . . . Well, once he went to Delphi and made so bold as to ask the oracle this question; and, gentlemen, don't make a disturbance at what I say; for he asked if there were anyone wiser than I. Now the Pythia[9] replied that there was no one wiser. And about these things his brother here will bear you witness, since Chaerephon is dead.

But see why I say these things; for I am going to tell you from where the prejudice against me has arisen. For when I heard this, I thought to myself: "What in the world does the god mean, and what riddle is he propounding?[10] For I am conscious that I am not wise to any degree. What then does he mean by declaring that I am the wisest? He certainly cannot be lying, for that is not possible for him." And for a long time I was at a loss as to what he meant; then with great reluctance I proceeded to investigate him somewhat as follows.

I went to one of those who had a reputation for wisdom, thinking that there, if anywhere, I should prove the utterance wrong and should show the oracle "This man is wiser than I, but you said I was wisest." So examining this man—for I need not call him by name, but it was one of the public men with regard to whom I had this kind of experience, men of Athens—and conversing with him, this man seemed to me to seem to be wise to many other people and especially to himself,

---

Plato, *Apologia*, in F. J. Church, trans., *The Trial and Death of Socrates* (London: Macmillan, 1880).

[7] **Delphi:** The location of the most important oracle in the Greek world, which was dedicated to the god Apollo.

[8] **your democratic party:** Socrates did not support Athens's democratic faction.

[9] **Pythia:** The priestess at Delphi who spoke for the god Apollo.

[10] **what riddle . . . propounding?:** The Pythia at Delphi was known for answering a question with a riddle.

but not to be so; and then I tried to show him that he thought he was wise, but was not. As a result, I became hateful to him and to many of those present; and so, as I went away, I thought to myself, I am wiser than this man; for neither of us really knows anything fine and good, but this man thinks he knows something when he does not, whereas I, as I do not know anything, do not think I do either. I seem, then, in just this little thing to be wiser than this man at any rate, that what I do not know I do not think I know either." From him I went to another of those who were reputed to be wiser than he, and these same things seemed to me to be true; and there I became hateful both to him and to many others. . . .

Now from this investigation, men of Athens, many enmities have arisen against me, and such as are most harsh and grievous, so that many prejudices have resulted from them and I am called a wise man. For on each occasion those who are present think I am wise in the matters in which I confute someone else; but the fact is, gentlemen, it is likely that the god is really wise and by his oracle means this: "Human wisdom is of little or no value." And it appears that he does not really say this of Socrates, but merely uses my name, and makes me an example, as if he were to say: "This one of you, O human beings, is wisest, who, like Socrates, recognizes that he is in truth of no account in respect to wisdom."

Therefore I am still even now going about and searching and investigating at the god's behest anyone, whether citizen or foreigner, who I think is wise; and when he does not seem so to me, I give aid to the god and show that he is not wise. And by reason of this occupation I have no leisure to attend to any of the affairs of the state worth mentioning, or of my own, but am in vast poverty on account of my service to the god.[11]

And in addition to these things, the young men who have the most leisure, the sons of the richest men, accompany me of their own accord, find pleasure in hearing people being examined, and often imitate me themselves, and then they undertake to examine others; and then, I fancy, they find a great plenty of people who think they know something, but know little or nothing. As a result, therefore, those who are examined by them are angry with me, instead of being angry with themselves, and say that "Socrates is a most abominable person and is corrupting the youth."

And when anyone asks them "by doing or teaching what?" they have nothing to say, but they do not know, and that they may not seem to be at a loss, they say these things that are handy to say against all the philosophers, "the things in the air and the things beneath the Earth" and "not to believe in the gods" and "to make the weaker argument the stronger." For they would not, I fancy, care to say the truth, that it is being made very clear that they pretend to know, but know nothing. . . . If you should say to me . . . "Socrates, this time we will not do as Anytus[12] says, but we will let you go, on this condition, however, that you no longer spend

---

[11] **my service to the god:** Socrates performed his civic duty for Athens as a soldier and as an officeholder.

[12] **Anytus:** The person who brought charges against Socrates.

our time in this investigation or in philosophy ["love of wisdom"], and if you are caught doing so again you shall die"; if you should let me go on this condition which I have mentioned, I should say to you, "Men of Athens, I respect and love you, but I shall obey the god [Apollo] rather than you, and while I live and am able to continue, I shall never give up philosophy or stop exhorting you and pointing out the truth to any one of you whom I may meet, saying in my accustomed way: "Most excellent man, are you who are a citizen of Athens, the greatest of cities and the most famous for wisdom and power, not ashamed to care for the acquisition of wealth and for reputation and honor, when you neither care nor take thought for wisdom and truth and the perfection of your soul?" And if any of you argues the point, and says he does care, I shall not let him go at once, nor shall I go away, but I shall question and examine and cross-examine him, and if I find that he does not possess virtue, but says he does, I shall rebuke him for scorning the things that are of most importance and caring more for what is of less worth. This I shall do to whomever I meet, young and old, foreigner and citizen, but most to the citizens, inasmuch as you are more nearly related to me. For know that the god commands me to do this, and I believe that no greater good ever came to pass in the city than my service to the god. For I go about doing nothing else than urging you, young and old, not to care for your persons or your property more than for the perfection of your souls, or even so much; and I tell you that virtue does not come from money, but from virtue comes money and all other good things to man, both to the individual and to the state. If by saying these things I corrupt the youth, these things must be injurious, but if anyone asserts that I say other things than these, he says what is untrue. Therefore I say to you, men of Athens, either do as Anytus tells you, or not, and either acquit me, or not, knowing that I shall not change my conduct even if I am to die many times over. . . .

For know that if you kill me, I being such a man as I say I am, you will not injure me so much as yourselves. . . . And so, men of Athens, I am now making my defense not for my own sake, as one might imagine, but far more for yours, that you may not by condemning me err in your treatment of the gift the god gave you. For if you put me to death, you will not easily find another, who, to use a rather absurd figure, attaches himself to the city as a gadfly to a horse, which, though large and well bred, is sluggish on account of his size and needs to be aroused by stinging. I think the god fastened me upon the city in some such capacity, and I go about arousing, and urging and reproaching each one of you, constantly alighting upon you everywhere the whole day long. Such another is not likely to come to you, gentlemen; but if you take my advice, you will spare me. But you, perhaps, might be angry, like people awakened from a nap, and might slap me, as Anytus advises, and easily kill me; then you would pass the rest of your lives in slumber, unless the god, in his care for you, should send someone else to sting you. And that I am, as I say, a kind of gift from the god, you might understand from this; for I have neglected all my own affairs and have been enduring the neglect of my concerns all these years, but I am always busy in your interest, coming to each one of you individually like a father or an elder brother and urging you to care for virtue; now that is not like human conduct. If I derived any profit from this and received pay for these exhortations, there would be some sense in it; but now you yourselves see that my accusers, though they accuse me of everything else in such a shameless way, have not been able to work themselves up to such a pitch of shamelessness as to produce a witness to testify that I ever exacted or asked pay of anyone. For I think I have a sufficient witness that I speak the truth, namely, my poverty. . . .

I was never any one's teacher. If any one, whether young or old, wishes to hear me speaking and pursuing my mission, I have never objected, nor do I converse only when I am paid and not otherwise, but I offer myself alike to rich and poor; I ask questions, and whoever wishes may answer and hear what I say. And whether any of them turns out well or ill, I should not justly be held responsible, since I never promised or gave any instruction to any of them;[13] but if any man says that he ever learned or heard anything privately from me, which all the others did not, be assured that he is lying.

But why then do some people love to spend much of their time with me? You have heard the reason, men of Athens; for I told you the whole truth; it is because they like to listen when those are examined who think they are wise and are not so; for it is amusing.

READING AND DISCUSSION QUESTIONS

1. How does Socrates defend himself against the charges of impiety and corrupting the youth? Do you find his argument convincing? Explain.

2. How does Socrates define and seek wisdom?

3. What tactics did Socrates use to question people? Why might he have attracted so many followers? Conversely, what elements of Socrates's method might have created enemies?

5-3 | A Hellenistic King Embraces Hellenic Virtues
PLUTARCH, From *Life of Cleomenes III* (First Century C.E.)

The rise of Macedonia did not result in the immediate elimination of Greek social and political traditions. The citizens of Greek city-states continued to believe in the ideal of the polis, and the outward forms of Greek government often remained in place. Nonetheless, the Greek world had changed. Increasingly, power was concentrated in the hands of kings and autocrats, even if a pretense was sometimes maintained that this was not the case. In this document, the Roman historian Plutarch describes the lifestyle and policies of Cleomenes III (r. 235–222 B.C.E.),

---

Plutarch, *Plutarch's Lives*, ed. and trans. Sir Thomas North, vol. 8 (London: J. M. Dent and Company, 1894), 39–41.

[13] **I was never any one's teacher . . . them:** Socrates contrasts himself with the Sophists, who charged money for their instruction.

a Spartan king who sought to reorganize the Spartan state, claiming greater power for himself in the process. As you read it, pay particular attention to Cleomenes's use of Sparta's past to justify his current rule. How and why did he seek to connect himself to older traditions?

For of all the armies otherwise of the Grecians, or kings in all Greece, there was no army only but his, that was without players, minstrels, fools and jugglers: for his camp only was clean of such rabble and foolery, and all the young men fell to some exercise of their bodies, and the old men also to teach them. And if they chanced to have any vacant time, then they would pleasantly be one merry with another, in giving some pretty fine mock after the Laconian[14] manner. And what profit they got by that kind of exercise, we have written it at large in Lycurgus' life. But of all these things, the king himself was their schoolmaster and example, showing himself very temperate of life, and plain without curiosity, no more than any private soldier of all his camp: the which were great helps unto him in his enterprises he made in Greece. For the Grecians having cause of suit and negotiation with other kings and princes, did not wonder so much at their pomp and riches, as they did abhor and detest their pride and insolency: so disdainfully they would answer them that had to do with them. But contrarily when they went unto Cleomenes, who was a king in name and deed as they were, finding no purple robes nor stately mantles, nor rich-embroidered beds, nor a prince to be spoken to but by messengers, gentlemen ushers, and supplications, and yet with great ado: and seeing him also come plainly appareled unto them, with a good countenance, and courteously answering the matters they came for: he thereby did marvelously win their hearts and good-wills, that when they returned home, they said he only was the worthy king, that came of the race of Hercules. Now for his diet at his board, that was very straight and Laconian-like, keeping only three boards: and if he chanced to feast any ambassadors or other his friends that came to see him, he then added too, two other boards, and besides, made his men to see that his fare should be amended, not with pastry and conserves, but with more store of meat, and some better wine than ordinary. For he one day reproved one of his friends, that bidding strangers to supper, he gave them nothing but black broth, and brown bread only, according to the Laconian manner. Nay, said he, we may not use strangers so hardly after our manner. The board being taken up, another little table was brought with three feet, whereupon they set a bowl of copper full of wine, and two silver cups of a pottle apiece, and certain other few silver pots besides: so every man drank what they listed, and no man was forced to drink more than he would. Furthermore, there was no sport, nor any pleasant song sung to make the company merry, for it needed not. For Cleomenes self would entertain them with some pretty questions or pleasant tale: whereby, as his talk was not severe and without pleasure, so was it also pleasant without insolency. For he was of opinion, that to win men by gifts or money, as other kings and princes did, was but base and clown-like: but to seek their good-wills by

---

[14] **Laconian:** Spartan.

courteous means and pleasantness, and therewith to mean good faith, that he thought most fit and honorable for a prince. For this was his mind, that there was but no other difference betwixt a friend and a hireling: but that the one is won with money, and the other with civility and good entertainment.

READING AND DISCUSSION QUESTIONS

1. What kind of image did Cleomenes cultivate for himself? Why?
2. Why do you think it was so important to Cleomenes to root his lifestyle and policies in Sparta's history? What does this tell you about the continuing strength of Spartan traditions in the Hellenistic period?

VIEWPOINTS

Depicting the Human Form

Hellenic art celebrated the possibility of physical perfection. It offered an idealized version of the human form, one without blemishes, imperfections, or complex emotions. In contrast, Hellenistic artists produced works that were more genuinely naturalistic, displaying the human form in all of its diversity and adding an emotional element. While the subjects of Hellenic art often appear serene, even detached, in Hellenistic art we see the physical reflection of the subject's life experiences and emotional state. Indeed, the subject's inner life and outer appearance are portrayed as inseparable. The two sculptures included here are good examples of the essential differences between Hellenic and Hellenistic art. As you examine them, try to make connections between each sculpture and the society that created it. How would you explain the artistic shift that the two pieces represent?

5-4 | A Hellenic Depiction of Physical Perfection
Zeus from Artemisium (ca. 460 B.C.E.)

This bronze statue was discovered in a shipwreck off the coast of the Greek island Euboea. Bronze statues from antiquity are rare because they were normally melted down for their precious metal. This statue stands almost seven feet tall and is thought to represent Zeus. The statue probably originally held a thunderbolt in its right hand and is in position to strike. Ancient Greek statues are often figures in complete nudity, reflecting the Greeks' comfort with the nude human form. For example, participants in athletic competitions never wore clothes.

DEA/G. Nimatallah/De Agostini/Getty Images.

READING AND DISCUSSION QUESTIONS

1. Describe the position of the figure's arms, legs, and head. How would you explain the artist's choices in this regard?

2. What should we make of the fact that Zeus is depicted as a perfect human? What does this statue tell us about how the Greeks saw their gods?

5-5 | A Hellenistic Depiction of Human Suffering
The Dying Gaul (ca. 230–220 B.C.E.)

In 278 B.C.E, tribes from Gaul (modern France) invaded Greece and later attacked the Greek cities in Asia Minor. One of the Hellenistic kingdoms, Pergamum, defeated the Gauls and later set up a massive monument to commemorate their victory. The original bronze sculpture of this figure has been lost; this Roman copy was discovered during excavations in the seventeenth century. The warrior's only adornment, a torque, and his hairstyle identify him as a Gallic warrior.

FRATELLI ALINARI S.P.A./Pinacoteca Capitolina, Palazzo Conservatori, Rome, Italy/Bridgeman Images.

READING AND DISCUSSION QUESTIONS

1. What clues does the sculpture offer that its subject is dying and not merely wounded or resting? How can we tell this from his body and from his facial expression?

2. What emotions does this statue evoke? How might the viewer have been meant to respond to it?

VIEWPOINTS COMPARATIVE QUESTIONS

1. What aspect of each statue do you find most striking? Why?

2. How did each artist approach the depiction of the human body? What similarities, if any, do you see between the two works in this regard?

3. How do these two pieces relate to larger social and cultural trends in the Greek world?

■ COMPARATIVE QUESTIONS ■

1. Compare and contrast the gods that are depicted in these sources. Specifically, how are the gods in Plato's *Apologia* similar to or different from those in Homer's *Iliad*?

2. What aspects of everyday life are evident in these sources? What aspects are unexamined?

3. Greek civilization is often described as "rational." In what ways do each of these sources support or challenge that characterization?

4. What light do the sources in this chapter shed on the essential differences between Hellenic and Hellenistic society?

6

The World of Rome

ca. 1000 B.C.E.–400 C.E.

According to tradition, the twins Romulus and Remus, abandoned as infants, founded the city of Rome in 753 B.C.E. on the site where they were discovered and nurtured by a she-wolf. Rome was at first controlled by kings, the last of whom was overthrown in 509 B.C.E., but the founding of the republic put power in the hands of elected officials and the Senate. Over the next five centuries, Rome defeated Carthage and the Hellenistic states, taking complete control of the Mediterranean world. While these victories brought immense wealth to Rome, its powerful leaders plunged the republic into civil war. In 31 B.C.E., the adoptive son of Julius Caesar, who was later known as Augustus, founded the Roman Empire. The Roman Empire expanded its territory even further, moving west and north into Gaul (modern France) and Britain and eastward into Asia, while emperors consolidated power for themselves, slowly restricting the powers of the senatorial class.

6-1 | The Romans Set Their Basic Laws in Stone
The Twelve Tables (ca. 450 B.C.E.)

By tradition, Roman laws were not written down and were only interpreted by the patricians (upper-class men) and the priests. In 451 B.C.E., a panel of ten men was appointed to inscribe the laws on stone, possibly to placate plebeian (lower-class) hostility to arbitrary justice. The panel initially produced ten tables and added two more in 450. The original Twelve Tables were destroyed when the city of Rome was sacked by the Gauls in the early fourth century B.C.E. and were gradually superseded by later laws. For these reasons, only fragments of the Twelve Tables survive.

Oliver J. Thatcher, ed., *The Library of Original Sources*, vol. 3: *The Roman World* (Milwaukee, Wis.: University Research Extension, 1901), 9–11. Modernized by J. S. Arkenberg.

Table I

1. If anyone summons a man before the magistrate, he must go. If the man summoned does not go, let the one summoning him call the bystanders to witness and then take him by force.
2. If he shirks or runs away, let the summoner lay hands on him.
3. If illness or old age is the hindrance, let the summoner provide a team. He need not provide a covered carriage with a pallet unless he chooses.
4. Let the protector of a landholder be a landholder; for one of the proletariat, let anyone that cares, be protector. . . .
6–9. When the litigants settle their case by compromise, let the magistrate announce it. If they do not compromise, let them state each his own side of the case, in the *comitium*[1] of the forum before noon. Afterwards let them talk it out together, while both are present. After noon, in case either party has failed to appear, let the magistrate pronounce judgment in favor of the one who is present. If both are present the trial may last until sunset but no later.

Table II

2. He whose witness has failed to appear may summon him by loud calls before his house every third day.

Table III

1. One who has confessed a debt, or against whom judgment has been pronounced, shall have thirty days to pay it in. After that forcible seizure of his person is allowed. The creditor shall bring him before the magistrate. Unless he pays the amount of the judgment or some one in the presence of the magistrate interferes in his behalf as protector the creditor so shall take him home and fasten him in stocks or fetters. He shall fasten him with not less than fifteen pounds of weight or, if he choose, with more. If the prisoner choose, he may furnish his own food. If he does not, the creditor must give him a pound of meal daily; if he choose he may give him more.
2. On the third market day let them divide his body among them. If they cut more or less than each one's share it shall be no crime.
3. Against a foreigner the right in property shall be valid forever.

Table IV

1. A dreadfully deformed child shall be quickly killed.
2. If a father sell his son three times, the son shall be free from his father.

---

[1] **comitium:** A location in the forum, in front of the Senate building, where speeches were delivered and judicial business was conducted.

3. As a man has provided in his will in regard to his money and the care of his property, so let it be binding. If he has no heir and dies intestate, let the nearest agnate [male relative] have the inheritance. If there is no agnate, let the members of his gens [families belonging to one ancestral group] have the inheritance.
4. If one is mad but has no guardian, the power over him and his money shall belong to his agnates and the members of his gens.
5. A child born after ten months since the father's death will not be admitted into a legal inheritance.

Table V

1. Females should remain in guardianship even when they have attained their majority.

Table VI

1. When one makes a bond and a conveyance of property, as he has made formal declaration so let it be binding. . . .
3. A beam that is built into a house or a vineyard trellis one may not take from its place. . . .
5. *Usucapio* [obtaining ownership] of movable things requires one year's possession for its completion; but *usucapio* of an estate and buildings two years.
6. Any woman who does not wish to be subjected in this manner to the hand of her husband should be absent three nights in succession every year, and so interrupt the *usucapio* of each year.

Table VII

1. Let them keep the road in order. If they have not paved it, a man may drive his team where he likes. . . .
9. Should a tree on a neighbor's farm be bent crooked by the wind and lean over your farm, you may take legal action for removal of that tree.
10. A man might gather up fruit that was falling down onto another man's farm.

Table VIII

2. If one has maimed a limb and does not compromise with the injured person, let there be retaliation. If one has broken a bone of a freeman with his hand or with a cudgel, let him pay a penalty of three hundred coins. If he has broken the bone of a slave, let him have one hundred and fifty coins. If one is guilty of insult, the penalty shall be twenty-five coins.
3. If one is slain while committing theft by night, he is rightly slain.
4. If a patron shall have devised any deceit against his client, let him be accursed.
5. If one shall permit himself to be summoned as a witness, or has been a weigher, if he does not give his testimony, let him be noted as dishonest and incapable of acting again as witness. . . .

10. Any person who destroys by burning any building or heap of corn deposited alongside a house shall be bound, scourged [whipped], and put to death by burning at the stake provided that he has committed the said misdeed with malice aforethought; but if he shall have committed it by accident, that is, by negligence, it is ordained that he repair the damage or, if he be too poor to be competent for such punishment, he shall receive a lighter punishment. . . .
12. If the theft has been done by night, if the owner kills the thief, the thief shall be held to be lawfully killed.
13. It is unlawful for a thief to be killed by day . . . unless he defends himself with a weapon; even though he has come with a weapon, unless he shall use the weapon and fight back, you shall not kill him. And even if he resists, first call out so that someone may hear and come up. . . .
23. A person who has been found guilty of giving false witness shall be hurled down from the Tarpeian Rock.[2] . . .
26. No person shall hold meetings by night in the city.

Table IX

4. The penalty shall be capital [i.e., execution] for a judge or arbiter legally appointed who has been found guilty of receiving a bribe for giving a decision.
5. Treason: he who shall have roused up a public enemy or handed over a citizen to a public enemy must suffer capital punishment.
6. Putting to death of any man, whosoever he might be unconvicted is forbidden.

Table X

1. None is to bury or burn a corpse in the city. . . .
3. The women shall not tear their faces nor wail on account of the funeral. . . .
5. If one obtains a crown himself, or if his chattel does so because of his honor and valor, if it is placed on his head, or the head of his parents, it shall be no crime.

Table XI

1. Marriages should not take place between plebeians and patricians.

Table XII

2. If a slave shall have committed theft or done damage with his master's knowledge, the action for damages is in the slave's name. . . .
5. Whatever the people had last ordained should be held as binding by law.

---

[2] **Tarpeian Rock:** A cliff located on the Capitoline Hill close to the temple of Jupiter. Those convicted of murder or treason during the republic were thrown off of it.

READING AND DISCUSSION QUESTIONS

1. From reading the Twelve Tables, what impression do you get of the Roman family? What power did men have over their children and wives?

2. What do these laws reveal about the Roman social hierarchy? How did social status shape the administration of justice?

6-2 | Plutarch Describes a Man Who Would Be King

PLUTARCH, *On Julius Caesar, a Man of Unlimited Ambition* (ca. 44 C.E.)

Plutarch's *Parallel Lives* served as the greatest source of knowledge about the ancient world for people of the Renaissance and for Shakespeare, even though its original intent was not to preserve history, but rather to examine moral virtues and vices. Plutarch was committed to supporting the Roman Empire and later became a priest at the Greek oracle shrine at Delphi. The following document, written about 150 years after the death of Julius Caesar, describes Roman attitudes toward the power that Julius Caesar gained following a civil war victory against the general Pompey.

But that which brought upon him the most apparent and mortal hatred was his desire of being king,[3] which gave the common people the first occasion to quarrel with him, and proved the most specious pretense to those who had been his secret enemies all along. Those who would have procured him that title gave it out that it was foretold in the Sibyls' books[4] that the Romans should conquer the Parthians[5] when they fought against them under the conduct of a king, but not before. And one day, as Caesar was coming down from Alba to Rome, some were so bold as to salute him by the name of king; but he, finding the people disrelish it, seemed to resent it himself, and said his name was Caesar, not king. Upon this there was a general silence, and he passed on looking not very well pleased or contented. Another time, when the senate had conferred on him some extravagant honors, he chanced to receive the message as he was sitting on the rostra [podium], where, though the consuls [highest elected officials] and praetors [elected ministers of justice] themselves waited on him, attended by the whole body of the senate, he did not rise, but behaved himself to them as if they had been private men, and told them his honors wanted rather to be retrenched than increased. This treatment offended not only the senate, but the commonalty too,

---

Plutarch, *Parallel Lives*, "Julius Caesar," trans. John Dryden, rev. Arthur Hugh Clough (New York: Modern Library, n.d.), 888–890.

[3] **his desire of being king:** The Romans feared the tyranny of kings.

[4] **Sibyls' books:** Books of prophecy that were consulted in Rome during times of crisis.

[5] **Parthians:** The only civilized power on Rome's frontiers, the Parthians controlled Mesopotamia and Persia. They were famous horsemen and developed the "Parthian shot," which allowed them to shoot arrows while riding away from attackers.

as if they thought the affront upon the senate equally reflected upon the whole republic; so that all who could decently leave him went off, looking much discomposed. Caesar, perceiving the false step he had made, immediately retired home; and laying his throat bare, told his friends that he was ready to offer this to any one would give the stroke. But afterwards he made the malady from which he suffered [epilepsy] the excuse for his sitting, saying that those who are attacked by it lose their presence of mind if they talk much standing; that they presently grow giddy, fall into convulsions, and quite lose their reason. But this was not the reality, for he would willingly have stood up to the senate, had not Cornelius Balbus, one of his friends, or rather flatterers, hindered him. "Will you not remember," said he, "you are Caesar, and claim the honor which is due to your merit?"

He gave a fresh occasion of resentment by his affront to the tribunes.[6] The Lupercalia were then celebrated, a feast at the first institution belonging, as some writers say, to the shepherds, and having some connection with the Arcadian Lycae [a mountain in Greece]. Many young noblemen and magistrates run up and down the city with their upper garments off, striking all they meet with thongs of hide, by way of sport; and many women, even of the highest rank, place themselves in the way, and hold out their hands to the lash, as boys in a school do to the master, out of a belief that it procures an easy labor to those who are with child, and makes those conceive who are barren. Caesar, dressed in a triumphal robe, seated himself in a golden chair at the rostra to view this ceremony. Antony [i.e., Marc Antony, Caesar's closest ally], as consul, was one of those who ran this course, and when he came into the forum, and the people made way for him, he went up and reached to Caesar a diadem wreathed with laurel [like a king's crown]. Upon this there was a shout, but only a slight one, made by the few who were planted there for that purpose; but when Caesar refused it, there was universal applause. Upon the second offer, very few, and upon the second refusal, all again applauded. Caesar finding it would not take, rose up, and ordered the crown to be carried into the capitol. Caesar's statues were afterwards found with royal diadems on their heads. Flavius and Marullus, two tribunes of the people, went presently and pulled them off, and having apprehended those who first saluted Caesar as king committed them to prison. The people followed them with acclamations, and called them by the name of Brutus, because Brutus was the first who ended the succession of kings,[7] and transferred the power which before was lodged in one man into the hands of the senate and people. Caesar so far resented this, that he displaced Marullus and Flavius; and in urging his charges against them, at the same time ridiculed the

---

[6] **tribunes:** Tribunes of the Plebs, which were originally created to defend the plebian class of citizens against the patricians who dominated the early Roman government and which could veto actions and laws they thought would harm the plebians. By the time of Caesar, the Tribunes of the Plebs were often working for their own benefit.

[7] **was the first . . . kings:** In 509 B.C.E., Lucius Brutus removed the last king from Rome.

people, by himself giving the men more than once the names of Bruti and Cumaei.[8]

This made the multitude turn their thoughts to Marcus Brutus, who, by his father's side, was thought to be descended from that first Brutus, and by his mother's side from the Servilii, another noble family, being besides nephew and son-in-law to Cato. But the honors and favors he had received from Caesar took off the edge from the desires he might himself have felt for overthrowing the new monarchy. For he had not only been pardoned himself after Pompey's defeat at Pharsalia, and had procured the same grace for many of his friends, but was one in whom Caesar had a particular confidence. He had at that time the most honorable praetorship for the year, and was named for the consulship four years after, being preferred before Cassius, his competitor. Upon the question as to the choice, Caesar, it is related, said that Cassius had the fairer pretensions, but that he could not pass by Brutus. Nor would he afterwards listen to some who spoke against Brutus, when the conspiracy against him was already afoot, but laying his hand on his body, said to the informers, "Brutus will wait for this skin of mine," intimating that he was worthy to bear rule on account of his virtue, but would not be base and ungrateful to gain it. Those who desired a change, and looked on him as the only, or at least the most proper, person to effect it, did not venture to speak with him; but in the night-time laid papers about his chair of state, where he used to sit and determine causes, with such sentences in them as, "You are asleep, Brutus," "You are no longer Brutus." Cassius, when he perceived his ambition a little raised upon this, was more insistent than before to work him yet further, having himself a private grudge against Caesar[9] for some reasons that we have mentioned in the Life of Brutus.[10] Nor was Caesar without suspicions of him, and said once to his friends, "What do you think Cassius is aiming at? I don't like him, he looks so pale." And when it was told him that Antony and Dolabella[11] were in a plot against him, he said he did not fear such fat, luxurious men, but rather the pale, lean fellows, meaning Cassius and Brutus.

READING AND DISCUSSION QUESTIONS

1. What was the Roman attitude toward Caesar's becoming king? What was the difference between the views of the senators and those of the common people?

2. How did the plot against Caesar develop? What justification did Brutus and Cassius use to support their assassination of Caesar?

---

[8] **Bruti and Cumaei:** Both names suggest that Caesar was calling the people stupid. The name Brutus means "stupid" and people from Cumae were thought to lack intelligence.

[9] **a private grudge against Caesar:** Cassius was angry that Caesar had promoted Brutus over him.

[10] **Life of Brutus:** Another one of Plutarch's *Parallel Lives*.

[11] **Dolabella:** A general who originally sided with Pompey but later joined with Caesar, who rewarded him with the consulship.

6-3 | A Roman Villa Sheds Light on Roman Religion
Initiation into the Cult of Dionysus (ca. 60–50 B.C.E.)

Roman religion did not focus on doctrinal orthodoxy or even on exclusive devotion to one particular religious sect. Instead, Romans engaged in a variety of religious practices, picking and choosing the ones that best satisfied their practical, emotional, and spiritual needs. This fresco was painted on the wall of a Roman villa in the southern Italian resort town of Pompeii. It depicts an initiation ceremony into the cult of Dionysus. Like other so-called mystery religions, the cult of Dionysus promised initiates access to secret knowledge and a special, personal relationship with the divine being or beings at the center of the cult. Here, an initiate (right) carries an offering to Dionysus, while a young girl, with her mother seated behind her, reads the cult's catechism. A priestess (left) presides over the ritual. As you examine the fresco, ask yourself why cults like the one depicted here might have been especially appealing to Roman women. What did such cults offer women that other forms of Roman religion did not?

Villa dei Misteri, Pompeii, Italy/Bridgeman Images.

READING AND DISCUSSION QUESTIONS

1. How would you characterize the relationship between the mother and daughter at the center of the image? Why might a Roman mother have wanted her daughter to participate in the cult?

2. What does the image suggest about the appeal of mystery religions like the cult of Dionysus? How might the social and emotional bonds formed between cult members have differed from the bonds formed in everyday Roman life?

VIEWPOINTS

Christianity and the Roman State

In general, the Romans were tolerant of religious diversity, and in most cases when they moved into a new area they did not attempt to suppress local religious practices and beliefs. In fact, religion was an important element of cultural exchange in the Roman Empire, with local peoples adopting aspects of Roman religion and the Romans adopting aspects of the belief systems they encountered. Roman toleration had its limits, however. If a local religion seemed to take on a political dimension, or if its followers used their religion as a vehicle for expressing their opposition to Roman rule, it ceased to be a religion in the minds of Roman officials, becoming instead a form of criminality. The two documents included here illustrate the limits of toleration in the context of second-century Christianity. As you read them, think about how Christianity must have appeared to Roman leaders. Why might some Romans have seen Christianity as a genuine threat to Roman society and the Roman state?

6-4 | An Official Asks for Advice on Dealing with Christians

PLINY THE YOUNGER, *Letters to and from the Emperor Trajan on Christians* (111–113 C.E.)

The Emperor Trajan (ca. 98–117) sent the senator Pliny the Younger to the province of Bithynia (modern northwest Turkey) to deal with problems arising from bankrupt municipal finances and reports of illegal meetings and political activity. Pliny had previously served with distinction in the imperial service, even obtaining the political office of consul. Despite being distant from Rome, Pliny repeatedly asked the emperor for advice, as he does in this passage. In his investigations, he discovered that meetings were taking place illegally among people calling themselves Christians.

Pliny to the Emperor Trajan

It is my custom to refer all my difficulties to you, Sir, for no one is better able to resolve my doubts and to inform my ignorance.

I have never been present at an examination of Christians. Consequently, I do not know the nature of the extent of the punishments usually meted out to them, nor the grounds for starting an investigation and how far it should be pressed. Nor am I at all sure whether any distinction should be made between them on the grounds of age, or if young people and adults should be treated alike; whether a pardon ought to be granted to anyone retracting his beliefs, or if he has once professed Christianity, he shall gain nothing by renouncing it; and whether it is the mere name of Christian which is punishable, even if innocent of crime, or rather the crimes associated with the name.

For the moment this is the line I have taken with all persons brought before me on the charge of being Christians. I have asked them in person if they are Christians, and if they admit it, I repeat the question a second and third time, with a warning of the punishment awaiting them. If they persist, I order them to be led away for execution; for, whatever the nature of their admission, I am convinced that their stubbornness and unshakable obstinacy ought not to go unpunished. There have been others similarly fanatical who are Roman citizens. I have entered them on the list of persons to be sent to Rome for trial.

Now that I have begun to deal with this problem, as so often happens, the charges are becoming more widespread and increasing in variety. An anonymous pamphlet has been circulated which contains the names of a number of accused persons. Amongst these I considered that I should dismiss any who denied that they were or ever had been Christians when they had repeated after me a formula of invocation to the gods and had made offerings of wine and incense to your statue[12] (which I had ordered to be brought into court for this purpose along with the images of the gods), and furthermore had reviled the name of Christ: none of which things, I understand, any genuine Christian can be induced to do.

Others, whose names were given to me by an informer, first admitted the charge and then denied it; they said that they had ceased to be Christians two or more years previously, and some of them even twenty years ago. They all did reverence to your statue and the images of the gods in the same way as the others, and reviled the name of Christ. They also declared that the sum total of their guilt or error amounted to no more than this: they had met regularly before dawn on a fixed day to chant verses alternately amongst themselves in honor of Christ as if to a god, and also to bind themselves by oath, not for any criminal purpose, but to abstain from theft, robbery, and adultery, to commit no breach of trust and not to deny a deposit when called upon to restore it. After this ceremony it had

---

[12] **offerings of wine and incense to your statue:** All inhabitants of the Roman Empire were supposed to make sacrifices for the well-being of the emperor and the empire, usually of incense. Some groups, such as the Jews, were exempted.

been their custom to disperse and reassemble later to take food of an ordinary, harmless kind; but they had in fact given up this practice since my edict, issued on your instructions, which banned all political societies. This made me decide it was all the more necessary to extract the truth by torture from two slave-women, whom they call deaconesses. I found nothing but a degenerate sort of cult carried to extravagant lengths.

I have therefore postponed any further examination and hastened to consult you. The question seems to me to be worthy of your consideration, especially in view of the number of persons endangered; for a great many individuals of every age and class, both men and women, are being brought to trial, and this is likely to continue. It is not only the towns, but villages and rural districts too which are infected through contact with this wretched cult. I think though that it is still possible for it to be checked and directed to better ends, for there is no doubt that people have begun to throng the temples which had been almost entirely deserted for a long time; the sacred rites which had been allowed to lapse are being performed again, and flesh of sacrificial victims is on sale everywhere, though up till recently scarcely anyone could be found to buy it. It is easy to infer from this that a great many people could be reformed if they were given an opportunity to repent.

Trajan's Reply to Pliny

You have followed the right course of procedure, my dear Pliny, in your examination of the cases of persons charged with being Christians, for it is impossible to lay down a general rule to a fixed formula. These people must not be hunted out; if they are brought before you and the charge against them is proved, they must be punished, but in the case of anyone who denies that he is a Christian, and makes it clear that he is not by offering prayers to our gods, he is to be pardoned as a result of his repentance however suspect his past conduct may be. But pamphlets circulated anonymously must play no part in any accusation. They create the worst sort of precedent and are quite out of keeping with the spirit of our age.

READING AND DISCUSSION QUESTIONS

1. How does Pliny describe the Christian beliefs and activities that he discovered?

2. How did Pliny investigate those who were suspected of being Christians?

3. What instructions does Trajan give to Pliny regarding the treatment of Christians?

4. What does this passage reveal about the day-to-day governing of the Roman Empire?

6-5 | A Christian Defends His Religion Against Roman Persecution

TERTULLIAN, From *Apologia* (ca. 197 C.E.)

The earliest Christians originated in the Near East, and the entire New Testament of the Christian Bible was composed in the *koine* (common) Greek spoken throughout eastern provinces of the Roman Empire. However, by the late second century, Christianity had attracted a number of converts in the western half of the empire as well. One of these converts, Tertullian (ca. 160–240), was the first Christian of note who wrote in Latin. His most famous work, the *Apologia*, presents a defense of Christianity against Roman persecution and is excerpted below. Tertullian would exert enormous influence on later Christians in the West, including Saint Augustine.

Magistrates of the Roman Empire! You who are seated for the administration of justice in almost the highest position of the state[13] and under the gaze of everyone! If you are not allowed to conduct an open examination, face to face, into the truth regarding the Christians, if in this case alone you fear or are ashamed to exercise your authority to conduct a public investigation with the care that justice demands, if, finally, the extreme hatred shown this group (as happened recently in the domestic courts) has been raised to such a level that it inhibits their defense, then let the truth reach your ears by the secret pathway of silent literature. . . .

If it is certain that we are the most criminal of people, why do you treat us differently from others of our kind, namely all other criminals? The same crime should receive the same treatment. When others are charged with the same crimes imputed to us, they are permitted to use their own mouths and the hired advocacy of others to plead their innocence. They have full freedom to answer the charge and to cross-examine. In fact, it is against the law to condemn anyone without a defense and a hearing. Only Christians are forbidden to say anything in defense of the truth that would clear their case and assist the judge in avoiding an injustice. All that they care about (and this by itself is enough to arouse public hatred) is a confession to bearing the name "Christian," not an investigation of the charge. Now, let us assume you are trying any other criminal. If he confesses to the crime of murder, or sacrilege, or sexual debauchery, or treason—to cite the crimes of which we stand accused—you are not content to pass sentence immediately. Rather, you weigh the relevant circumstances: the nature of the deed; how often, where, how, and when it was committed; the co-conspirators and the partners-in-crime. Nothing of this sort is done in our case. Yet, whenever that false charge is brought against us, we should equally be made to confess: How

---

Rev. S. Thelwell, trans., *Ante-Nicene Fathers*, vol. 3 (Buffalo: Christian Literature Publishing, 1885–1886). Modernized by Walter Ward.

[13] **You who are seated . . . state:** In theory, a Roman citizen could appeal a judgment made by a provincial governor to the emperor.

many murdered babies has one eaten? How many illicit sexual acts has one performed under cover of darkness? Which cooks and which dogs were there? Oh, how great would be the glory of that governor who should bring to light a Christian who has already devoured 100 babies!

To the contrary, we find that it is forbidden to hunt us down. When Pliny the Younger was a provincial governor and had condemned some Christians to death and had intimidated others to abandon the steadfastness of their faith, he was still concerned by their sheer numbers and worried about what to do in the future. So he consulted Trajan, the reigning emperor [ca. 98–117]. Pliny explained that, other than their obstinate refusal to offer sacrifice, he had learned nothing else about their religious ceremonies, except that they met before daybreak to sing hymns to Christ and God and to bind themselves by oath to a way of life that forbids murder, adultery, fraud, treachery, and all other crimes. Trajan then wrote back that people of this sort should not be hunted down, but, when brought to court, they should be punished.

What a decision! How inevitably self-contradictory! He declares that they should not be hunted down, as though they are innocent. Then he prescribes that they be punished, as though they are guilty. He spares them, yet he directs his anger upon them. He pretends to shut his eyes, yet he calls attention to them. Judges, why do you tie yourself up in knots? If you condemn them why not hunt them down? If you do not hunt them down, why not also find them innocent?

Throughout all the provinces, soldiers are assigned by lot to hunt down bandits. When it comes to traitors and public enemies each person is a soldier. Inquiry extends even to one's associates and confederates. The Christian alone may not be hunted down, but he may be brought to court, as if hunting down led to anything other than being haled [hauled] into court. So, you condemn someone who is haled into court, although no one wished to seek him out. He has not merited punishment, I suppose, because he is guilty, but because, forbidden to be looked for, he was found! . . .

A person shouts out, "I am a Christian." He says what he is. You want to hear what he is not. You preside to extort the truth, yet in our case alone you take infinite pains to hear a lie. "I am," he says, "what you ask if I am. Why torture me to twist the fact around? I confess, and you torture me. What would you do if I denied?" Clearly when others deny you do not readily believe them. In our case, when we deny, you immediately believe us. . . .

Inasmuch as you treat us differently from all other criminals, which you do by concentrating on disassociating us from that name (for we are cut off from the name "Christian" only if we do what non-Christians do), you must know that there is no crime whatsoever in our case. It is only a name. . . .

So much for my preface, as it were, which is intended to beat into submission the injustice of the public hatred felt for us. Now I take the stand to plead our innocence. . . .

We are said to be the worst of criminals because of our sacramental baby-killing and the baby-eating that accompanies it and the sexual license that follows the banquet, where dogs are our pimps in darkness when they overturn candles and procure a certain modesty for our impious lusts.[14] We are always spoken of in this way, yet you take no pains to investigate the charges that you have made against us for so long. If you believe them, investigate them. Otherwise, stop believing what you do not investigate. The fact that you look the other way suggests that the evil that you yourselves dare not investigate does not exist. . . .

You say, "You do not worship the [traditional Greek and Roman] gods, and you do not offer sacrifices for the emperors." It follows logically that we do not offer sacrifices for others because we do not do so even for ourselves. All of this is a consequence of our not worshipping the gods. So we are accused of sacrilege and treason. This is the chief case against us. In fact, it is the whole case. . . . Your gods we cease to worship from the moment we recognize they are not gods. So that is what you ought to require us to prove—that those gods do not exist and for that reason should not be worshipped because they deserve worship only if they are gods.

READING AND DISCUSSION QUESTIONS

1. According to Tertullian, what proof was necessary to convict someone of being a Christian? Of what crimes were Christians accused?

2. What problems does Tertullian describe concerning the persecution of Christians? How were Christian court cases unique?

3. Why did the Christians refuse to make sacrifices to the emperors? How did the Roman authorities interpret this defiance?

VIEWPOINTS COMPARATIVE QUESTIONS

1. Compare and contrast the descriptions of Christian religious practices in the two documents. What does Pliny's description tell you about his general attitude toward Christianity?

2. How might Pliny have responded to Tertullian's critique of his policies toward Christians?

3. In your opinion, were the Christians guilty of a crime against the Roman state? If so, what crime?

---

[14] **where . . . impious lusts:** A rumor stated that dogs were used to extinguish the candles. Strings were attached to the dog's tails and to the candles so that when the dogs were thrown food the dogs would leap and cause the candles to fall over.

▪ COMPARATIVE QUESTIONS ▪

1. How do the laws enshrined in the Twelve Tables compare to the law codes you examined in previous chapters? (See Documents 2-2 and 3-4.)

2. Compare and contrast Plutarch's descriptions of Caesar (Document 6-2) and Cleomenes III (Document 5-3). Which of these men did Plutarch find most admirable? Why?

3. What light do the documents in this chapter shed on the nature of Roman religion and the limits of Roman religious toleration?

4. What kind of relationship did Christians have with the Roman state, according to Pliny and Tertullian?

7

East Asia and the Spread of Buddhism

221 B.C.E.–845 C.E.

The Qin Dynasty (221–206 B.C.E.) conquered the "warring states" of China and created what Qin Shihuangdi (259–210 B.C.E.) hoped would be an empire that would last for ten thousand years. However, the brutal strategies of control espoused by Legalism, a philosophy that called for strict adherence to laws and a ruler with absolute power, ended the dynasty in just fourteen years. When the Han Dynasty (206 B.C.E.–220 C.E.) took control of China, they maintained a traditional focus on Confucianism and rejected the Qin's harsh punishments. Following the Han's collapse, nomadic groups from Central Asia took power in northern China, while southern China was ruled by a succession of unsuccessful dynasties. Buddhism became increasingly influential in this Age of Division (220–589 C.E.); Islam and Christianity also appeared in China but were less popular. When the Sui (581–618 C.E.) and Tang (618–907 C.E.) Dynasties reestablished formal control over all of China, neighboring societies in Korea, Tibet, Vietnam, and Japan began to imitate Chinese rule and culture.

7-1 | A Chinese Historian Describes a Nomadic People

SIMA QIAN, From *The Records of the Historian: On the Xiongnu* (ca. 109–86 B.C.E.)

Sima Qian is considered the founder of Chinese historical writing. By interviewing eyewitnesses, traveling, and collecting old records, he hoped to write a history of China and its neighbors from the beginning of Chinese civilization. He had access to official documents

Thomas R. Martin, *Herodotus and Sima Qian: The First Great Historians of Greece and China* (Boston: Bedford/St. Martin's, 2010), 129–131. Reprinted by permission of the publisher.

from his position in the imperial government, but he lost favor when he defended a scapegoat for military disasters against the Xiongnu (nomads north of China). His punishment was castration. In the following passage, Sima Qian describes the customs of the Xiongnu.

The ancestor of the Xiongnu descended from the ruler of the Xia dynasty, whose name was Qun Wei. From before the time of Emperors Yao and Shun [third millennium B.C.E.], there have been barbarians . . . living in northern uncivilized areas and wandering around herding animals. They herd mainly horses, cattle, and sheep, but also some unusual animals, such as camels, donkeys, mules, and wild horses. . . . They move around looking for water and pasture and have no walled settlements or permanent housing. They do not farm, but they do divide their land into separate holdings under different leaders. They have no writing, and all contracts are verbal. When their children can ride a sheep, they begin to use bows and arrows to shoot birds and rodents. When they are older, they shoot foxes and rabbits for food. In this way, all the young men are easily able to become archers and serve as cavalry. It is their custom when times are easy to graze their animals and hunt with the bow for their living, but when hard times come, they take up weapons to plunder and raid. This is their innate nature. Their long-range weapons are bows and arrows; they use swords and spears in close combat. When they have the advantage in battle, they advance, but if not, they retreat, since there is no shame in running away. They are only concerned with self-interest, knowing nothing of proper behavior or justice.

Everyone, including the chiefs, eats the meat of their domesticated animals and wears clothing of hides and coats of fur. The men who are in their prime eat the fattiest and best food, while the elderly eat what is left over, since the Xiongnu treasure the strong and healthy but place little value on the weak and old. When his father dies, a son marries his stepmother, and when brothers die, the surviving brothers marry their widows. They have personal names but no family names or additional names. . . .

[By 221 B.C.E.] the state of Qin had finally defeated the other six states of China [to create a unified empire]. The First Emperor of Qin sent General Meng Tian with 100,000 men to attack the barbarians in the north. He won control of all the lands south of the Yellow River and made the river into a defended border. Meng Tian built forty-four walled settlements along the river and filled them with convicts sentenced to labor and sent to the border to do garrison duty. He also constructed the direct road from Jiuyuan to Yunyang. In this way, he used the slopes of the mountain and the valleys to create a defended border, erecting ramparts and fortifications at needed points. The entire line of defense stretched over two thousand miles from Lintao to Liaodong and even crossed the Yellow River, running through Yangshan and Beijia. . . .

The chief of the Xiongnu was named Touman. Too weak to resist the army of Qin, Touman had retreated to the far north, where he held out with his subjects for more than a decade. Following Meng Tian's death, the revolt of the subordinate lords against the Qin dynasty created conflict and unrest in China. The convict laborers that the Qin dynasty had sent to garrison the border seized this opportunity to return home. When the Xiongnu discovered that no one was defending the border, they crossed the Yellow River southward into their old territory and established themselves along China's previous border.

Touman's oldest son and heir apparent as chief of the Xiongnu was named Maodun, but Touman also had a younger son from a different mother whom he had married later. Touman loved this woman very much and decided to eliminate Maodun, to make the younger son his heir. Touman therefore sent Maodun as a diplomatic hostage held by the Yuezhi.[1] As soon as Maodun reached the Yuezhi, Touman suddenly attacked them. They were on the verge of executing Maodun in revenge for the attack when he stole one of their best horses and got away. When he made his way home, his courage so impressed Touman that he made Maodun the commander of a cavalry unit of ten thousand men.

Maodun had arrows made that whistled in flight and trained his men to shoot their bows as they were riding. He ordered, "He who does not shoot where my whistling arrow hits will be executed!" He then went out hunting birds and animals, and if any of his men failed to shoot at what he shot at with his whistling arrow, he immediately beheaded them. Next, he shot a whistling arrow at his own favorite horse. Some of his men hesitated, not daring to shoot the horse. Maodun beheaded them. A little later, he used a whistling arrow to shoot at his favorite wife. Again, some of his men, perhaps because they were afraid, did not dare to shoot. Once more, Maodun beheaded them. Later, he went hunting with his men and shot his father's best horse. All his men shot it, too. Then Maodun knew that he could rely on his troops. Accompanying Touman on a hunting trip, he shot a whistling arrow at his father. All his followers shot where the whistling arrow struck and killed the chief. Next, Maodun murdered his stepmother, his younger brother, and all the senior officers who refused to follow his commands. So Maodun made himself the chief [in 209 B.C.E.].

READING AND DISCUSSION QUESTIONS

1. How did the Xiongnu sustain themselves? What was their society like?
2. How did Maodun take charge of the Xiongnu?
3. How might the Chinese have viewed the Xiongnu at this time?

---

[1] **Yuezhi:** A nomadic people who lived northwest of Han China.

7-2 | What Makes a Good Woman?
BAN ZHAO, From *Lessons for Women* (ca. 80 C.E.)

Although women in traditional Confucian society were regarded as subservient to men, a few women achieved distinction in their literary pursuits and roles in government. Ban Zhao (ca. 45–120 C.E.) was the daughter of a famous writer and administrator and sister to Ban Gu, who served as the court historian for Emperor He (r. 89–105 C.E.). The privileged Ban Zhao was educated at an early age. When Ban Gu died, Ban Zhao finished his history of the Han Dynasty and served as an adviser to Emperor He and the Empress Deng. Ban Zhao's best-known work, *Lessons for Women*, served as an advice manual for women in China until the twentieth century.

I, the unworthy writer, am unsophisticated, unenlightened, and by nature unintelligent, but I am fortunate both to have received not a little favor from my scholarly father, and to have had a cultured mother and instructresses upon whom to rely for a literary education as well as for training in good manners. More than forty years have passed since at the age of fourteen I took up the dustpan and the broom in the Cao family.[2] During this time with trembling heart I feared constantly that I might disgrace my parents, and that I might multiply difficulties for both the women and the men of my husband's family. Day and night I was distressed in heart, but I labored without confessing weariness. Now and hereafter, however, I know how to escape from such fears.

Being careless, and by nature stupid, I taught and trained my children without system. Consequently I fear that my son Gu may bring disgrace upon the Imperial Dynasty by whose Holy Grace he has unprecedentedly received the extraordinary privilege of wearing the Gold and the Purple,[3] a privilege for the attainment of which by my son, I a humble subject never even hoped. Nevertheless, now that he is a man and able to plan his own life, I need not again have concern for him. But I do grieve that you, my daughters, just now at the age for marriage, have not at this time had gradual training and advice; that you still have not learned the proper customs for married women. I fear that by failure in good manners in other families you will humiliate both your ancestors and your clan. I am now seriously ill, life is uncertain. As I have thought of you all in so untrained a state, I have been uneasy many a time for you. At hours of leisure I have composed . . . these instructions under the title, "Lessons for Women." In order that you may have something wherewith to benefit your persons, I wish every one of you, my daughters, each to write out a copy for yourself.

From this time on every one of you strive to practice these lessons.

Nancy Lee Swann, trans., *Pan Chao: Foremost Woman Scholar of China* (New York: Century Co., 1932), 111–114. © The East Asian Library and the Gest Collection, Princeton University. Reprinted by permission.

[2] **took up the dustpan . . . family:** Ban Zhao had become a wife.
[3] **the Gold and the Purple:** The colors worn by the elite administrants of the Chinese realm.

Humility

On the third day after the birth of a girl the ancients observed three customs: first to place the baby below the bed; second to give her a potsherd [shard of pottery] with which to play; and third to announce her birth to her ancestors by an offering. Now to lay the baby below the bed plainly indicated that she is lowly and weak, and should regard it as her primary duty to humble herself before others. To give her potsherds with which to play indubitably signified that she should practice labor and consider it her primary duty to be industrious. To announce her birth before her ancestors clearly meant that she ought to esteem as her primary duty the continuation of the observance of worship in the home.

These three ancient customs epitomize a woman's ordinary way of life and the teachings of the traditional ceremonial rites and regulations. Let a woman modestly yield to others; let her respect others; let her put others first, herself last. Should she do something good, let her not mention it; should she do something bad, let her not deny it. Let her bear disgrace; let her even endure when others speak or do evil to her. Always let her seem to tremble and to fear. When a woman follows such maxims as these, then she may be said to humble herself before others.

Let a woman retire late to bed, but rise early to duties; let her not dread tasks by day or by night. Let her not refuse to perform domestic duties whether easy or difficult. That which must be done, let her finish completely, tidily, and systematically. When a woman follows such rules as these, then she may be said to be industrious.

Let a woman be correct in manner and upright in character in order to serve her husband. Let her live in purity and quietness of spirit, and attend to her own affairs. Let her love not gossip and silly laughter. Let her cleanse and purify and arrange in order the wine and the food for the offerings to the ancestors. When a woman observes such principles as these, then she may be said to continue ancestral worship.

No woman who observes these three fundamentals of life has ever had a bad reputation or has fallen into disgrace. If a woman fails to observe them, how can her name be honored; how can she but bring disgrace upon herself?

Husband and Wife

The Way of husband and wife is intimately connected with *Yin* and *Yang*,[4] and relates the individual to gods and ancestors. Truly it is the great principle of Heaven and Earth, and the great basis of human relationships. Therefore the "Rites"[5] honor union of man and woman; and in the "Book of Poetry"[6] the "First

---

[4] **Yin and Yang:** An important concept in Chinese culture that originated in Daoism. Yin and yang are oppositional forces that are bound together and create each other.

[5] **the "Rites":** The *Book of Rites* is one of the five classics of Confucianism. It deals with li, or "rules of conduct," and provides instructions for the correct observation of rituals.

[6] **"Book of Poetry":** The *Book of Songs* is another of the five classics of Confucianism.

Ode" manifests the principle of marriage. For these reasons the relationship cannot but be an important one.

If a husband is unworthy, then he possesses nothing by which to control his wife. If a wife is unworthy, then she possesses nothing with which to serve her husband. If a husband does not control his wife, then the rules of conduct manifesting his authority are abandoned and broken. If a wife does not serve her husband, then the proper relationship between men and women and the natural order of things are neglected and destroyed. As a matter of fact the purpose of these two [the controlling of women by men, and the serving of men by women] is the same.

Now examine the gentlemen of the present age. They only know that wives must be controlled, and that the husband's rules of conduct manifesting his authority must be established. They therefore teach their boys to read books and study histories. But they do not in the least understand that husbands and masters must also be served, and that the proper relationship and the rites should be maintained.

Yet only to teach men and not to teach women — is that not ignoring the essential relation between them? According to the "Rites," it is the rule to begin to teach children to read at the age of eight years, and by the age of fifteen years they ought then to be ready for cultural training. Only why should it not be that girls' education as well as boys' be according to this principle?

Respect and Caution

As *Yin* and *Yang* are not of the same nature, so man and woman have different characteristics. The distinctive quality of the *Yang* is rigidity; the function of the *Yin* is yielding. Man is honored for strength; a woman is beautiful on account of her gentleness. Hence there arose the common saying: "A man though born like a wolf may, it is feared, become a weak monstrosity; a woman though born like a mouse may, it is feared, become a tiger."

Now for self-culture nothing equals respect for others. To counteract firmness nothing equals compliance. Consequently it can be said that the Way of respect and acquiescence is woman's most important principle of conduct. So respect may be defined as nothing other than holding on to that which is permanent; and acquiescence nothing other than being liberal and generous. Those who are steadfast in devotion know that they should stay in their proper places; those who are liberal and generous esteem others, and honor and serve them.

If husband and wife have the habit of staying together, never leaving one another, and following each other around within the limited space of their own rooms, then they will lust after and take liberties with one another. From such action improper language will arise between the two. This kind of discussion may lead to licentiousness. Out of licentiousness will be born a heart of disrespect to the husband. Such a result comes from not knowing that one should stay in one's proper place.

Furthermore, affairs may be either crooked or straight; words may be either right or wrong. Straightforwardness cannot but lead to quarreling; crookedness cannot but lead to accusation. If there are really accusations and quarrels, then undoubtedly there will be angry affairs. Such a result comes from not esteeming others, and not honoring and serving them.

If wives suppress not contempt for husbands, then it follows that such wives rebuke and scold their husbands. If husbands stop not short of anger, then they are certain to beat their wives. The correct relationship between husband and wife is based upon harmony and intimacy, and conjugal love is grounded in proper union. Should actual blows be dealt, how could matrimonial relationship be preserved? Should sharp words be spoken, how could conjugal love exist? If love and proper relationship both be destroyed, then husband and wife are divided.

Womanly Qualifications

A woman ought to have four qualifications: (1) womanly virtue; (2) womanly words; (3) womanly bearing; and (4) womanly work. Now what is called womanly virtue need not be brilliant ability, exceptionally different from others. Womanly words need be neither clever in debate nor keen in conversation. Womanly appearance requires neither a pretty nor a perfect face and form. Womanly work need not be work done more skillfully than that of others.

To guard carefully her chastity; to control circumspectly her behavior; in every motion to exhibit modesty; and to model each act on the best usage, this is womanly virtue.

To choose her words with care; to avoid vulgar language; to speak at appropriate times; and not to weary others with much conversation, may be called the characteristics of womanly words.

To wash and scrub filth away; to keep clothes and ornaments fresh and clean; to wash the head and bathe the body regularly; and to keep the person free from disgraceful filth, may be called the characteristics of womanly bearing.

With whole-hearted devotion to sew and to weave; to love not gossip and silly laughter; in cleanliness and order to prepare the wine and food for serving guests, may be called the characteristics of womanly work.

These four qualifications characterize the greatest virtue of a woman. No woman can afford to be without them. In fact they are very easy to possess if a woman only treasure them in her heart. The ancients had a saying: "Is Love afar off? If I desire love, then love is at hand!" So can it be said of these qualifications. . . .

Implicit Obedience

Whenever the mother-in-law says, "Do not do that," and if what she says is right, unquestionably the daughter-in-law obeys. Whenever the mother-in-law says, "Do that," even if what she says is wrong, still the daughter-in-law submits unfailingly to the command.

Let a woman not act contrary to the wishes and the opinions of parents-in-law about right and wrong; let her not dispute with them what is straight and what is crooked. Such docility may be called obedience which sacrifices personal opinion. Therefore the ancient book, "A Pattern for Women," says: "If a daughter-in-law who follows the wishes of her parents-in-law is like an echo and a shadow, how could she not be praised?"

READING AND DISCUSSION QUESTIONS

1. What does the document suggest about the status of women in Chinese society? How does the treatment of infant daughters convey this status?

2. What, in Ban Zhao's opinion, constitutes the perfect marriage? What role should each partner play?

3. What, in Ban Zhao's opinion, constitutes the perfect woman? Why does she argue that women need to be educated if they are to achieve this ideal?

7-3 | Cultural Fusion in Medieval Japan

Hachiman, Shinto God of War, in the Guise of a Buddhist Monk (ca. 1100–1300 C.E.)

The introduction of Buddhism from China into Japan had a profound impact on Japanese society and culture, shaping cultural, political, and social developments from that point forward. Buddhism was part of a larger pattern of Chinese cultural influence on Japan, each component of which tended to reinforce the others. However, it would be inaccurate to say that Chinese culture supplanted or displaced traditional Japanese values and beliefs. Instead, Chinese and Japanese cultural elements were fused, creating new cultural hybrids. This statue from a Buddhist temple in Nara, Japan, exemplifies this process. As you examine it, consider its implications. What does it tell you about the fusion of Buddhism and Shintoism in ancient Japan?

DE AGOSTINI EDITORE/Bridgeman Images.

READING AND DISCUSSION QUESTIONS

1. Does it surprise you that a Shinto god of war was integrated into Japanese Buddhism? Why or why not?

2. To what groups in Japanese society might such a hybrid deity appeal?

VIEWPOINTS

Buddhism in China

The rapid spread of Buddhism in China in the centuries following the fall of the Han Dynasty is a testimony both to its wide appeal and to the support it received from Chinese elites. In an age of chaos and uncertainty, Buddhism's message of compassion and its direct engagement with the problem of human suffering resonated with many people, rich and poor, male and female. While this intrinsic appeal was essential to Buddhism's success, it was not the only important factor in the establishment of Chinese Buddhism. The financial and political support of elites was also critical. Without such support, it would not have been possible to build and maintain the thousands of Buddhist temples and monasteries that had sprung up by the end of the fifth century. The importance of elite patronage is underscored by the consequences of the withdrawal of that support under the Tang Dynasty. While Buddhism itself survived Tang-era persecution, the Buddhist monastic establishment was dealt a blow from which it never recovered. As you read the documents included here, think about the factors that shaped the changing place of Buddhism in Chinese society. What role did social, economic, and political factors play in this context?

7-4 | Reconciling Buddhism with Traditional Chinese Values

HAN YU, From *Lives of the Eminent Monks: Zhu Seng Du* (ca. 550 C.E.)

Buddhism entered China during the Han Dynasty, spreading from Central Asia along the Silk Road. Although conversion to Buddhism was slow at first, later dynasties such as the Wei (386–534 C.E.) adopted and promoted Buddhism. The continued political division of China and concurrent chaos prompted many to seek spiritual refuge in the Buddha. The transformation of Buddhism so that it appealed more readily to the Chinese was a long process. *Lives of the Eminent Monks*, for example, was composed in a traditional Chinese style of biography, but the content is clearly Buddhist. One of the most important features of the following life is the defense of Buddhist customs that seem to challenge traditional Chinese ways of life.

Zhu Seng Du was originally named Wang Xi (Xuanzong) and came from Donghuan, in Guangdong, South China. He came from a lesser literati family but was a very presentable young man. When he was sixteen his spirit soared high and his character stood out among his peers. His personality was mild and he was well loved by his neighbors. He lived with his mother and was a filial son to the last letter of the Confucian code. He courted the daughter of Mr. Yang Deshen in the same village. The Yang family was also respectable. Their daughter, Tiaohua, had a comely face and proper poise. She was versed in the apocryphal literature and was the same age as Du. The day he proposed to her, she accepted. However, not soon afterwards and before the marriage was set, Tiaohua's mother died. Tiaohua's father soon followed. Meanwhile, Du's mother also passed away. Suddenly realizing the transience of this world, Du left it behind and entered a monastic order, changing his name to Seng Du, Du, the follower of Sakyamuni.[7] He left his trace beyond the world of dust and wandered, as a student, in faraway places. Tiaohua, after having tended to the mourning rites for her parents, realized that there was no place in society for a woman like her without anyone on whom to depend, neither parents, husband, nor child. Therefore she wrote to Du, "According to the Confucian norms of filial piety the hair and skin of one's body, being something received from one's parents, should not be harmed [for example, by tonsure]. The ancestral temples should not be abandoned as you, Du, the monk, have done. Moreover, considering the teaching of Confucian society you should abandon your lofty hermit ideal, and arousing your talents make a name for yourself in the world. Through your success you should let shine the spirit and glory of your ancestors and be a comfort to those close to you, fulfilling the expectations of both man and the spirits." She also wrote five poems. . . .

Seng Du responded, "Serving the king, as demanded by Confucianism, is to assist in the ruling of one's country. That cannot be compared with pursuing the Buddhist path for all peoples. Serving one's parents means to establish a family of one's own; but that cannot be compared with following the Buddhist path for the sake of all beings in the three realms. The dictum 'Never to harm your body or hair' is the narrow advice of those committed to the world. I am ashamed that my present virtue has not extended itself to cover even that filial duty. However, small baskets of earth add up to a mountain: all beginnings are small. Thus I put on my monk's gown, drink the pure water, and laud the wisdom of the Buddhas. Although the dress of princes, the food of the eight rarities, the sound of music and the color of glories are all fine, I would not trade my lot for them. If our minds are in tune to one another, we will meet in nirvana. However, people's hearts are different, just as their faces are. Your distaste for the hermit's way is like my indifference to the world. Dear one, let this be the last parting and let all the karmic ties from ten thousand years past that brought us together end here. Time is running short. The student of the dharma must learn to daily eliminate his attachment to the world of action. Men and women of the world, however, should adapt themselves to the times. You are, in age and virtue, in your prime, so you should pursue what you desire and admire. Do not keep this man who is

---

[7] **Sakyamuni:** Another name for the Buddha.

committed to Buddhism in your mind and thereby lose the best years of your life." Du further wrote five poems in reply. . . .

Du's mind was made up and, like a rock, it could not be swayed. Touched by his reply, Tiaohua also entered an order and became a nun.

READING AND DISCUSSION QUESTIONS

1. According to this document, what features of Buddhism were out of place in traditional Chinese culture?

2. How does Seng Du defend Buddhism against its critics?

7-5 | Emperor Wuzong Cracks Down on Buddhism

EMPEROR WUZONG, *Edict on the Suppression of Buddhism* (845 C.E.)

Despite Buddhism's success, or perhaps because of it, a movement within China began to advocate the removal of Buddhist influences in China. The most famous thinker of this age, Han Yu (768–824), urged a return to traditional Confucian values. Although Wuzong's writings did not lead to tangible results during his lifetime, the later Emperor Wuzong (r. 841–846) issued the following edict, which severely damaged Buddhism's standing in China but did not eliminate the religion. Ironically, Wuzong seems to have been less influenced by Confucian scholars such as Han Yu than he was by Daoist priests, who promised him immortality for eliminating the rival Buddhist belief in China.

Edict of the Eighth Month

We have heard that up through the Three Dynasties the Buddha was never spoken of. It was only from the Han and Wei on that the religion of idols gradually came to prominence. So in this latter age it has transmitted its strange ways, instilling its infection with every opportunity, spreading like a luxuriant vine, until it has poisoned the customs of our nation; gradually, and before anyone was aware, it beguiled and confounded men's minds so that the multitude have been increasingly led astray. It has spread to the hills and plains of all the nine provinces and through the walls and towers of our two capitals. Each day finds its monks and followers growing more numerous and its temples more lofty. It wears out the strength of the people with constructions of earth and wood, pilfers their wealth for ornaments of gold and precious objects, causes men to abandon their lords and parents for the company of teachers, and severs man and

---

William Theodore de Bary, ed., *Sources of East Asian Tradition*, vol. 1: *Premodern Asia* (New York: Columbia University Press, 2008), 585–586. Copyright © 2008 Columbia University Press. Reprinted with permission of the publisher.

wife with its monastic decrees. In destroying law and injuring mankind, indeed, nothing surpasses this doctrine!

Now if even one man fails to work the fields, someone must go hungry; if one woman does not tend her silkworms, someone will be cold. At present there are an inestimable number of monks and nuns in the empire, each of them waiting for the farmers to feed him and the silkworms to clothe him, while the public temples and private chapels have reached boundless numbers, all with soaring towers and elegant ornamentation sufficient to outshine the imperial palace itself. . . .

Having thoroughly examined all earlier reports and consulted public opinion on all sides, we no longer have the slightest doubt in Our mind that this evil should be eradicated. Loyal ministers of the court and provinces have lent their aid to Our high intentions, submitting most apt proposals that We have found worthy of being put into effect. Presented with an opportunity to suppress this source of age-old evil and fulfill the laws and institutions of the ancient kings, to aid mankind and bring profit to the multitude, how could We forbear to act?

The temples of the empire that have been demolished number more than 4,600; 260,500 monks and nuns have been returned to lay life and enrolled as subject to the Twice-a-Year Tax;[8] more than 40,000 privately established temples have been destroyed, releasing 30 or 40 million *qing*[9] of fertile, top-grade land and 150,000 male and female servants who will become subject to the Twice-a-Year Tax. Monks and nuns have been placed under the jurisdiction of the Director of Aliens to make it perfectly clear that this is a foreign religion. Finally, We have ordered more than 3,000 men of the Nestorian and Mazdean[10] religions to return to lay life and to cease polluting the customs of China.

Alas, what had not been carried out in the past seemed to have been waiting for this opportunity. If Buddhism is completely abolished now, who will say that the action is not timely? Already more than 100,000 idle and unproductive Buddhist followers have been expelled, and countless of their gaudy, useless buildings destroyed. Henceforth We may guide the people in stillness and purity, cherish the principle of doing nothing [*wuwei*], order Our government with simplicity and ease, and achieve a unification of customs so that the multitudes of all realms will find their destination in Our august rule.

READING AND DISCUSSION QUESTIONS

1. How is the spread of Buddhism described? How does it conflict with the traditional activities of Chinese society?

2. How does Wuzong describe the Buddhist monks and nuns?

3. What actions did Wuzong order to suppress Buddhism?

---

[8] **Twice-a-Year Tax:** Tax paid by all inhabitants of the Chinese Empire.

[9] *qing*: Chinese unit of land, equal to 100 square meters.

[10] **Mazdean:** A follower of Zoroastrianism.

VIEWPOINTS COMPARATIVE QUESTIONS

1. How might Zhu Seng Du have responded to Emperor Wuzong's edict? What arguments would Du make?

2. What aspects of traditional Chinese life were at the center of the debate over its compatibility with Buddhism?

■ COMPARATIVE QUESTIONS ■

1. What role did the Chinese government play in promoting religion throughout China?

2. How does the status and daily life of women in China, as described by Ban Zhao, compare with that of women in India, according to *The Laws of Manu* (Document 3-4)?

3. What features of Buddhism made it successful throughout East Asia?

4. Why would people in less developed areas of the world at this time, such as Sri Lanka and Japan, want to borrow cultural, religious, and political ideas from their more advanced neighbors?

8

Continuity and Change in Europe and Western Asia
250–850

In the fourth century, the Roman emperor Constantine legalized Christianity, and by the fifth century it was the official religion of the empire. This change transformed the previously illegal and persecuted religion into the most important cultural force throughout the Mediterranean world. While Christian devotion flourished during the fifth century, the Roman Empire at large began to disintegrate. Rome was sacked twice, and by the end of the century the western portion of the empire was in the hands of Germanic-speaking Christian peoples such as the Goths, Lombards, and Franks. These usurping kingdoms encouraged the spread of Christianity into new territories, such as Saxony in modern Germany. Despite Rome's loss of the western Mediterranean, the eastern part of the empire, called the Byzantine Empire by modern scholars, endured until the Ottoman Turks captured Constantinople in 1453.

8-1 | Rules for a Religious Community
SAINT BENEDICT OF NURSIA, From *The Rule of Saint Benedict: Work and Pray* (529)

Christian monasticism developed in the Egyptian desert at the turn of the fourth century C.E. as a solitary activity of self-denial. In the early fourth century, however, groups of monks began to come together to live in self-sufficient communities. These groups required regulation, leading to the creation of monastic "rules." Saint Benedict (480–547), who turned his country estate at Monte Cassino, Italy, into a monastery, developed the most important rule for western European monks. It guided medieval monasticism and helped shape the early Catholic Church.

E. F. Henderson, ed., *Select Historical Documents of the Middle Ages* (London: G. Bell, 1892; rept., New York: AMS Press, 1968), 274–275, 288–289, 597–598.

Concerning the kinds of monks and their manner of living. It is manifest that there are four kinds of monks. The cenobites are the first kind; that is, those living in a monastery, serving under a rule or an abbot. Then the second kind is that of the anchorites; that is, the hermits,—those who, not by the new fervor of a conversion but by the long probation of life in a monastery, have learned to fight against the devil, having already been taught by the solace of many. They, having been well prepared in the army of brothers for the solitary fight of the hermit, being secure now without the consolation of another, are able, God helping them, to fight with their own hand or arm against the vices of the flesh or of their thoughts.

But a third very bad kind of monks are the sarabaites, approved by no rule, experience being their teacher, as with the gold which is tried in the furnace. But, softened after the manner of lead, keeping faith with the world by their works, they are known through their tonsure to lie to God. These being shut up by twos or threes, or, indeed, alone, without a shepherd, not in the Lord's but in their own sheep-folds—their law is the satisfaction of their desires. For whatever they think good or choice, this they call holy; and what they do not wish, this they consider unlawful. But the fourth kind of monks is the kind which is called gyratory. During their whole life they are guests, for three or four days at a time, in the cells of the different monasteries, throughout the various provinces; always wandering and never stationary, given over to the service of their own pleasures and the joys of the palate, and in every way worse than the sarabaites. Concerning the most wretched way of living of all of such monks it is better to be silent than to speak. These things therefore being omitted, let us proceed, with the aid of God, to treat of the best kind, the cenobites. . . .

Concerning the utensils or property of the monastery. For the belongings of the monastery in utensils, or garments, or property of any kind, the abbot shall provide brothers of whose life and morals he is sure; and to them as he shall see fit he shall consign the different things to be taken care of and collected. Concerning which the abbot shall keep a list, so that when in turn the brothers succeed each other in the care of the things assigned, he may know what he gives or what he receives. If moreover any one have soiled or treated negligently the property of the monastery, he shall be rebuked; but if he do not amend, he shall be subjected to the discipline of the Rule.

Whether the monks should have any thing of their own. More than any thing else is this special vice to be cut off root and branch from the monastery, that one should presume to give or receive anything without the order of the abbot, or should have anything of his own. He should have absolutely not anything: neither a book, nor tablets, nor a pen—nothing at all.—For indeed it is not allowed to the monks to have their own bodies or wills in their own power. But all things necessary they must expect from the Father of the monastery; nor is it allowable to have anything which the abbot did not give or permit. All things shall be common to all, as it is written: "Let not any man presume or call anything his own." But if any one shall have been discovered delighting in this most evil vice: being warned once and again, if he do not amend, let him be subjected to punishment. . . .

Concerning the daily manual labor. Idleness is the enemy of the soul. And therefore, at fixed times, the brothers ought to be occupied in manual labor; and again, at fixed times, in sacred reading. Therefore we believe that, according to this disposition, both seasons ought to be arranged; so that, from Easter until the Calends of October,[1] going out early, from the first until the fourth hour they shall do what labor may be necessary. Moreover, from the fourth hour until about the sixth, they shall be free for reading. After the meal of the sixth hour, moreover, rising from table, they shall rest in their beds with all silence; or, perchance, he that wishes to read may so read to himself that he do not disturb another. And the nona[2] shall be gone through with more moderately about the middle of the eighth hour; and again they shall work at what is to be done until Vespers.[3] But, if the exigency or poverty of the place demands that they be occupied by themselves in picking fruits, they shall not be dismayed: for then they are truly monks if they live by the labors of their hands; as did also our fathers and the apostles. Let all things be done with moderation, however, on account of the faint-hearted. . . . [There follows a slightly different schedule for the winter months from October to Easter.] But in the days of Lent,[4] from dawn until the third full hour, they shall be free for their readings; and, until the tenth full hour, they shall do the labor that is enjoined on them. In which days of Lent they shall all receive separate books from the library; which they shall read entirely through in order. These books are to be given out on the first day of Lent. Above all there shall certainly be appointed one or two elders, who shall go round the monastery at the hours in which the brothers are engaged in reading, and see to it that no troublesome brother chance to be found who is open to idleness and trifling, and is not intent on his reading; being not only of no use to himself, but also stirring up others. If such a one — may it not happen — be found, he shall be admonished once and a second time. If he do not amend, he shall be subject under the Rule to such punishment that the others may have fear. . . . On feeble or delicate brothers such a labor or art is to be imposed, that they shall neither be idle, nor shall they be so oppressed by the violence of labor as to be driven to take flight. Their weakness is to be taken into consideration by the abbot.

READING AND DISCUSSION QUESTIONS

1. What are the four kinds of monks? Which did Benedict consider the best kind?

2. Describe the daily life of a monk. Why might so many people have found this lifestyle admirable and appealing?

3. Why might there have been so much emphasis on reading in the monastery? Why did Benedict believe it necessary to balance reading and prayer with manual labor?

---

[1] **Calends of October:** The first day of the month of October.
[2] **nona:** The second meal of the day.
[3] **Vespers:** Evening prayers.
[4] **Lent:** The forty days leading up to Easter, normally spent in self-denial, fasting, and prayer.

8-2 | A Germanic People Create a Code of Law
The Law of the Salian Franks (ca. 500–600)

As the institutions of Roman government in the West faltered and then crumbled, the power and reach of Roman law also declined. This is not to say that Roman law disappeared in the West or that the West descended into utter lawlessness. The Germanic peoples whose migrations played such an important role in precipitating Rome's fall brought with them their own systems of law and justice. As Germanic peoples settled in the West and established kingdoms, those systems were written down and codified. Such was the case with *The Law of the Salian Franks*, first published in written form in the early sixth century at the order of Clovis I (ca. 466–511). As you read this excerpt, consider what it reveals about Frankish society. What kinds of problems did the laws address? How did ideas about social status and gender shape the laws?

Title I. Concerning Summonses

1. If any one be summoned before the "Thing" by the king's law, and do not come, he shall be sentenced to 600 denars, which make 15 shillings (solidi).
2. But he who summons another, and does not come himself, shall, if a lawful impediment have not delayed him, be sentenced to 15 shillings, to be paid to him whom he summoned.
3. And he who summons another shall walk with witnesses to the home of that man, and, if he be not at home, shall bid the wife or any one of the family to make known to him that he has been summoned to court.
4. But if he be occupied in the king's service he can not summon him.
5. But if he shall be inside the hundred[5] seeing about his own affairs, he can summon him in the manner explained above.

Title II. Concerning Thefts of Pigs, etc.

1. If any one steal a sucking pig, and it be proved against him, he shall be sentenced to 120 denars, which make three shillings.
2. If any one steal a pig that can live without its mother, and it be proved on him, he shall be sentenced to 40 denars — that is, 1 shilling. . . .
14. If any one steal 25 sheep where there were no more in that flock, and it be proved on him, he shall be sentenced to 2500 denars — that is, 62 shillings.

Title III. Concerning Thefts of Cattle

4. If any one steal that bull which rules the herd and never has been yoked, he shall be sentenced to 1800 denars, which make 45 shillings.

E. F. Henderson, trans. and ed., *Select Historical Documents of the Middle Ages* (London: G. Bell, 1892), 176–181.

[5] **inside the hundred:** Governing body.

5. But if that bull is used for the cows of three villages in common, he who stole him shall be sentenced to three times 45 shillings.

6. If any one steal a bull belonging to the king he shall be sentenced to 3600 denars, which make 90 shillings.

Title IV. Concerning Damage Done Among Crops or in Any Enclosure

1. If any one finds cattle, or a horse, or flocks of any kind in his crops, he shall not at all mutilate them.

2. If he do this and confess it, he shall restore the worth of the animal in place of it, and shall himself keep the mutilated one.

3. But if he have not confessed it, and it have been proved on him, he shall be sentenced, besides the value of the animal and the fines for delay, to 600 denars, which make 15 shillings.

Title XI. Concerning Thefts or Housebreakings of Freemen

1. If any freeman steal, outside of the house, something worth 2 denars, he shall be sentenced to 600 denars, which make 15 shillings.

2. But if he steal, outside of the house, something worth 40 denars, and it be proved on him, he shall be sentenced, besides the amount and the fines for delay, to 1400 denars, which make 35 shillings.

3. If a freeman break into a house and steal something worth 2 denars, and it be proved on him, he shall be sentenced to 15 shillings.

4. But if he shall have stolen something worth more than 2 denars, and it have been proved on him, he shall be sentenced, besides the worth of the object and the fines for delay, to 1400 denars, which make 35 shillings.

5. But if he have broken, or tampered with, the lock, and thus have entered the house and stolen anything from it, he shall be sentenced, besides the worth of the object and the fines for delay, to 1800 denars, which make 45 shillings.

6. And if he have taken nothing, or have escaped by flight, he shall, for the housebreaking alone, be sentenced to 1200 denars, which make 30 shillings.

Title XII. Concerning Thefts or Housebreakings on the Part of Slaves

1. If a slave steal, outside of the house, something worth two denars, he shall, besides paying the worth of the object and the fines for delay, be stretched out and receive 120 blows.

2. But if he steal something worth 40 denars, he shall either be castrated or pay 6 shillings. But the lord of the slave who committed the theft shall restore to the plaintiff the worth of the object and the fines for delay.

Title XIII. Concerning Rape Committed by Freemen

1. If three men carry off a free born girl, they shall be compelled to pay 30 shillings.

2. If there are more than three, each one shall pay 5 shillings.

3. Those who shall have been present with boats shall be sentenced to three shillings.
4. But those who commit rape shall be compelled to pay 2500 denars, which make 63 shillings.
5. But if they have carried off that girl from behind lock and key, or from the spinning room, they shall be sentenced to the above price and penalty.
6. But if the girl who is carried off be under the king's protection, then the "frith" (peace-money) shall be 2500 denars, which make 63 shillings.
7. But if a bondsman of the king, or a leet, should carry off a free woman, he shall be sentenced to death.
8. But if a free woman have followed a slave of her own will, she shall lose her freedom.
9. If a freeborn man shall have taken an alien bondswoman, he shall suffer similarly.
10. If any body take an alien spouse and join her to himself in matrimony, he shall be sentenced to 2500 denars, which make 63 shillings.

Title XIV. Concerning Assault and Robbery

1. If any one have assaulted and plundered a free man, and it be proved on him, he shall be sentenced to 2500 denars, which make 63 shillings.
2. If a Roman have plundered a Salian Frank, the above law shall be observed.
3. But if a Frank have plundered a Roman, he shall be sentenced to 35 shillings.
4. If any man should wish to migrate, and has permission from the king, and shall have shown this in the public "Thing": whoever, contrary to the decree of the king, shall presume to oppose him, shall be sentenced to 8000 denars, which make 200 shillings.

Title XV. Concerning Arson

1. If any one shall set fire to a house in which men were sleeping, as many free-men as were in it can make complaint before the "Thing"; and if any one shall have been burned in it, the incendiary shall be sentenced to 2500 denars, which make 63 shillings.

Title XVII. Concerning Wounds

1. If any one have wished to kill another person, and the blow have missed, he on whom it was proved shall be sentenced to 2500 denars, which make 63 shillings.
2. If any person have wished to strike another with a poisoned arrow, and the arrow have glanced aside, and it shall be proved on him: he shall be sentenced to 2500 denars, which make 63 shillings.
3. If any person strike another on the head so that the brain appears, and the three bones which lie above the brain shall project, he shall be sentenced to 1200 denars—which make 30 shillings.

4. But if it shall have been between the ribs or in the stomach, so that the wound appears and reaches to the entrails, he shall be sentenced to 1200 denars—which make 30 shilling—besides five shillings for the physician's pay.
5. If any one shall have struck a man so that blood falls to the floor, and it be proved on him, he shall be sentenced to 600 denars, which make 15 shillings.
6. But if a freeman strike a freeman with his fist so that blood does not flow, he shall be sentenced for each blow—up to 3 blows—to 120 denars, which make 3 shillings.

Title XVIII. Concerning Him Who, Before the King, Accuses an Innocent Man

If any one, before the king, accuse an innocent man who is absent, he shall be sentenced to 2500 denars, which make 63 shillings.

Title XIX. Concerning Magicians

1. If any one have given herbs to another so that he die, he shall be sentenced to 200 shillings (or shall surely be given over to fire).
2. If any person have bewitched another, and he who was thus treated shall escape, the author of the crime, who is proved to have committed it, shall be sentenced to 2500 denars, which make 63 shillings.

Title XXIV. Concerning the Killing of Little Children and Women

1. If any one have slain a boy under 10 years—up to the end of the tenth—and it shall have been proved on him, he shall be sentenced to 24000 denars, which make 600 shillings. . . .
3. If any one have hit a free woman who is pregnant, and she dies, he shall be sentenced to 28000 denars, which make 700 shillings. . . .
6. If any one have killed a free woman after she has begun bearing children, he shall be sentenced to 24000 denars, which make 600 shillings.
7. After she can have no more children, he who kills her shall be sentenced to 8000 denars, which make 200 shillings.

Title XXX. Concerning Insults

3. If any one, man or woman, shall have called a woman harlot, and shall not have been able to prove it, he shall be sentenced to 1800 denars, which make 45 shillings.
4. If any person shall have called another "fox," he shall be sentenced to 3 shillings.
5. If any man shall have called another "hare," he shall be sentenced to 3 shillings.
6. If any man shall have brought it up against another that he have thrown away his shield, and shall not have been able to prove it, he shall be sentenced to 120 denars, which make 3 shillings.
7. If any man shall have called another "spy" or "perjurer," and shall not have been able to prove it, he shall be sentenced to 600 denars, which make 15 shillings.

READING AND DISCUSSION QUESTIONS

1. Based on these laws, how would you characterize life in a Frankish community?

2. What might explain the fact that most crimes were punished with fines?

3. What do the laws tell us about the status and role of women in Frankish society?

4. What might explain Clovis's decision to publish a written version of the laws? What does this decision suggest about the development of Frankish society and government?

VIEWPOINTS

Justinian's Deeds and His Critics

Justinian (ca. 482–565) has a justifiable claim to having been the greatest of the Byzantine emperors. At his direction, Roman law was systematically reformed and codified. The resulting *Corpus Juris Civilis* would have a profound effect on European legal systems for centuries to come. While his military efforts did not result in long-term gains, during his lifetime Justinian's armies recaptured significant territory in the West that had previously been lost to Germanic peoples. His extensive building programs, particularly in Constantinople, produced some of the most spectacular structures the world has ever seen. The best-known account of his reign, however, paints a very different picture. As Procopius's *Secret History* tells it, Justinian and his wife, Theodora, were evil incarnate, capable of the most vicious and depraved acts. As you examine the documents included below, think about this apparent contradiction. Given Justinian's accomplishments, what might Procopius's motive have been for vilifying him in the *Secret History*? How might Justinian have responded to Procopius's charges?

8-3 | The Greed and Immorality of a Byzantine Emperor
PROCOPIUS, From the *Secret History* (ca. 550–562)

The Byzantine scholar and nobleman Procopius (ca. 500–565) lived in a time of enormous uncertainty and turmoil. In his view, Byzantine society was on the verge of collapse, an opinion that was not so far-fetched given events in Rome in the previous century. The *Secret History* was Procopius's effort to draw connections between the policies and personalities of Byzantium's rulers and the rapid decline that he perceived. As you read this excerpt, consider what connections Procopius might have wanted readers to make between his descriptions of

---

G. A. Williamson, trans., *Procopius: The Secret History* (London: Penguin Books, 1966, 1981), 94–95, 101–103. Copyright © 1966 G. A. Williamson. Reprinted by permission of David Higham Associates Ltd.

Justinian and Theodora and the problems and challenges his society faced. On what basis did he hold them responsible for Byzantium's ills?

When Justinian ascended the throne it took him a very little while to bring every-thing into confusion. Things hitherto forbidden by law were one by one brought into public life, while established customs were swept away wholesale, as if he had been invested with the forms of majesty on condition that he would change all things to new forms. Long established offices were abolished, and new ones set up to run the nation's business; the laws of the land and the organization of the army were treated in the same way, not because justice required it or the general interest urged him to it, but merely that everything might have a new look and might be associated with his name. If there was anything which he was not in a position to transform then and there, even so he would at least attach his own name to it.

Of the forcible seizure of property and the murder of his subjects he could never have enough: when he had looted innumerable houses of wealthy people he was constantly on the look-out for others, immediately squandering on one foreign tribe or another, or on crazy building schemes, all that he had amassed by his earlier looting. And when he had without any excuse got rid of thousands and thousands of people, or so it would seem, he promptly devised schemes for doing the same to others more numerous still. . . .

Until the "Nika" insurrection[6] took place, they [Justinian and Theodora] were content to annex the estates of the well-to-do one at a time; but after it took place, as I related in an earlier volume, from then on they confiscated at a single stroke the possessions of nearly all the senators. On all movable property and on the most attractive landed estates they laid their hands just as they fancied; but they set aside properties liable to oppressive and crushing taxation, and with sham gener-osity sold them to their previous owners! These in consequence were throttled by the tax-collectors and reduced to penury by the never-ending interest on their debts, dragging out a miserable existence that was no more than a lingering death.

In view of all this I, like most of my contemporaries, never once felt that these two were human beings: they were a pair of blood-thirsty demons and what the poets call "plaguers of mortal men." For they plotted together to find the easiest and swiftest means of destroying all races of men and all their works, assumed human shape, became man-demons, and in this way con-vulsed the whole world. Proof of this could be found in many things, but espe-cially in the power manifested in their doings. For the actions of demons are unmistakably different from those of human beings. In the long course of time there have doubtless been many men who by chance or by nature have inspired the utmost fear, and by their unaided efforts have ruined cities or countries or whatever it might be; but to bring destruction on all mankind and calamities on

---

[6]**"Nika" insurrection:** In 532, riots began at the chariot races in Constantinople's hippodrome. The riots almost pushed Justinian out of the city, and many important buildings, such as Hagia Sophia (see Document 8-4), were damaged. In the end, Justinian retained his throne through bribery and the slaughter of thousands.

the whole world has been beyond the power of any but these two, who were, it is true, aided in their endeavors by chance, which collaborated in the ruin of mankind; for earthquakes, pestilences, and rivers that burst their banks brought widespread destruction at this time, as I shall explain shortly. Thus it was not by human but by some very different power that they wrought such havoc.

It is said that Justinian's own mother told some of her close friends that he was not the son of her husband Sabbatius or of any man at all. For when she was about to conceive she was visited by a demon, who was invisible but gave her a distinct impression that he was really there with her like a man in bodily contact with a woman. Then he vanished like a dream.

Some of those who were in the Emperor's company late at night, conversing with him (evidently in the Palace)—men of the highest possible character— thought that they saw a strange demonic form in his place. One of them declared that he more than once rose suddenly from the imperial throne and walked round and round the room; for he was not in the habit of remaining seated for long. And Justinian's head would momentarily disappear, while the rest of his body seemed to continue making these long circuits. The watcher himself, thinking that something had gone seriously wrong with his eyesight, stood for a long time distressed and quite at a loss. But later the head returned to the body, and he thought that what a moment before had been lacking was, contrary to expectation, filling out again. A second man said that he stood by the Emperor's side as he sat, and saw his face suddenly transformed to a shape-less lump of flesh: neither eyebrows nor eyes were in their normal position, and it showed no other distinguishing feature at all; gradually, however, he saw the face return to its usual shape. I did not myself witness the events I am describ-ing, but I heard about them from men who insist that they saw them at the time.

READING AND DISCUSSION QUESTIONS

1. How does Procopius describe Justinian and Theodora? What evidence does he provide that they might not have been fully human?

2. What does the *Secret History* tell you about how Procopius saw his own society? What might explain his deep pessimism?

8-4 | Constantinople's Crowning Glory
Hagia Sophia (537)

At the beginning of Justinian's reign, rioters in the Nika revolt burned Hagia Sophia, the church dedicated to Holy Wisdom. Justinian decided to replace it with an extravagant struc-ture and spared no expense. The crowning achievement was the large dome, designed by Anthemius of Tralles, which Procopius described as seeming to be "suspended from heaven by a fabled golden chain." When the church was dedicated, Justinian claimed to have out-done Solomon's construction of the first temple of Jerusalem. The structure awed all visitors to Constantinople for centuries, and when the Ottomans took the city in 1453, they con-verted it into a mosque and added the minarets that can be seen in this image.

Murat Taner/Getty Images.

DE AGOSTINI EDITORE/Bridgeman Images.

READING AND DISCUSSION QUESTIONS

1. Describe the structure of the Hagia Sophia.

2. Why would Justinian have wanted to build such an impressive church?

3. What does the Hagia Sophia suggest about the relationship between church and state in the Byzantine Empire during the reign of Justinian?

VIEWPOINTS COMPARATIVE QUESTIONS

1. Compare Procopius's description of Justinian in the *Secret History* with the construction of the Hagia Sophia. In what ways does the Hagia Sophia confirm Procopius's description, and in what ways does this building challenge Procopius?

2. How would you reconcile the apparent discrepancy between Justinian's accomplishments and Procopius's description of him? What evidence can you produce to support your position?

8-5 | Einhard Describes Charlemagne, the Man

EINHARD, From *The Life of Charlemagne* (829–836)

During the collapse of the western half of the Roman Empire in the fifth century, the Franks took control of northern Gaul (now called France). By the middle of the eighth century, the Franks had become the most powerful of the Germanic kingdoms. Charlemagne (747–814), or Charles the Great, amassed such a large empire in what is now France, Germany, and Italy that he was crowned Roman Emperor on Christmas Day in 800 by Pope Leo III, who was seeking allies against the Byzantine Empire. One of Charlemagne's closest friends and advisers, Einhard, composed these passages, which describe Charlemagne's building projects and his personal characteristics.

However much energy Charlemagne may have expended in enlarging his realm and conquering foreign nations, and despite all the time which he devoted to this preoccupation, he nevertheless set in hand many projects which aimed at making his kingdom more attractive and at increasing public utility. Some of these projects he completed. Outstanding among these, one might claim, are the great church of the Holy Mother of God at Aachen, which is a really remarkable construction, and the bridge over the Rhine at Mainz, which is five hundred feet long, this being the width of the river at that point. The bridge was burned down

Lewis Thorpe, trans., *Two Lives of Charlemagne: Einhard and Notker the Stammerer* (London: Penguin Classics, 1969), 71, 78–80. Copyright © 1989 Professor Lewis Thorpe. Reproduced by permission of Penguin Books Ltd.

just one year before Charlemagne's death. He planned to rebuild it in stone instead of wood, but his death followed so quickly that the bridge could not be restored in time. He also began the construction of two magnificent palaces: one not far from the city of Mainz, near the township called Ingelheim; and the other at Nimeguen, on the River Waal, which flows along the southern shore of the Betuwa peninsula. More important still was the fact that he commanded the bishops and churchmen in whose care they were to restore sacred edifices which had fallen into ruin through their very antiquity, wherever he discovered them throughout the whole of his kingdom; and he instructed his representatives to see that these orders were carried out. . . .

He was moderate in his eating and drinking, and especially so in drinking; for he hated to see drunkenness in any man, and even more so in himself and his friends. All the same, he could not go long without food, and he often used to complain that fasting made him feel ill. He rarely gave banquets and these only on high feast days, but then he would invite a great number of guests. His main meal of the day was served in four courses, in addition to the roast meat which his hunters used to bring in on spits and which he enjoyed more than any other food. During his meal he would listen to a public reading or some other entertainment. Stories would be recited for him, or the doings of the ancients told again. He took great pleasure in the books of Saint Augustine and especially in those which are called *The City of God*.

He was so sparing in his use of wine and every other beverage that he rarely drank more than three times in the course of his dinner. In summer, after his midday meal, he would eat some fruit and take another drink; then he would remove his shoes and undress completely, just as he did at night, and rest for two or three hours. During the night he slept so lightly that he would wake four or five times and rise from his bed. When he was dressing and putting on his shoes he would invite his friends to come in. Moreover, if the Count of the Palace told him that there was some dispute which could not be settled without the Emperor's personal decision, he would order the disputants to be brought in there and then, hear the case as if he were sitting in tribunal and pronounce a judgement. If there was any official business to be transacted on that day, or any order to be given to one of his ministers, he would settle it at the same time.

He spoke easily and fluently, and could express with great clarity whatever he wanted to say. He was not content with his own mother tongue, but took the trouble to learn foreign languages. He learnt Latin so well that he spoke it as fluently as his own tongue; but he understood Greek better than he could speak it. He was eloquent to the point of sometimes seeming almost garrulous.

He paid the greatest attention to the liberal arts; and he had great respect for men who taught them, bestowing high honors upon them. When he was learning the rules of grammar he received tuition from Peter the Deacon of Pisa, who by then was an old man, but for all other subjects he was taught by Alcuin, surnamed Albinus, another Deacon, a man of the Saxon race who came from Britain and was the most learned man anywhere to be found. Under him the emperor spent much time and effort in studying rhetoric, dialectic and especially astrology. He applied himself to mathematics and traced the course of the stars with great attention and care. He also tried to learn to write. With this object in view he used to keep writing-tablets and notebooks under the pillows on his bed, so that he could try his hand at forming letters during his leisure moments; but, although he tried very hard, he had begun too late in life and he made little progress.

Charlemagne practiced the Christian religion with great devotion and piety, for he had been brought up in this faith since earliest childhood. This explains why he built a cathedral of such great beauty at Aachen, decorating it with gold and silver, with lamps, and with lattices and doors of solid bronze. He was unable to find marble columns for his construction anywhere else, and so he had them brought from Rome and Ravenna.

As long as his health lasted he went to church morning and evening with great regularity, and also for early-morning Mass, and the late-night hours. He took the greatest pains to ensure that all church ceremonies were performed with the utmost dignity, and he was always warning the sacristans to see that nothing sordid or dirty was brought into the building or left there. He donated so many sacred vessels made of gold and silver, and so many priestly vestments, that when service time came even those who opened and closed the doors, surely the humblest of all church dignitaries, had no need to perform their duties in their everyday clothes.

He made careful reforms in the way in which the psalms were chanted and the lessons read. He was himself quite an expert at both of these exercises, but he never read the lesson in public and he would sing only with the rest of the congregation and then in a low voice.

He was most active in relieving the poor and in that form of really disinterested charity which the Greeks call *eleemosyna*. He gave alms not only in his own country and in the kingdom over which he reigned, but also across the sea in Syria, Egypt, Africa, Jerusalem, Alexandria and Carthage. Wherever he heard that Christians were living in want, he took pity on their poverty and sent them money regularly. It was, indeed, precisely for this reason that he sought the friendship of kings beyond the sea, for he hoped that some relief and alleviation might result for the Christians living under their domination.

READING AND DISCUSSION QUESTIONS

1. What features of Charlemagne's personal habits would have made him a good ruler?

2. Describe Charlemagne's personality. What were his religious beliefs?

3. What does this source tell us about life in post-Roman Europe?

▪ COMPARATIVE QUESTIONS ▪

1. What do the documents in this chapter reveal about the political, cultural, and religious changes that had taken place since the time of ancient Rome (Chapter 6)?

2. Compare and contrast *The Law of the Salian Franks* with other law codes included in this reader (Documents 2-2, 3-4, and 6-1). What similarities and differences do you note?

3. Why does Procopius's description of Justinian seem so different from Einhard's description of Charlemagne? Compare the two rulers.

4. Compare and contrast Einhard's description of Charlemagne with Plutarch's description of Cleomenes III (Document 5-3). What similarities and differences do you note?

9

The Islamic World
600–1400

In the sixth century, the city of Mecca rose to prominence in the Arabian peninsula because of the popularity of its religious shrine, the Ka'ba, and its trade with the Byzantine and Persian Empires. The Prophet Muhammad (ca. 570–632) began his adult life working Mecca's caravans, but on turning forty he began to have revelations that formed the basis for the Qur'an. In 622, Muhammad was forced out of Mecca and led his followers to Medina, where he settled disputes between Jewish merchant groups and eventually became the leader of the city. Muhammad later captured the city of Mecca and united the nomadic tribes of the Arabian peninsula. Under Muhammad's successors, the caliphs, Islamic armies conquered the Middle East, North Africa, Spain, and portions of northern India. In so doing, the Muslims encountered Jews and Christians—honored as fellow "people of the book"—as well as polytheists, whom they persecuted. During the Umayyad (661–750) and the Abbasid (750–1258) Dynasties, the Islamic caliphate dominated the world in economic activity, scientific development, and culture.

VIEWPOINTS

Islam and the People of the Book

As monotheists, Jews and Christians living in Muslim lands were considered "protected peoples." They were not forced to convert to Islam, were allowed to maintain churches and synagogues in Muslim towns and cities, and faced no undue restrictions on their social and economic activities. Without question, the experience of Jews and Christians living in Muslim society compared favorably to that of Jews and other religious minorities living in Christian Europe. Nonetheless, toleration was not the same as full equality. Christians and Jews were seen as members of distinct communities, separate from and inferior to the larger Islamic community, and their protected status was contingent on their acknowledgment of Muslim political authority. Moreover, their religious views and practices, while tolerated, were seen by the Muslim majority as corrupted versions of their own much purer truth. The documents included here offer an opportunity to further explore Islamic views of other "people of the book." As you read them, consider what they reveal about the scriptural foundations of Islamic policies toward religious minorities.

9-1 | Muslims, Christians, and Jews in the Qur'an
MUHAMMAD, *Qur'an* (ca. 650)

The Prophet Muhammad urged "submission" (Islam) to God (Allah), and he demanded that the nomadic Arab tribes of the Arabian peninsula convert from polytheism. His revelations (Qur'an) delivered by the angel Gabriel accepted the authority of Jewish prophets and the teachings of Jesus, who was also considered a prophet. However, according to the Qur'an, most Jews and Christians had lost sight of the truths their prophets revealed. Thus, their special status as "people of the book" was more a reflection of their potential for spiritual perfection than a statement about the truthfulness of Christianity and Judaism as actually practiced. As you read these passages from the Qur'an, pay particular attention to the light they shed on Muslim views of the relationship between Islam, Judaism, and Christianity. What potential sources of tension do they reveal between Muslims and the Jews and Christians who lived in Muslim domains?

In the Name of God, the Compassionate, the Merciful

Praise be to God, the Lord of the Worlds!
    The Compassionate, the Merciful!
    King of the day of judgment!
    Thee we worship, and Thee we ask for help.
    Guide us in the straight way,
    The way of those to whom Thou art gracious;
    Not of those upon whom is Thy wrath, nor of the erring.
    In the name of the merciful and compassionate God. That is the book! There is no doubt therein; a guide to the pious, who believe in the unseen, and are

N. J. Dawood, trans., *The Koran: With a Parallel Arabic Text* (London: Penguin Books, 1990), 28–29, 76–77, 81. Copyright © 1956, 1959, 1966, 1968, 1974, 1990, 1993, 1997, 1999, 2003 N. J. Dawood. Reproduced by permission of Penguin Books Ltd.

steadfast in prayer, and of what we have given them expend in alms; who believe in what is revealed to thee, and what was revealed before thee, and of the hereafter they are sure. These are in guidance from their Lord, and these are the prosperous.

Verily, those who misbelieve, it is the same to them if ye warn them or if ye warn them not, they will not believe. God has set a seal upon their hearts and on their hearing; and on their eyes is dimness, and for them is grievous woe. There are, indeed, those among men who say, "We believe in God and in the last day"; but they do not believe. They would deceive God and those who do believe; but they deceive only themselves and they do not perceive. In their hearts is a sickness, and God has made them still more sick, and for them is grievous woe because they lied. . . .

And if ye are in doubt of what we have revealed unto our servant, then bring a chapter like it, and call your witnesses other than God if ye tell truth. But if ye do it not, and ye shall surely do it not, then fear the fire, whose fuel is men and stones, prepared for misbelievers. But bear the glad tidings to those who believe and work righteousness, that for them are gardens beneath which rivers flow. Whenever they are provided with fruit therefrom they say, "This is what we were provided with before, and they shall be provided with the like; and there are pure wives for them therein, and they shall dwell therein for aye [forever]." . . .

In the Name of God, the Compassionate, the Merciful

Have we not made the earth as a bed? And the mountains as tent-pegs? and created you in pairs, and made you sleep for rest, and made the night for a mantle, and made the day for breadwinning, and built above you seven firmaments, and put therein a burning lamp, and sent down water pouring from the squeezed clouds to bring forth grain and herb withal, and gardens thick with trees?

Lo! the Day of Decision is appointed—the day when there shall be a blowing of the trumpet, and ye shall come in troops, and the heavens shall be opened, and be full of gates, and the mountains shall be removed, and turn into [mist]. Verily hell lieth in wait, the goal for rebels, to abide therein for ages; they shall not taste therein coolness nor drink, save scalding water and running sores,—a meet reward! Verily they did not expect the reckoning, and they denied our signs with lies; but everything have we recorded in a book:—

Then the people of the right hand—what people of good omen! And the people of the left hand—what people of ill omen! And the outstrippers, still outstripping:—these are the nearest [to God], in gardens of delight; a crowd of the men of yore, and a few of the latter days; upon inwrought couches, reclining thereon face to face. Youths ever young shall go unto them round about with goblets and ewers [pitchers] and a cup of flowing wine,—their heads shall not ache with it, neither shall they be confused; and fruits of their choice, and flesh of birds of their desire; and damsels with bright eyes like hidden pearls,—a reward for what they have wrought. They shall hear no folly therein, nor any sin, but only the greeting, "Peace! peace!"

And the people of the right hand—what people of good omen! Amid thorn-less lote-trees,[1] and bananas laden with fruit, and shade outspread, and water flowing, and fruit abundant, never failing, nor forbidden. . . . But the people of the left hand—what people of ill omen!—amid burning wind and scalding water, and a shade of black smoke, not cool or grateful! Verily before that they were prosperous; but they persisted in the most grievous sin, and used to say, "When we have died, and become dust and bones, shall we indeed be raised again, and our fathers, the men of yore." Say: Verily those of yore and of the lat-ter days shall surely be gathered to the trysting-place of a day which is known. Then ye, O ye who err and call it a lie, shall surely eat of the tree of Zakkum,[2] and fill your bellies with it, and drink upon it scalding water,—drink like the thirsty camel:—this shall be their entertainment on the Day of Judgment! . . .

On Violence, Unbelievers, and the People of the Book

In the month of Ramaḍān the Qur'an was revealed, a book of guidance for man-kind with proofs of guidance distinguishing right from wrong. Therefore who-ever of you is present in that month let him fast. But he who is ill or on a journey shall fast a similar number of days later on.

God desires your well-being, not your discomfort. He desires you to fast the whole month so that you may magnify God and render thanks to Him for giving you His guidance.

If My servants question you about Me, tell them that I am near. I answer the prayer of the suppliant when he calls to Me; therefore let them answer My call and put their trust in Me, that they may be rightly guided.

It is now lawful for you to lie with your wives on the night of the fast; they are a comfort to you as you are to them. God knew that you were deceiving your-selves. He has relented towards you and pardoned you. Therefore you may now lie with them and seek what God has ordained for you. Eat and drink until you can tell a white thread from a black one in the light of the coming dawn. Then resume the fast till nightfall and do not approach them, but stay at your prayers in the mosques.

These are the bounds set by God: do not approach them. Thus He makes known His revelations to mankind that they may guard themselves against evil.

Do not devour one another's property by unjust means, nor bribe the judges with it in order that you may wrongfully and knowingly usurp the possessions of other men.

They question you about the phases of the moon. Say: "They are seasons fixed for mankind and for the pilgrimage."

---

[1] **lote-trees:** Mythical trees representing the boundary between humans and Allah and beyond which no mortal can pass; they mark the uppermost limit of human knowledge.

[2] **Zakkum:** A tree in hell that causes a burning sensation when eaten. People in hell are forced to eat from it.

Righteousness does not consist in entering your dwellings from the back.[3] The righteous man is he that fears God. Enter your dwellings by their doors and fear God, so that you may prosper.

Fight for the sake of God those that fight against you, but do not attack them first. God does not love aggressors.

Slay them wherever you find them. Drive them out of the places from which they drove you. Idolatry is more grievous than bloodshed. But do not fight them within the precincts of the Holy Mosque unless they attack you there; if they attack you put them to the sword. Thus shall the unbelievers be rewarded: but if they mend their ways, know that God is forgiving and merciful.

Fight against them until idolatry is no more and God's religion reigns supreme. But if they desist, fight none except the evil-doers.

A sacred month for a sacred month: sacred things too are subject to retaliation. If anyone attacks you, attack him as he attacked you. Have fear of God, and know that God is with the righteous.

Give generously for the cause of God and do not with your own hands cast yourselves into destruction. Be charitable; God loves the charitable.

Make the pilgrimage and visit the Sacred House for His sake. If you cannot, send such offerings as you can afford and do not shave your heads until the offerings have reached their destination. But if any of you is ill or suffers from an ailment of the head, he must do penance either by fasting or by almsgiving or by offering a sacrifice. . . .

The People of the Book ask you to bring down for them a book from heaven. Of Moses they demanded a harder thing than that. They said to him: "Show us God distinctly." And for their wickedness the thunderbolt smote them. They worshipped the calf after clear signs had been revealed to them; yet We forgave them that, and bestowed on Moses clear authority.

When We made a covenant with them We raised the Mount above them and said: "Enter the gates in adoration. Do not break the Sabbath." We took from them a solemn covenant. But they broke their covenant, denied the revelations of God, and killed the prophets unjustly. They said: "Our hearts are sealed."

It is God who has sealed their hearts, on account of their unbelief. They have no faith, except a few of them.

They denied the truth and uttered a monstrous falsehood against Mary. They declared: "We have put to death the Messiah, Jesus son of Mary, the apostle of God." They did not kill him, nor did they crucify him, but they thought they did.

God made a covenant with the Israelites and raised among them twelve chieftains. God said: "I shall be with you. If you attend to your prayers and render the alms levy; if you believe in My apostles and assist them and give God a generous loan, I shall forgive you your sins and admit you to gardens watered by running streams. But he that hereafter denies Me shall stray from the right path."

---

[3] **entering your dwellings from the back:** The pre-Islamic Arabs would enter their houses from the back when they had completed a pilgrimage.

But because they broke their covenant We laid on them Our curse and hardened their hearts. They have tampered with words out of their context and forgotten much of what they were enjoined. You will ever find them deceitful, except for a few of them. But pardon them and bear with them. God loves those who do good.

With those who said they were Christians We made a covenant also, but they too have forgotten much of what they were exhorted to do. Therefore We stirred among them enmity and hatred, which shall endure till the Day of Resurrection, when God will declare to them all that they have done.

People of the Book! Our apostle has come to reveal to you much of what you have hidden of the Scriptures, and to forgive you much. A light has come to you from God and a glorious Book, with which God will guide to the paths of peace those that seek to please Him; He will lead them by His will from darkness to the light; He will guide them to a straight path.

Unbelievers are those who declare: "God is the Messiah, the son of Mary." Say: "Who could prevent God, if He so willed, from destroying the Messiah, the son of Mary, his mother, and all the people of the earth? God has sovereignty over the heavens and the earth and all that lies between them. He creates what He will; and God has power over all things."

The Jews and the Christians say: "We are the children of God and His loved ones." Say: "Why then does He punish you for your sins? Surely you are mortals of His own creation. He forgives whom He will and punishes whom He pleases. God has sovereignty over the heavens and the earth and all that lies between them. All shall return to Him."

Those that disagreed about him were in doubt concerning him; they knew nothing about him that was not sheer conjecture; they did not slay him for certain. God lifted him up to Him; God is mighty and wise. There is none among the People of the Book but will believe in him before his death; and on the Day of Resurrection he will bear witness against them.

Because of their iniquity, We forbade the Jews wholesome things which were formerly allowed them; because time after time they have debarred others from the path of God; because they practice usury—although they were forbidden it—and cheat others of their possessions. Woeful punishment have We prepared for those that disbelieve. But those of them that have deep learning, and those that truly believe in what has been revealed to you and what was revealed before you; who attend to their prayers and render the alms levy and have faith in God and the Last Day—these shall be richly recompensed.

We have revealed Our will to you as We revealed it to Noah and to the prophets who came after him; as We revealed it to Abraham, Ishmael, Isaac, Jacob, and the tribes; to Jesus, Job, Jonah, Aaron, Solomon and David,[4] to whom We gave the Psalms. Of some apostles We have already told you, but there are others of whom We have not yet spoken (God spoke directly to Moses): apostles

---

[4] **Abraham, Ishmael, . . . Solomon and David:** People mentioned in the Hebrew Bible.

who brought good news to mankind and admonished them, so that they might have no plea against God after their coming. God is mighty and wise.

READING AND DISCUSSION QUESTIONS

1. How is God (Allah) described in these passages? What Muslim religious practices do they reveal?

2. What is the fate for believers and unbelievers? In what ways does this contradict or support the idea of a compassionate, merciful God?

3. What does this selection say about religious violence? What about nonreligious violence?

4. How does the Qur'an describe Jews and Christians? How does this selection criticize their beliefs? How is Islam connected to Judaism and Christianity?

9-2 | Muhammad Signs a Treaty with the Jews of Medina

MUHAMMAD, *The Constitution of Medina* (ca. 625)

In 622, Muhammad was invited by the Jewish tribes of Yathrib (Medina) to settle disputes that caused continual fighting among them. Because Muhammad's teaching faced growing persecution in Mecca, his entire community followed him to Medina. This "flight" (*hijra*) marks the beginning of the Islamic calendar. Muhammad became the most important leader in Medina as many of the Jewish tribes converted to Islam. Around 625, Muhammad and the remaining Jewish tribes signed the following treaty, which was originally recorded by the eighth-century Arabic historian Ibn Ishaq and preserved in the text of the ninth-century writer Ibn Hisham.

The Messenger of God [Muhammad] wrote a document, concerning the emigrants from Mecca and the helpers of Medina, in which he reconciled the Jews and covenanted with them, letting them act freely in the religion and possessions which they had, and stated reciprocal obligations.

In the Name of God, the Merciful, the Compassionate!

This document is from Muhammad the Prophet, governing relations among the Believers and the Muslims of Quraysh [Mecca] and Yathrib (Medina) and those who followed them and joined with them and struggled with them.

1. They are one Community (*umma*) to the exclusion of all other men. . . .

11. The Believers shall not desert any poor person among them, but shall pay his redemption or blood-money, as is proper.

J. A. Williams, *Themes in Islamic Civilization* (Berkeley and Los Angeles: University of California Press, 1971), 11–15. Reprinted with the permission of John Alden Willliams.

12. No Believer shall seek to turn the auxiliary of another Believer against him.

13. God-fearing Believers will be against whoever among them is rebellious or whoever seeks to sow injustice or sin or enmity among the Believers; every man's hand shall be against him, though he were the son of one of them.

14. No Believer shall kill a Believer for the sake of an unbeliever, or aid an unbeliever against a Believer.

15. The protection of God is one: even the least of them may extend it to a stranger. The Believers are friends to each other, to the exclusion of all other men.

16. The Jews who follow us shall have aid and equality, except those who do wrong or aid the enemies of the Muslims.

17. The peace of the Believers is one: no Believer shall make peace separately where there is fighting for God's sake. Conditions (of peace) must be just and equitable to all.

18. In every raid, the riders shall ride close together.

19. And the Believers shall avenge one another's blood, if shed for God's sake, for the God-fearing have the best and strongest guidance.

20. No idolator [polytheist] (of Medina) shall take Qurayshi property or persons under his protection, nor shall he turn anyone against a Believer.

21. Whoever kills a Believer shall also be killed, unless the next of kin of the slain man is otherwise satisfied, and the Believers shall be against him altogether; no one is permitted to act otherwise.

22. No Believer who accepts this document and believes in God and Judgment is permitted to aid a criminal or give him shelter. The curse of God and His wrath on the Day of Judgment shall fall upon whoever aids or shelters him, and no repentance or compensation shall be accepted from him if he does.

23. Whenever you differ about a case, it shall be referred to God and to Muhammad.

24. The Jews shall bear expenses with the Muslims as long as they fight along with them.

25. The Jews of the Banu 'Awf [one Jewish tribe] are one community with the Believers; the Jews have their religion and the Muslims have theirs. This is so for them and their clients, except for one who does wrong or treachery; he hurts only himself and his family. . . .

46. Everyone shall have his portion from the side to which he belongs; the Jews of al-Aws [another Jewish tribe], their clients and themselves, are in the same position as the people of this document. Honorable dealing is without treachery.

47. Whoever acquires any (guilt) does not acquire it for any but himself. God is the most just and loyal fulfiller of what is in this document. This writing will not protect a wrongdoer or a traitor. Whoever goes out is safe, and he who stays at home is safe in the town, unless he has done wrong or treachery. God is the protecting neighbor (*jar*) of whoever does good and fears Him, and Muhammad is the Messenger of God. Verily God is wrathful when His covenant is broken. Peace be upon you.

READING AND DISCUSSION QUESTIONS

1. What is the role of religion in administering justice for Muhammad and the tribes of Medina?

2. How is the relationship between Jews and Muslims defined here? What could negatively affect that relationship?

3. Muhammad, unlike Jesus, was a secular ruler in addition to being a religious teacher. How may this have affected his teachings?

VIEWPOINTS COMPARATIVE QUESTIONS

1. How does Muhammad characterize Jews and Christians? What distinction does he make between non-Muslim monotheists and polytheists or "idolaters"?

2. What day-to-day evidence of Muslim-Jewish and Muslim-Christian relations is revealed in these documents? How might practical considerations have shaped Islamic policies toward Christians and Jews living in Muslim lands?

9-3 | A Spanish Jew Visits Baghdad

BENJAMIN BEN JONAH OF TUDELA, From *Book of Travels* (ca. 1159–1172)

By the twelfth century, cultures throughout the Mediterranean were coming into contact with one another, largely as a consequence of the Crusades that began in 1095. Following in the paths of merchant vessels from Italian city-states and Crusader armies, travelers and pilgrims began to cross from Europe to the Middle East. One such traveler, Benjamin ben Jonah of Tudela, left his home in Christian-controlled Spain and visited Jewish communities throughout Europe and the Middle East. Benjamin's record of his journeys, the *Book of Travels*, describes the social and religious customs at his various stops.

Baghdad [is] . . . the royal residence of the Caliph[5] Emir al-Muminin al-Abbasi (1160–1170) of the family of Muhammad [Abbasid Dynasty]. He is at the head of the Muslim religion, and all the kings of Islam obey him; he occupies a similar position to that held by the pope over the Christians. He has a palace in Baghdad three miles in extent, wherein is a great park with all varieties of trees,

---

Benjamin ben Jonah, *The Itinerary of Benjamin of Tudela,* trans. Marcus N. Adler (London: H. Frowde, 1907), 35–42.

[5] **Caliph:** A successor of Muhammad; the title denotes the secular and religious leader of the Islamic community, or *umma*.

fruit-bearing and otherwise, and all manner of animals. . . . There the great king, al-Abbasi the Caliph holds his court, and he is kind unto Israel [the Jewish people], and many belonging to the people of Israel are his attendants; he knows all languages, and is well versed in the Law of Israel. He reads and writes the holy language [Hebrew]. . . . He is truthful and trusty, speaking peace to all men. . . .

In Baghdad there are about forty thousand Jews,[6] and they dwell in security, prosperity, and honor under the great Caliph, and among them are great sages, the heads of Academies engaged in the study of the Law [Jewish law: the Torah and the Talmud]. In this city there are ten Academies. . . . And at the head of them all is Daniel the son of Hisdai, who is styled "Our Lord the Head of the Captivity of all Israel." He possesses a book of pedigrees going back as far as David, King of Israel (ca. 1000–965 B.C.E.). The Jews call him "Our Lord, Head of the Captivity," and the Muslims call him "Saidna ben Daoud," ["Lord, son of David"] and he has been invested with authority over all the congregations of Israel at the hands of the Emir al-Muminin, the Lord of Islam. For thus Muhammad [not the Prophet, but a later Abbasid ruler of Baghdad] commanded concerning him and his descendants; and he granted him a seal of office over all the congregations that dwell under his rule, and ordered that every one, whether Muslim or Jew, or belonging to any other nation in his dominion, should rise up before him and salute him, and that any one who should refuse to rise up should receive one hundred stripes [public lashes].

And every fifth day when he goes to pay a visit to the great Caliph, horsemen, gentiles as well as Jews, escort him, and heralds proclaim in advance, "Make way before our Lord, the son of David, as is due unto him," the Arabic words being "Amilu tarik la Saidna ben Daud." He is mounted on a horse, and is attired in robes of silk and embroidery with a large turban on his head. . . . Then he appears before the Caliph and kisses his hand, and the Caliph rises and places him on a throne which Muhammad had ordered to be made for him, and all the Muslim princes who attend the court of the Caliph rise up before him. And the Head of the Captivity is seated on his throne opposite to the Caliph, in compliance with the command of Muhammad. . . . The authority of the Head of the Captivity extends over all the communities of Shinar,[7] Persia, Khurasan, and Sheba which is El-Yemen, and Diyar Kalach and the land of Aram Naharaim, and over the dwellers in the mountains of Ararat and the land of the Alans. . . . His authority extends also over the land of Siberia, and the communities in the land of the Togarmim unto the mountains of Asveh and the land of Gurgan, the inhabitants of which are called Gurganim who dwell by the river Gihon, and these are the Girgashites [Nubians and Ethiopians] who follow the Christian religion.

---

[6] **forty thousand Jews:** Some of these Jews were the descendants of families deported by Nebuchadnezzar during the Babylonian captivity (586–537 B.C.E.).

[7] **the communities of Shinar:** The Head of the Captivity's reach extended through great stretches of Mesopotamia, northeastern Iran, around the Black Sea, all the way to a city in Central Asia along the Silk Road, then to Tibet and India.

Further it extends to the gates of Samarkand, the land of Tibet, and the land of India. In respect of all these countries the Head of the Captivity gives the communities power to appoint Rabbis and Ministers who come unto him to be consecrated and to receive his authority. They bring him offerings and gifts from the ends of the earth. He owns hospices, gardens, and plantations in Babylon, and much land inherited from his fathers, and no one can take his possessions from him by force. He has a fixed weekly revenue arising from the hospices of the Jews, the markets and the merchants, apart from that which is brought to him from far-off lands. The man is very rich, and wise in the Scriptures as well as in the Talmud,[8] and many Israelites dine at his table every day.

At his installation, the Head of the Captivity gives much money to the Caliph, to the Princes, and to the Ministers. On the day that the Caliph performs the ceremony of investing him with authority, he rides in the second of the royal carriages, and is escorted from the palace of the Caliph to his own house with timbrels and fifes. The Exilarch [leader of the exile, Daniel the son of Hisdai] appoints the Chiefs of the Academies by placing his hand upon their heads, thus installing them in their office. The Jews of the city are learned men and very rich.

In Baghdad there are twenty-eight Jewish Synagogues, situated either in the city itself or in al-Karkh on the other side of the Tigris; for the river divides the metropolis into two parts. The great synagogue of the Head of the Captivity has columns of marble of various colors overlaid with silver and gold, and on these columns are sentences of the Psalms in golden letters. And in front of the ark are about ten steps of marble; on the topmost step are the seats of the Head of the Captivity and of the Princes of the House of David. The city of Baghdad is twenty miles in circumference, situated in a land of palms, gardens and plantations, the like of which is not to be found in the whole land of Shinar.

READING AND DISCUSSION QUESTIONS

1. What is the relationship between the Jewish and Muslim communities of Baghdad, as described by Benjamin ben Jonah?

2. Describe the Jewish community and the social status of Daniel the son of Hisdai.

3. In this account, ben Jonah appears to have exaggerated the power of the caliph, who had delegated authority to sultans throughout the caliphate. Why might ben Jonah have portrayed the caliphate as more powerful than it really was?

4. What seems to be ben Jonah's opinion of Baghdad? What does it suggest about the purpose of his travels?

---

[8] **Talmud:** Writings that date after the Torah but have a high authority. One collection was written in Babylon during the captivity, and the other was compiled later in Palestine.

9-4 | Geometry and Islamic Design

Great Mosque of Córdoba, Spain, and Gate of Al Hakam II, Detail (987)

Unlike the cathedrals of medieval Christian Europe, the great mosques of Muslim cities contained no representations of humans, since the inclusion of such images in a place of worship was considered a form of idolatry. Thus, there are no images of the prophets, no scenes from the life of Muhammad, no pictures of angels or demons, no depictions of God. Despite this limitation, Islamic artists and architects proved remarkably successful at using the mosque as a vehicle for explaining to believers the essence of their faith. The two images included here are of the interior of the Great Mosque of Córdoba, Spain, and a detail of the mosque's exterior. As you examine them, think about how the mosque's creators used geometry to convey the Islamic message. What do the design and decoration of the mosque tell you about Islamic ideas about the nature of God?

Ken Welsh / Bridgeman Images.

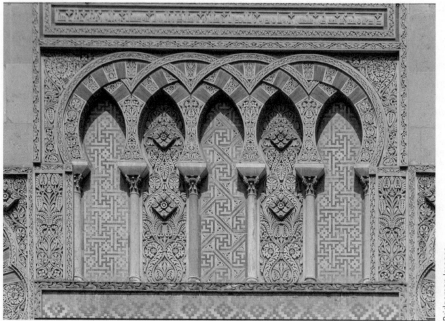

Bridgeman Images.

READING AND DISCUSSION QUESTIONS

1. How is the design of the interior of the mosque echoed in the decoration of its exterior? What religious significance might the mosque's creators have attached to the repetition of geometric motifs?

2. How do Muslims describe the nature of God? What connections can you make between this vision of the divine and geometry and mathematics?

9-5 | A Muslim Scholar Explores the History of Islam

IBN KHALDŪN, From *Prolegomenon to History: On Shi'ite Succession* (1377)

Ibn Khaldūn (1332–1406) was one of the most learned people of his day and is credited as being one of the first scholars of sociology, demography, economics, and the philosophy of history. Born in North Africa, he received a traditional Muslim education in the Qur'an. At age twenty he began a career working for Muslim rulers in North Africa and Spain. He later became a professor in Egypt and even negotiated with the Mongol general Timur. His *Prolegomenon to History* is considered the first book on the philosophy of history. In this passage, he describes the Shi'ite view of succession after the death of Muhammad. In Islam, Sunnis such as Ibn Khaldūn often consider Shi'ites a heretical group.

Franz Rosenthal, trans., *Ibn Khaldūn, the Muqaddimah: An Introduction to History* (New York: Pantheon, 1958), 403–408. © 1958, 1967 Princeton University Press/Bollingen. Reprinted by permission of Princeton University Press.

Shī'ah Tenets Concerning the Question of the Imamate[9]

It should be known that, linguistically, *Shī'ah* means "companions and follow-ers." In the customary usage of old and modern jurists and speculative theologians, the word is used for the followers and descendants of 'Alī. The tenet on which they all agree is that the imamate is not a general (public) interest to be delegated to the Muslim nation for consideration and appointment of a person to fill it. (To the Shī'ah,) it is a pillar and fundamental article of Islam. No prophet is permitted to neglect it or to delegate (the appointment of an imam) to the Muslim nation. It is incumbent upon him to appoint an imam for the (Muslims). The imam cannot commit sins either great or small. 'Alī is the one whom Muḥammad appointed. The (Shī'ah) transmit texts (of traditions) in support of (this belief), which they interpret so as to suit their tenets. The authorities on the Sunnah and the transmitters of the religious law do not know these texts. Most of them are supposititious, or some of their transmitters are suspect, or their (true) interpretation is very different from the wicked interpretation that (the Shī'ah) give to them. . . .

Another tradition of this sort is the following statement of (Muḥammad): "Your best judge is 'Alī." Imamate means exclusively the activity of judging in accordance with the divine laws. (The activity of) judging and being a judge is (what is) meant by "the people in authority" whom God requires us to obey in the verse of the Qur'ān: "Obey God, and obey the Messenger and the people in authority among you." Therefore, 'Alī and no other was arbitrator in the question of the imamate on the day of the Saqīfah.[10]

Another statement of this sort is the following statement by (Muḥammad): "He who renders the oath of allegiance to me upon his life is my legatee and the man who will be in charge of this authority here after me." Only 'Alī rendered the oath of allegiance to him (in this manner).

An implied (argument), according to the Shī'ah, is the fact that the Prophet sent 'Alī to recite the *sūrat al-Barā'ah*[11] at the festival (in Mecca) when it had (just) been revealed. He first sent Abū Bakr with it. Then it was revealed to Muḥammad that "a man from you,"—or: ". . . from your people"—"should transmit it." Therefore, he sent 'Alī to transmit it. As they say, this proves that 'Alī. was preferred (by Muḥammad). Furthermore, it is not known that Muḥammad ever preferred anyone to 'Alī, while he preferred Usāmah b. Zayd and 'Amr b. al-'Āṣ to both Abū Bakr and 'Umar[12] during two different raids. According to (the Shī'ah), all these things prove that 'Alī and no one else was appointed (by Muḥammad) to the caliphate. However, some of the statements quoted are little known, and others require an interpretation very different from that which (the Shī'ah) give.

---

[9] **imamate:** The lead Muslim religious authority.
[10] **Saqīfah:** The council that decided who would succeed Muhammad.
[11] *sūrat al-Barā'ah*: Ninth chapter in the Qur'an, issued during a time of war.
[12] **Abū Bakr and 'Umar:** Abū Bakr was the first successor of Muhammad, 'Umar the second.

Some (Shī'ah) hold the opinion that these texts prove both the personal appointment of 'Alī and the fact that the imamate is transmitted from him to his successors. They are the Imāmīyah. They renounce the two *shaykhs* (Abū Bakr and 'Umar), because they did not give precedence to 'Alī and did not render the oath of allegiance to him, as required by the texts quoted. The Imāmīyah do not take the imamates (of Abū Bakr and 'Umar) seriously. But we do not want to bother with transmitting the slanderous things said about (Abū Bakr and 'Umar) by (Imāmīyah) extremists. They are objectionable in our opinion and (should be) in theirs. . . .

The Shī'ah differ in opinion concerning the succession to the caliphate after 'Alī. Some have it passed on among the descendants of Fātimah[13] in succession, through testamentary determination (*nass*). We shall mention that later on. They (who believe this) are called the Imāmīyah, with reference to their statement that knowledge of the imam and the fact of his being appointed are an article of the faith. That is their fundamental tenet. . . .

Some (Shī'ah) consider as successors to the imamate, after 'Alī—or after his two sons, Muhammad's grandsons (al-Hasan and al-Husayn), though they disagree in this respect—(al-Hasan's and al-Husayn's) brother, Muhammad b. al-Hanafīyah, and then the latter's children. They are the Kaysānīyah, so named after Kaysān, a client of ('Alī's).

There are many differences among these sects which we have omitted here for the sake of brevity.

There are also (Shī'ah) sects that are called "Extremists" (*ghulāh*). They transgress the bounds of reason and the faith of Islam when they speak of the divinity of the imams. They either assume that the imam is a human being with divine qualities, or they assume that he is God in human incarnation. This is a dogma of incarnation that agrees with the Christian tenets concerning Jesus. 'Alī himself had these (Shī'ah) who said such things about him burned to death. Muhammad b. al-Hanafīyah was very angry with al-Mukhtār b. Abī 'Ubayd when he learned that al-Mukhtār had suggested something along these lines concerning him. He cursed and renounced al-Mukhtār openly. Ja'far as-Sādiq did the same thing with people about whom he had learned something of the sort.

Some (Shī'ah) extremists say that the perfection the imam possesses is possessed by nobody else. When he dies, his spirit passes over to another imam, so that this perfection may be in him. This is the doctrine of metempsychosis.

Some extremists stop (w—q—f) with one of the imams and do not go on. (They stop with the imam) whom they consider (to have been) appointed as the (last one). They (who believe this) are the Wāqifīyah. Some of them say that the (last imam) is alive and did not die, but is removed from the eyes of the people. As a proof for that (theory), they adduce the problem of al-Khidr.[14] . . .

---

[13] **Fātimah:** Daughter of Muhammad and wife to Ali.

[14] **al-Khidr:** "The Green One," thought to be a companion of Moses. He was said to have obtained eternal life and illumination directly from God.

The extremist Imāmīyah, in particular the Twelvers, hold a similar opinion. They think that the twelfth of their imams, Muḥammad b. al-Ḥasan al-'Askarī, to whom they give the epithet of al-Mahdī, entered the cellar of their house in al-Ḥillah and was "removed" when he was imprisoned (there) with his mother. He has remained there "removed." He will come forth at the end of time and will fill the earth with justice. The Twelver Shī'ah refer in this connection to the tradition found in the collection of at-Tirmidhī regarding the Mahdī. The Twelver Shī'ah are still expecting him to this day. Therefore, they call him "the Expected One." Each night after the evening prayer, they bring a mount and stand at the entrance to the cellar where (the Mahdī is "removed"). They call his name and ask him to come forth openly. They do so until all the stars are out. Then, they disperse and postpone the matter to the following night. They have continued that custom to this time.

Some of the Wāqifīyah say that the imam who died will return to actual life in this world. They adduce as a proof (for the possibility of this assumption) the story of the Seven Sleepers, the one about the person who passed by a village, and the one about the murdered Israelite who was beaten with the bones of the cow that (his people) had been ordered to slaughter, all of them stories included in the Qur'ān. They further adduce similar wonders that occurred in the manner of (prophetical) miracles. However, it is not right to use those things as proof for anything except where they properly apply.

READING AND DISCUSSION QUESTIONS

1. Who do Shi'ites think should have been the successor of Muhammad?

2. What, according to the Wāqifīyah, happened to the last of the imams?

3. How does Ibn Khaldūn feel about the Shi'ites? Is Ibn Khaldūn a trustworthy source about their beliefs? Why or why not?

▪ COMPARATIVE QUESTIONS ▪

1. How do Muslims understand their relationship to God? How do their views on this subject compare to those of Jews and Christians?

2. Drawing on the documents in this chapter, what evidence is there to explain the success of Islam? What factors might have influenced people to convert to Islam?

3. How does the architectural style of the Great Mosque of Córdoba compare to the Hagia Sophia (Document 8–4)? What are the notable similarities and differences?

10

African Societies and Kingdoms

1000 B.C.E.–1500 C.E.

The history of Africa is as richly diverse as the continent itself. By the fifteenth century, Islam was dominant in the north, several major kingdoms had emerged in the west, and the Bantu-speaking people had migrated through the interior of the continent. Although written records for the period are often from the perspective of outsiders, such as Muslim merchants, they nonetheless point to the vitality and strength of African culture and society. The selections for this chapter reveal the critical role that trade routes played in the development of Africa, bringing African societies into contact with one another and connecting Africa to the larger world. The readings also document the introduction of Islam and Christianity to the continent, both of which significantly influenced the direction of the early kingdoms of Africa.

VIEWPOINTS

Outsiders' Views of Sub-Saharan Africa

Much of the written records of sub-Saharan Africa from this period were written by outsiders. This does not mean that such accounts are necessarily untrustworthy or that they do not reveal useful information about African society. It does mean, however, that the writers' beliefs, priorities, and previous experiences played a major role in shaping their vision of Africa. For example, we might begin by noting that the vast majority of firsthand written descriptions of sub-Saharan Africa from this period were written by Muslims and that Muslims were drawn to sub-Saharan Africa primarily by a desire for trade. Thus, Muslim accounts of Africa almost always stress the trade goods available in particular towns and regions, as well as local trade policies and taxes. Muslim authors and their readers also possessed a deep knowledge of northern Africa and East Africa, developed in the many centuries that followed Islamic expansion and conquest in the region. Thus, when Muslim writers turned their attention to sub-Saharan Africa, they did so with clear points of comparison. As you read the selections included in this feature, keep such issues in mind. What does each account reveal about the attitudes and assumptions of its author?

10-1 | A Muslim Traveler Describes Ghana and Mali

ABU UBAYDALLAH AL-BAKRI, From *The Book of Routes and Realms* (ca. 1067–1068)

For centuries, the expansive Sahara desert isolated northern and western Africa from each other. In the fifth century c.e., the introduction of the Arabian camel allowed for the establishment of regular trade routes across the Sahara. This trans-Sahara trade accelerated in the seventh and eight centuries as Arab Muslim forces conquered North Africa and turned to the western Sudan region for gold and slaves. In exchange for their precious goods, West Africans received items such as horses and salt, as well as exposure to the tenets of the Islamic faith. Excepted here are accounts by a Spanish Muslim of the West African kingdoms of Ghana and Mali.

Ghana is a title given to their kings; the name of the region is Awkar, and their king today, namely in the year 460, is Tunka Manin. He ascended the throne in 455 [1063 c.e.]. The name of his predecessor was Basi and he became their ruler at the age of 85. He led a praiseworthy life on account of his love of justice and friendship for the Muslims. At the end of his life he became blind, but he concealed this from his subjects and pretended that he could see. When something was put before him he said: "This is good" or "This is bad." His ministers deceived the people by indicating to the king in cryptic words what he should say, so that the commoners could not understand. Basi was a maternal uncle of Tunka Manin. This is their custom and their habit, that the kingship is inherited only by the son of the king's sister. He has no doubt that his successor is a son of his sister, while he is not certain that his son is in fact his own, and he is not convinced of the genuineness of his relationship to him. This Tunka Manin is powerful, rules an enormous kingdom, and possesses great authority. . . .

Around the king's town are domed buildings and groves and thickets where the sorcerers of these people, men in charge of the religious cult, live. In them too are their idols and the tombs of their kings. These woods are guarded and none

---

N. Levtzion and J. F. P. Hopkins, eds., *Corpus of Early Arabic Sources for West African History,* trans. J. R. Hopkins (Cambridge: Cambridge University Press, 1981), 78–83, 85–87.

may enter them and know what is there. In them also are the king's prisons. If somebody is imprisoned there no news of him is ever heard. The king's inter-preters, the official in charge of his treasury and the majority of his ministers are Muslims. Among the people who follow the king's religion[1] only he and his heir apparent (who is the son of his sister) may wear sewn clothes. All other people wear robes of cotton, silk, or brocade, according to their means. All of them shave their beards, and women shave their heads. . . .

Their religion is paganism and the worship of idols. When their king dies they construct over the place where his tomb will be an enormous dome of wood. Then they bring him on a bed covered with a few carpets and cushions and place him beside the dome. At his side they place his ornaments, his weapons, and the vessels from which he used to eat and drink, filled with various kinds of food and beverages. They place there too the men who used to serve his meals. They close the door of the dome and cover it with mats and furnishings. Then the peo-ple assemble, who heap earth upon it until it becomes like a big hillock and dig a ditch around it until the mound can be reached at only one place.

They make sacrifices to their dead and make offerings of intoxicating drinks.

On every donkey-load of salt when it is brought into the country their king levies one golden dinar, and two dinars when it is sent out. From a load of copper the king's due is five mithqals,[2] and from a load of other goods ten mithqals. The best gold found in his land comes from the town of Ghiyaru, which is eighteen days' traveling distant from the king's town over a country inhabited by tribes of the Sudan whose dwellings are continuous.

The nuggets found in all the mines of his country are reserved for the king, only this gold dust being left for the people. But for this the people would accu-mulate gold until it lost its value. The nuggets may weigh from an ounce to a pound. It is related that the king owns a nugget as large as a big stone. . . .

The king of Ghana, when he calls up his army, can put 200,000 men[3] into the field, more than 40,000 of them archers. . . .

On the opposite bank of the Nil [the Niger River] is another great kingdom, stretching a distance of more than eight days' marching, the king of which has the title of Daw. The inhabitants of this region use arrows when fighting. Beyond this country lies another called Malal [later Mali], the king of which is known as *al-musulmani* ["the Muslim"]. He is thus called because his country became afflicted with drought one year following another; the inhabitants prayed for rain, sacrificing cattle till they had exterminated almost all of them, but the drought and the misery only increased. The king had as his guest a Muslim who used to read the Quran and was acquainted with the Sunna [Islamic traditions].

---

[1] **the king's religion:** The king was not a Muslim. He followed the traditional religion of the Soninke.

[2] **dinar . . . mithqals:** A dinar was a standard gold coin in the Islamic kingdom. It weighed one *mithqal*, or 4.72 grams.

[3] **200,000 men:** Surely an exaggeration. Ghana had no standing army.

To this man the king complained of the calamities that assailed him and his people. The man said: "O King, if you believed in God (who is exalted) and testified that He is One, and testified as to the prophetic mission of Muhammad (God bless him and give him peace) and if you accepted all the religious laws of Islam, I would pray for your deliverance from your plight and that God's mercy would envelop all the people of your country and that your enemies and adversaries might envy you on that account." Thus he continued to press the king until the latter accepted Islam and became a sincere Muslim. The man made him recite from the Quran some easy passages and taught him religious obligations and practices which no one may be excused from knowing. Then the Muslim made him wait till the eve of the following Friday [the Islamic day of rest], when he ordered him to purify himself by a complete ablution, and clothed him in a cotton garment which he had. The two of them came out towards a mound of earth, and there the Muslim stood praying while the king, standing at his right side, imitated him. Thus they prayed for a part of the night, the Muslim reciting invocations and the king saying "Amen." The dawn had just started to break when God caused abundant rain to descend upon them. So the king ordered the idols to be broken and expelled the sorcerers from his country. He and his descendants after him as well as his nobles were sincerely attached to Islam, while the common people of his kingdom remained polytheists. Since then their rulers have been given the title of *al-musulmani.*

READING AND DISCUSSION QUESTIONS

1. What evidence does al-Bakri provide to suggest that the king of Ghana wielded significant power and authority in his territory?

2. Describe the presence of Islam in Ghana. Who practiced Islam? How was the spread of Islam encouraged? What potential obstacles were there to the growth of Islam in Ghana?

3. Based on this account, what aspects of life in Ghana were most interesting to al-Bakri and his readers? Why do you think he focused on the subjects that he did?

10-2 | Fact and Fiction in an Account of Sub-Saharan Africa
ABŪ HĀMID MUHAMMAD AL-ANDALUSĪ AL-GHARNĀTĪ, From *Gift of the Spirit* (ca. 1120–1170)

The Muslim traveler Abū Hāmid Muhammad al-Andalusī al-Gharnātī (ca. 1080–1170) was born in Spain but left in his twenties, never to return. He visited numerous Muslim-controlled regions of the world, such as North Africa, Egypt, Syria, and Central Asia. It is unknown if he

N. Levtzion and J. F. P. Hopkins, eds., J. F. P. Hopkins, trans., *Corpus of Early Arabic Sources for West African History* (New York: Cambridge University Press, 1981), 132–134.

actually visited sub-Saharan Africa. Regardless, he preserves much information that was circulating about sub-Saharan Africa, but he embellishes it with legends and writings from previous authors, including the Greeks.

The inhabited earth has an extent of one hundred years' travelling of which fourteen belong to the various peoples of the Sūdān. Their country lies next to the Upper West (*al-Maghrib al-A'lā*), which adjoins Ṭanja, stretching along the Sea of Darkness[4] (*Baḥr al Ẓulumāt*).

It is said that kings of five of their tribes have adopted Islam. The nearest of them is Ghāna, where gold of extraordinary [purity] (*al-dhahab al-tibr al-ghāya*) grows in the sand, and is in abundance. Merchants carry to them on camels blocks of rock salt. They set out from a town called Sijilmāsa, at the farthest end of the Upper West. They travel over sands like seas, led by guides who direct themselves over the wastes according to the stars and the mountains. They carry supplies for six months with them. When they arrive in Ghāna, they sell the salt at one weight for one weight of gold, or sometimes they sell it at one weight for two weights or more, according to whether traders are many or few.

The people of Ghāna, of all the Sūdān, have the best way of living, are the best looking, and have the least crinkled hair. They possess intelligence and understanding, and they go on the Pilgrimage to Mecca. As for the Fāwah (var. Qitāwa), the Qūqū, the Malī, the Takrūr and the Ghadāmis,[5] they are brave people but there are no blessings in their lands, nor anything good, nor do they possess religion or intelligence. The worst of them are the Qūqū, who have short necks, flattened noses, and red eyes. Their hair is like peppercorns, and their smell is abominable, resembling burnt horn. They shoot arrows poisoned with the blood of yellow snakes. Within one hour the flesh begins to fall off the bones of anyone struck with such an arrow, be it elephant or any other animal. For these people vipers and all other kinds of snakes are like fish, which they eat, paying no attention to the venom of the vipers and serpents, with the exception of the yellow snake which is found in their country. This they fear, and take its blood for their arrows. Their bows, which I have seen in the Maghrib, are short and so are their arrows. I saw that their bows have strings made from the fibres of a tree that grows in their country. Their arrows are short, each one span in length, and have points made of tree thorns as strong as iron, which they fasten to their arrows with the fibres of a tree. [When shooting] they [can] hit the pupil of the eye. They are the worst kind of the Sūdān. The other Sūdān are useful as slaves and laborers, but not the Qūqū, who have no good qualities, except in war. They possess small wooden tablets, with holes partly drilled through them, on which they whistle, and produce strange tones, thus causing all sorts of snakes, vipers and serpents to come out. Then they take these reptiles and eat them. Some of them tie these snakes round their middles as one ties a cummerbund, others use a long serpent in the guise of a turban, and enter the market,

---

[4] **Sea of Darkness:** The Atlantic Ocean.
[5] **Fāwah . . . Ghadāmis:** Peoples of the Sudan; the Ghadāmis, however, were from North Africa.

while nobody pays attention [to them]. Then they take off their clothes and throw upon people various serpents and vipers. People give them something to go away, for otherwise they would throw some of these snakes into their shops.

Various kinds of goatskins dyed in a marvellous manner are exported from the land of the Sūdān, each skin being tough, thick and pliant, and in a pleasing color from violet to black. One skin may weigh twenty *mann*. They are used to make boots for kings. They do not let the water through, nor do they damage easily or perish, despite their pliability and softness and their pleasant smell. One such skin is sold for ten dinars. The thread with which the shoe is sown perishes, but the leather does not, nor does it crack. It may be washed in a bath of hot water, and again becomes as new. The owner may have inherited it from his grandfather through his father. It is one of the marvels of the world.

In the country of these people lives an animal called *lamṭ*, resembling a big bull. It has horns like spears, stretching along its back, and growing as long as its body. If it strikes an animal with them, the latter is killed instantly. It has a broad neck, and from its hide shields called *al-daraq al-lamṭiyya* are made, called after the animal. The shields are three cubits long, light and pliable, and cannot be pierced by an arrow, nor does a sword make any impression on them. They are white like paper, and they are one of the best kinds of shield, being flat like a flat cake of bread, and cover the knight and his horse.

In the land of the Sūdān exist people without heads. They are mentioned by al-Sha'bī in his book *Siyar al-Mulūk* [*Rules for Kings*]. It is also said that in the deserts of the Maghrib there are a people of the progeny of Adam, consisting solely of women. There are no men among them, nor does any of the male sex live in that land. These women enter a certain water by which they become pregnant. Each woman gives birth to a girl, never to a boy. Tubba' Dhū 'l-Manār arrived in their country when he was trying to reach the Darkness (*al-ẓulumāt*), which Dhū 'l-Qarnayn had entered. God knows best. And [it is also said] that his son, Ifrīqisūn b. Tubba' Dhū 'l-Manār was the one who founded the town of Ifrīqiya, and called it after himself. And that his father, Tubba', reached Wādī al-Sabt (the River of Saturday), which is a river in the Maghrib, where sands flow like flood-water, and no living being may enter it without perishing. When he reached there, he hastened back. As for Dhū 'l-Qarnayn, on his arrival there he stayed until the day of Saturday, when the flow of the sand stopped, and then he crossed it, and marched until he reached the Darkness. This is what is said, but God knows best. These headless people have eyes in their shoulders, and mouths in their chests. They form many nations, and are numerous like beasts. They reproduce and do not harm anyone, and they have no intelligence. God knows best.

READING AND DISCUSSION QUESTIONS

1. How does al-Gharnātī describe the people of Ghana and their neighbors? How does he describe the people of Sudan?

2. What importance should we attach to the fact that he includes elements in his account which are clearly fictional? Why might al-Gharnātī and his readers have

believed that there really were groups with no heads and tribes made up entirely of women?

3. Would al-Gharnātī be likely to describe any of the groups he discussed as "civilized"? Why or why not?

10-3 | Leo Africanus Describes Timbuktu to a European Audience

LEO AFRICANUS (AL-HASAN IBN MUHAMMAD AL-WAZZAN AL-FASI), From *The History and Description of Africa* (1526)

Al-Hasan ibn Muhammad al-Wazzan al-Fasi (ca. 1494–1554), better known as Leo Africanus, was born in Granada to a wealthy and important Muslim family. His family left Spain and moved to the northern African city of Fez sometime in the mid-1490s, and it was there that Leo Africanus grew up. As a young man, he attended university and entered the diplomatic service of the Sultan of Fez. In this capacity he traveled the length and breadth of the Muslim world. In 1520, while on a diplomatic mission, he was captured by Spanish pirates in the Mediterranean and taken to Rome, where he was presented to Pope Leo X. Leo freed him, had him baptized, and commissioned him to write a detailed account of Africa based on his extensive travels. In the passage from his *History and Description of Africa* included here, Leo Africanus described the famous Ghanaian city of Timbuktu. As you read the selection, think about the aspects of the city that Leo Africanus chose to emphasize. How might his account have been influenced by the fact that it was written for a European audience?

Of the Kingdome of Tombuto

This name was in our times (as some thinke) imposed upon this kingdome from the name of a certain towne so called, which (they say) king *Mense Suleiman* founded in the yeere of the Hegeira 610, and it is situate within twelve miles of a certaine branch of Niger, all the houses whereof are now changed into cottages built of chalke, and covered with thatch. Howbeit there is a most stately temple to be seene, the wals whereof are made of stone and lime; and a princely palace also built by a most excellent workeman of Granada. Here are many shops of artificers, and merchants, and especially of such as weave linnen and cotton cloth. And hither do the Barbarie-merchants bring cloth of Europe. All the women of this region except maid-servants go with their faces covered, and sell all necessarie victuals. The inhabitants, & especially strangers there residing, are exceeding rich, insomuch, that the king that now is, married both his daughters unto two rich merchants. Here are many wels, containing most sweete water; and so often as the river Niger overfloweth, they conveigh the water thereof by certaine sluces into

---

Leo Africanus, *History and Description of Africa*, trans. John Pory (1600), ed. Robert Brown (London: Hakluyt Society, 1896), 824–826.

the towne. Corne, cattle, milke, and butter this region yeeldeth in great abundance: but salt is verie scarce heere; for it is brought hither by land from Tegaza, which is five hundred miles distant. When I my selfe was here, I saw one camels loade of salt sold for 80 ducates. The rich king of Tombuto hath many plates and scepters of gold, some whereof weigh 1300 poundes: and he keepes a magnificent and well furnished court. When he travelleth any whither he rideth upon a camell, which is lead by some of his noblemen; and so he doth likewise when hee goeth to warfar, and all his souldiers ride upon horses. Whosoever will speake unto this king must first fall downe before his feete, & then taking up earth must sprinkle it upon his owne head & shoulders: which custom is ordinarily observed by them that never saluted the king before, or come as ambassadors from other princes. He hath alwaies three thousand horsemen, and a great number of footmen that shoot poysoned arrowes, attending upon him. They have often skirmishes with those that refuse to pay tribute, and so many as they take, they sell unto the merchants of Tombuto. Here are verie few horses bred, and the merchants and courtiers keepe certaine little nags which they use to travell upon: but their best horses are brought out of Barbarie. And the king so soone as he heareth that any merchants are come to towne with horses, he commandeth a certaine number to be brought before him, and chusing the best horse for himselfe, he payeth a most liberall price for him. He so deadly hateth all Jewes, that he will not admit any into his citie: and whatsoever Barbarie merchants he understandeth have any dealings with the Jewes, he presently causeth their goods to be confiscate. Here are great store of doctors, judges, priests, and other learned men, that are bountifully maintained at the kings cost and charges. And hither are brought divers manuscripts or written bookes out of Barbarie, which are sold for more money than any other merchandize. The coine of Tombuto is of gold without any stampe or superscription: but in matters of smal value they use certaine shels brought hither out of the kingdome of Persia, fouer hundred of which shels are worth a ducate: and six peeces of their golden coine with two third parts weigh an ounce. The inhabitants are people of a gentle and chereful disposition, and spend a great part of the night in singing and dancing through all the streets of the citie: they keep great store of men and women slaves, and their towne is much in danger of fire: at my second being there halfe the town almost was burnt in five houers space. Without the suburbs there are no gardens nor orchards at all.

Of the Towne of Cabra

This large towne built without walles in manner of a village, standeth about twelve miles from Tombuto upon the river Niger: and here such merchants as travel unto the kingdomes of Ghinea and Melli embarke themselves. Neither are the people or buildings of this towne any whit inferiour to the people and buildings of Tombuto; and hither the Negros resort in great numbers by water. In this towne the king of Tombuto appointeth a judge to decide all controversies; for it were tedious to goe thither so oft as need should require. I my selfe am acquainted with *Abu Bacr*, sirnamed *Pargama*, the kings brother, who is blacke in colour, but most beautifull in minde and conditions. Here breed many diseases which exceedingly diminish the people; and that by reason of the fond and loathsome mixture of their meats; for they mingle fish, milke, butter, and flesh altogither. And this is the ordinarie food also in Tombuto.

Of the Towne and Kingdome of Gago

The great towne of Gago being unwalled also, is distant southward from Tombuto almost fouer hundred miles, and enclineth somewhat to the southeast. The houses thereof are but meane, except those wherein the king and his courtiers remaine. Here are exceeding rich merchants: and hither continually resort great store of Negros which buy cloth here brought out of Barbarie and Europe. This towne aboundeth with corne and flesh, but is much destitute of wine, trees, and fruits. Howbeit here is plentie of melons, citrons, and rice: here are many welles also containing most sweete and holesome water. Here is likewise a certaine place where slaves are to be sold, especially upon such daies as the merchants use to assemble; and a yoong slave of fifteene yeeres age is sold for sixe ducates, and so are children sold also. The king of this region hath a certaine private palace wherein he maintaineth a great number of concubines and slaves, which are kept by eunuches: and for the guard of his owne person he keepeth a sufficient troupe of horsemen and footmen. Betweene the first gate of the palace and the inner part thereof, there is a place walled round about wherein the king himselfe decideth all his subjects controversies: and albeit the king be in this function most diligent, and performeth all things thereto appertayning, yet hath he about him his counsellors & other officers, as namely his secretaries, treasurers, factors, and auditors. It is a woonder to see what plentie of Merchandize is dayly brought hither, and how costly and sumptuous all things be. Horses bought in Europe for ten ducates, are here sold againe for fortie and sometimes for fiftie ducates a piece. There is not any cloth of Europe so course, which will not here be sold for fouer ducates an elle, and if it be anything fine they will give fifteene ducates for an ell: and an ell of the scarlet of Venice or of Turkie-cloath is here worth thirtie ducates. A sword is here valued at three or fouer crownes, and so likewise are spurs, bridles, with other like commodities, and spices also are sold at an high rate: but of al other commodities salt is most extremelie deere. The residue of this kingdome containeth nought but villages and hamlets inhabited by husbandmen and shepherds, who in winter cover their bodies with beasts skins; but in sommer they goe all naked save their privie members; and sometimes they weare upon their feet certaine shooes made of camels leather. They are ignorant and rude people, and you shall scarce finde one learned man in the space of an hundred miles. They are continually burthened with grievous exactions, so that they have scarce any thing remaining to live upon.

READING AND DISCUSSION QUESTIONS

1. What does this account tell you about the importance of trade to Timbuktu?

2. What importance should we attach to Leo Africanus's report that in Timbuktu books were "sold for more money than any other merchandise"? What does this tell you about the culture of Timbuktu and its connections to the larger Islamic world?

3. How might European readers have responded to this description of Timbuktu? What aspects of the account might they have found most interesting? Why?

VIEWPOINTS COMPARATIVE QUESTIONS

1. What aspects of West African life do all three authors emphasize?

2. Which of the three accounts seems most reliable to you? Why?

3. What do the three accounts tell you about the influence of Islam on West African life?

10-4 | A History of West Africa by West Africans
From *Epic of Sundiata* (ca. 1250)

Very little literature of West Africa was written down prior to European imperialism in the nineteenth century; instead, literature and culture were handed down orally. This passage, a selection from the *Epic of Sundiata*, was passed on by oral poets called griots. The *Epic of Sundiata* covers the life of Mali's first ruler, Sundiata Keita (ca. 1217–1255), and contains a wealth of information about the rise of Mali's power and everyday life in the kingdom. This passage narrates the wedding ceremony between Maghan Konfara and Sogolon, Sundiata's parents.

Alone, she went and sat on her husband's bed.
If they had not finished with the sorcery,
That is why when a new bride is brought,
If you see her sitting in a chair,
If she does not sit on her husband's bed, she has something on her mind.
She does not want to marry this man;
She has another man's name to confess.
(You heard it?)
It is good for a new bride to want to be with her husband. . . .

When the bridal drum was played in the town circle,
The celebration was at its peak.

Sunjata: A West African Epic of the Mande Peoples, translated by David C. Conrad, copyright 2004. Reprinted by permission of Hackett Publishing Company, Inc. All rights reserved.

The celebration with the bridal drum surpassed the one of circumcision.
(You heard it?)
When they came to the town circle, all the women were there in force.
Sogolon Condé said to her husband, "Simbon,
If you agree,
I would like to go and see the people,
As they dance for the bride in the town circle."
She said, "I would like to go and see the people,
While they dance in the circle for the bride."
Maghan Konfara said, "Eh!"
He said, "Condé woman,
That might be what they do in Dò ni Kiri,
The home of the Condé,
But here in Manden,
Women do not see the bride's dance circle."
She said, "Un un, I will not go in person.
If you agree,
I will stay here behind you and see them in the circle."
That is how sorcery was used.
(You heard it?)
If you should be told
That Sunjata's mother was pregnant for seven years,
That she did not deliver for seven years,
That when he was finally born he did not walk,
It was all the result of that one night.
She said, "I will stay behind you,
But I will go and see them."
Simbon said, "Ah, if you will not go there in person,
You and I are finished with what we were doing.
There is no sorcery you can show me,
That will be worse than that with which you started.
If you keep your body here but can still see them,
I will not say 'no.'"
She said, "Very well."
(You heard it?)

She put her left hand on her husband.
She was lying behind him on the bed.
She stretched her right arm,
She stretched her right hand,
It passed through the straw of the roof.
She stretched her arm,
She stretched her hand to reach the dance circle,
She laid her hand up in the *dubalen* tree.
She pointed two fingers down;

Light was coming out of them.
The circle was suddenly full of light, *wa*!
And she was still lying behind her husband.
From behind her husband she said, "Heeeh,
Mande people know how to do it.
Heeeh," she said.
"Jonmusoni Manyan really knows how to dance!
Heeeh, Tunku Manyan Diawara has a good voice!
Heeh, Tassisi Gbandimina knows how to dance!
Heeh, Maramajan Tarawelé is dancing!
Heeh, Flaba Naabi, heeya, she knows!"
While they were dancing,
Jonmusoni Manyan raised her head.
She saw that the inner circle was all lit up,
But there were no torches.
When she saw it was lit up,
She looked up and saw the two fingers hanging down.
They were shedding light like a pressure lamp.
She said, "Big sister Sansun Bereté,
Big sister Maramajan Tarawelé,
Lift up your eyes.
This is the one about whom we said
That we would not need to be jealous of her.
This is a sprouting tree,
And when it grows to extend its branches,
It will take Manden away from us.
Hee! The new bride is lying behind her husband,
But she is watching us with her two fingers, look!
Do you see the two fingers with eyes?
Mande women, if you are real women,
You had better get ready.
This one must not be successful here."
(You heard it?)
They suddenly stopped the wedding dance.
All the women felt chilled.
They all went home.
They all dipped their hands into their *dalilu*.[6]

When Sogolon came to Maghan Konfara, she was still a virgin.
After three days her bloody virgin cloth was taken out.
The following month, she became pregnant with Sunjata.
That is how Sunjata was conceived.
(You heard it?)

---

[6] *dalilu*: Magic.

READING AND DISCUSSION QUESTIONS

1. Describe the wedding ceremony.

2. What does the passage tell you about religious beliefs in thirteenth-century Mali? How might a Muslim Malian listener from this time period have responded to this portion of the epic?

■ COMPARATIVE QUESTIONS ■

1. What role did the introduction of Christianity and Islam play in the development of the kingdoms of Ghana and Mali? How did these religions influence the actions of the kings? How did they influence the economies of the territories?

2. Describe al-Bakri's, al-Gharnāti's, and Leo Africanus's impressions of the sub-Saharan kingdoms of Ghana and Mali. What do they admire about these kingdoms? What local traditions do they criticize?

3. How does the role of women in society in these passages compare to other societies that you have read about, such as those of India and China?

11

The Americas
3200 B.C.E.–1500 C.E.

Written records of premodern societies in both Africa and the Americas typically come from the perspective of outsiders. While Muslim explorers and merchants created a record of African civilizations, European conquerors and missionaries wrote accounts of the American experience. These same Europeans also destroyed many of the writings of native American civilizations to discourage traditional practices and beliefs that opposed the spread of Christianity. This chapter explores the cultures of the Western Hemisphere, specifically the Mississippian societies of North America, the Maya and Mexica of Mesoamerica, and the Inca in South America. European colonization of these peoples was so successful that little evidence from the precontact period survives. Thus, the most important information concerning these societies comes from discoveries in archaeological excavations or from the writings of Europeans, some of whom attempted to preserve native languages and cultures.

11-1 | An Artist Uses Archaeological Evidence to Imagine an Ancient City
Moundville (ca. 1000–1450 C.E.)

The Mississippian cultures of North America shared much in common with the larger and better-known civilizations of Mesoamerica. Archaeological evidence points to a hierarchical society with a priest and warrior elite, intensive cultivation of maize, a lively trade in luxury goods, and tribute systems in which more powerful groups exacted resources and slaves from less powerful ones. The artist's reconstruction included here shows the Mississippian settlement of Moundville as it might have appeared in its heyday. Located in present-day Alabama, Moundville had a population of about 1,000 in the settlement itself, with a total population in the settlement and surrounding agricultural lands of about 10,000. As you examine the artist's reconstruction, look for clues about Moundville's social, political, and economic life. What can you deduce about Mississippian culture from the people, objects, and buildings included in the picture?

H. Tom Hall (1932–2010)/NATIONAL GEOGRAPHIC SOCIETY/Bridgeman Images.

READING AND DISCUSSION QUESTIONS

1. What evidence does the picture provide of social hierarchy? How did the people of Moundville display their status?

2. What role does trade appear to have played in Moundville life? What evidence does the picture provide of labor specialization?

3. What does the decision of Moundville's people to build the massive pyramid in the center of the settlement tell you about their society? What must have been true about their society to make such an achievement possible?

11-2 | A Spanish Conquistador Describes Inca Government

PEDRO DE CIEZA DE LEÓN, From *Chronicles: On the Inca* (ca. 1535)

From the fifteenth to the early sixteenth century, the large Inca empire in western South America spanned an area that included modern-day Peru. Compared with other civilizations in the Americas, the Inca had a sophisticated bureaucracy. Their empire had four provinces that were each headed by a governor who reported back to the king, or Sapa Inca (God Emperor). In the following account, Pedro de Cieza de León (1520–1554), a Spanish conquistador who came to admire the Inca culture, describes the administration of the empire. In the case of the Inca, historians are particularly dependent on the Spanish record because no civilization from South America developed a form of writing.

It is told for a fact of the rulers of this kingdom that in the days of their rule they had their representatives in the capitals of all the provinces, ... for in all these places there were larger and finer lodgings than in most of the other cities of this great kingdom, and many storehouses. They served as the head of the provinces or regions, and from every so many leagues around the tributes were brought to one of these capitals, and from so many others, to another. This was so well organized that there was not a village that did not know where it was to send its tribute. In all these capitals the Incas had temples of the sun, mints, and many silversmiths who did nothing but work rich pieces of gold or fair vessels of silver; large garrisons were stationed there, and, as I have said, a steward or representative who was in command of them all, to whom an accounting of everything that was brought in was made, and who, in turn, had to give one of all that was issued. And these governors could in no way interfere with the jurisdiction of another who held a similar post, but within his own, if there were any disorder or disturbance, he had authority to punish it[s perpetrators], especially if it were in the nature of a conspiracy or a rebellion, or failure to obey the Inca [i.e., Sapa Inca], for full power resided in these governors. And if the Incas had not had the foresight to appoint them and to establish the *mitimaes*,[1] the natives would have often revolted and shaken off the royal rule; but with the many troops and the abundance of provisions, they could not effect this unless they had all plotted such treason or rebellion together. This happened rarely, for these governors who were named were of complete trust, all of them *Orejones* [elite, and typically blood relations of the king], and most of them had their holdings, or *chacaras*, in

---

Pedro de Cieza de León, *Chronicles*, from *The Incas of Pedro de Cieza de León*, ed. Victor Wolfgang von Hagen, trans. Harriet de Onis (Norman: University of Oklahoma Press, 1959), 165–167, 169–174, 177–178. Copyright 1959 by the University of Oklahoma Press. Reproduced with permission. All rights reserved.

[1] **establish the *mitimaes*:** A reference to the practice of relocating the populations of recently conquered territories. By moving the population of the empire around, the Inca hoped to break down local customs and practices and create a unified culture for the entire empire.

the neighborhood of *Cuzco* [the capital city], and their homes and kinfolk. If one of them did not show sufficient capacity for his duties, he was removed and another put in his place.

When one of them came to Cuzco on private business or to see the Inca, he left a lieutenant in his place, not one who aspired to the post, but one he knew would faithfully carry out what he was ordered to do and what was best for the service of the Inca. And if one of these governors or delegates died while in office, the natives at once sent word to the Inca how and of what he had died, and even transported the body by the post road if this seemed to them advisable. The tribute paid by each of these districts where the capital was situated and that turned over by the natives, whether gold, silver, clothing, arms, and all else they gave, was entered in the accounts of . . . [those] who kept the *quipus* [knotted strings used for accounting] and did everything ordered by the governor in the matter of finding the soldiers or supplying whomever the Inca ordered, or making delivery to Cuzco; but when they came from the city of Cuzco to go over the accounts, or they were ordered to go to Cuzco to give an accounting, the accountants themselves gave it by the quipus, or went to give it where there could be no fraud, but everything had to come out right. Few years went by in which an accounting of all these things was not made. . . .

Realizing how difficult it would be to travel the great distances of their land where every league and at every turn a different language was spoken, and how bothersome it would be to have to employ interpreters to understand them, these rulers, as the best measure, ordered and decreed, with severe punishment for failure to obey, that all the natives of their empire should know and understand the language of Cuzco, both they and their women. This was so strictly enforced that an infant had not yet left its mother's breast before they began to teach it the language it had to know. And although at the beginning this was difficult and many stubbornly refused to learn any language but their own, the Incas were so forceful that they accomplished what they had proposed, and all had to do their bidding. This was carried out so faithfully that in the space of a few years a single tongue was known and used in an extension of more than 1,200 leagues, yet, even though this language was employed, they all spoke their own [languages], which were so numerous that if I were to list them it would not be credited. . . .

[The Indians] had a method of knowing how the tributes of food supplies should be levied on the provinces when the Lord-Inca came through with his army, or was visiting the kingdom; or, when nothing of this sort was taking place, what came into the storehouses and what was issued to the subjects, so nobody could be unduly burdened. . . . This involved the quipus, which are long strands of knotted strings, and those who were the accountants and understood the meaning of these knots could reckon by them expenditures or other things that had taken place many years before. By these knots they counted from one to ten and from ten to a hundred, and from a hundred to a thousand. On one of these strands there is the account of one thing, and on the other of another, in such a way that what to us is a strange, meaningless account is clear to them. In the capital of each province there were accountants whom they called *quipu-camayocs*, and by these knots they kept the account of the tribute to be paid by the natives of that district in silver, gold, clothing, flocks, down to wood and other more insignificant things, and by these same quipus at the end of a year, or ten, or twenty years, they gave a report to the one whose duty it was to check the account so exact that not even a pair of sandals was missing. . . .

The *Orejones* of Cuzco who supplied me with information are in agreement that in olden times, in the days of the Lord-Incas, all the villages and provinces of Peru were notified that a report should be given to the rulers and their representatives each year of the men and women who had died, and all who had been born, for this was necessary for the levying of the tributes as well as to know how many were available for war and those who could assume the defense of the villages. This was an easy matter, for each province at the end of the year had a list by the knots of the quipus of all the people who had died there during the year, as well as of those who had been born. At the beginning of the new year they came to Cuzco, bringing their quipus, which told how many births there had been during the year, and how many deaths. This was reported with all truth and accuracy, without any fraud or deceit. In this way the Inca and the governors knew which of the Indians were poor, the women who had been widowed, whether they were able to pay their taxes, and how many men they could count on in the event of war, and many other things they considered highly important.

As this kingdom was so vast, as I have repeatedly mentioned, in each of the many provinces there were many storehouses filled with supplies and other needful things; thus, in times of war, wherever the armies went they drew upon the contents of these storehouses, without ever touching the supplies of their confederates or laying a finger on what they had in their settlements. And when there was no war, all this stock of supplies and food was divided up among the poor and the widows. These poor were the aged, or the lame, crippled, or paralyzed, or those afflicted with some other diseases; if they were in good health, they received nothing. Then the storehouses were filled up once more with the tributes paid the Inca. If there came a lean year, the storehouses were opened and the provinces were lent what they needed in the way of supplies; then, in a year of abundance, they paid back all they had received. Even though the tributes paid to the Inca were used only for the aforesaid purposes, they were employed to advantage, for in this way their kingdom was opulent and well supplied.

No one who was lazy or tried to live by the work of others was tolerated; everyone had to work. Thus on certain days each lord went to his lands and took the plow in hand and cultivated the earth, and did other things. Even the Incas themselves did this to set an example, for everybody was to know that there should be nobody so rich that, on this account, he might disdain or affront the poor. And under their system there was none such in all the kingdom, for, if he had his health, he worked and lacked for nothing; and if he was ill, he received what he needed from the storehouses. And no rich man could deck himself out in more finery than the poor, or wear different clothing, except the rulers and headmen, who, to maintain their dignity, were allowed great freedom and privilege, as well as the *Orejones*, who held a place apart among all the peoples.

READING AND DISCUSSION QUESTIONS

1. Describe the Inca bureaucracy. How did it enable the king to rule this large territory?

2. What role did the *quipu* play in the administration of the Inca Empire?

3. Cieza mentions a law requiring that every person in the empire learn the Inca language. What does this law tell you about the priorities of the Inca government?

4. What services did the Inca government provide for the people of the empire? How were they able to offer such services?

11-3 | Diego Durán Describes Mexica Customs

DIEGO DURÁN, From *Book of the Gods and Rites* (ca. 1576–1579)

The Mexica, or Aztecs, occupied a large section of modern-day central Mexico. Like their Maya and Toltec predecessors in the area, the Mexica practiced human sacrifice. This tradition drew on Mesoamerican creation myths, which often involved gods making the first sacrifice by offering their own blood to create humanity. Victims of human sacrifice were usually captured enemy soldiers sold in slave markets. In this excerpt, the Dominican priest Diego Durán (1537–1588) describes the role of the marketplace in Mexica society, as well as the practice of human sacrifice.

The markets in this land were all enclosed by walls and stood either in front of the temples of the gods or to one side. Market day in each town was considered a main feast in that town or city. And thus in that small shrine where the idol of the market stood were offered ears of corn, chili, tomatoes, fruit, and other vegetables, seeds, and breads—in sum, everything sold in the *tianguiz* [marketplace]. Some say that (these offerings) were left there until they spoiled; others deny this, saying that all was gathered up by the priests and ministers of the temples.

But, to return to what I said about the market day being a feast day, the following is the truth. One day I was informed in a personal way, and now I shall tell what took place between me and a lord of a certain village. When I begged him to finish a part of the church that was under construction, he answered: "Father, do you not know that tomorrow is a great feast in this town? How can you expect them to work? Leave it for another day." Then, very carefully, I looked at the calendar to see which saint's day it was, and I found none. Laughing at me, (the lord) said: "Do you not know that tomorrow is the feast of the *tianguiz*

---

of this town? (Do you not know) that not a man or a woman will fail to pay it its due honor?" From these words I realized (how important) a feast and solemnity the market is for them. . . .

Furthermore, a law was established by the state prohibiting the selling of goods outside the market place. Not only were there laws and penalties connected with this, but there was a fear of the supernatural, of misfortune, and of the ire and wrath of the god of the market. No one ventured, therefore, to trade outside (the market limits), and the custom has survived until these days. Many a time have I seen a native carry two or three hens or a load of fruit for sale in the market. On the road he meets a Spaniard who wants to buy them from him. The Spaniard offers the price which he would have received in the market. The native refuses and is unwilling to sell, even though he would save himself a league or two of walking. He begs the Spaniard to go to the market place to buy them there. . . . Even today, though they are Christians, the awe and fear of their ancient law is still strong. It must also be said that the planting of this awe and nonsense in these people brought a certain income from all that which was sold in the markets (in the form of taxes), which was divided between the lord and the community.

In this land the sovereigns had set up a regulation regarding the markets: they were to take the form of fairs or markets specializing in the selling of certain things. Some markets, therefore, became famous and popular for these reasons: it was commanded that slaves were to be sold at the fair in Azcapotzalco and that all the people of the land who had slaves for sale must go there and to no other place to sell. The same can be said of Itzocan. Slaves could be sold in these two places only. It was at these two fairs that slaves were sold so that those who needed them would go there and no other place to buy. In other places, such as Cholula, it was ordered that the merchandise must consist of jewels, precious stones, and fine featherwork. At others, such as Tetzcoco, cloth and fine gourds were sold, together with exquisitely worked ceramics, splendidly done in the native way. . . .

I would like to say some things regarding the slaves sold in the two markets I have mentioned, Azcapotzalco and Itzocan. Some things worthy of remembering can be said about these slaves. In the first place, it should be known that in honor of the gods (as has been noted) men and women were slain on all the feast days. Some of these were slaves bought in the market place for the special purpose of representing gods. When they had performed the representation, when those slaves had been purified and washed—some for an entire year, others for forty days, others for nine, others for seven—after having been honored and served in the name of the god they impersonated, at the end they were sacrificed by those who owned them.

Captives of another type were those taken as prisoners in war. These served exclusively as sacrifices for the man who had impersonated the god whose feast was being celebrated. Thus these were called the "delicious food of the gods." I do not have to deal with all of these, but only with the slaves who were sold in the market place for having broken the law or for the reasons

I shall describe later. These were bought by rich merchants and by important chieftains, some to glorify their own names and others to fulfill their customary vows.

The masters took the slaves to the *tianguiz*: some took men, others women, others boys or girls, so that there would be variety from which to choose. So that they would be identified as slaves, they wore on their necks wooden or metal collars with small rings through which passed rods about one yard long. In its place I shall explain the reason for putting these collars on them. At the site where these slaves were sold (which stood at one side of the *tianguiz*, according to market regulations) the owners kept (the slaves) dancing and singing so that merchants would be attracted by the charm of their voices and their (dance) steps and buy them quickly. If one possessed this facility, therefore, he found a master immediately. This was not the case for those who lacked grace and were inept in these things. Thus they were presented many times at market places without anyone paying attention to them, though (occasionally) some bought them to make use of them (as domestic servants), since they were unfit to represent the gods. Singers and dancers were in demand because when they were garbed in the raiment of the gods they went about singing and dancing in the streets and the houses during the time of their impersonation. They entered (the houses) and the temples and (climbed to) the flat roofs of the royal houses and those of their masters. They were given all the pleasures and joys of the world—foods, drink, feasts—as if they had been the gods themselves. So it was that the merchants wished that, aside from being good dancers and singers, they were healthy, without blemish or deformity. . . . (These slaves) were therefore made to strip, and were examined from head to foot, member by member. They were forced to extend their hands and lift their feet (as is done today with) Negro (slaves), to determine whether they were crippled. If one was found healthy, he was bought; otherwise, no. For it was desired that the slaves to be purified to represent the gods (this ceremony belonging to their rites, religion and precepts) were healthy and without blemish, just as we read in the Holy Writ about the sacrifices of the Old Testament which were to be without blemish. These slaves were not strangers or foreigners or prisoners of war, as some have declared, but were natives of the same town.

READING AND DISCUSSION QUESTIONS

1. What rules did the Mexica government establish to regulate the marketplaces?

2. What role did the markets play in Mexica society? Why would work stop on the day of the market?

3. How were slaves selected for human sacrifice? What qualities did they need to exhibit?

4. How were slaves treated before being sacrificed?

VIEWPOINTS

The Importance of the Ball Game in Maya Society

The Maya ball game tlachtli was much more than a spectator sport. Matches and their outcomes had social, political, and religious significance. Tlachtli courts were some of the most important structures in Maya cities. Their size demonstrated the power and authority of the city, while decorative carvings highlighted key aspects of Maya religion and myth. While winners became heroes, losers were typically sacrificed to the Maya gods. The two documents included here offer contrasting accounts of tlachtli. The first, written by Antonio de Herrera y Tordesillas, emphasizes the rules of the game and tells us very little about its social and cultural implications. The second, written by a Spanish priest, represents a genuine effort to preserve and relate Maya religious stories and beliefs. As you read the two documents, think about the differences between them. What does each have to tell us about tlachtli?

11-4 | The Rules and Objectives of a Maya Ball Game

ANTONIO DE HERRERA Y TORDESILLAS, *On the Maya Ball Game Tlachtli* (ca. 1598)

Antonio de Herrera y Tordesillas (1549–1626) was the chief chronicler of Castile and the Americas during the reigns of Philip II and Philip III of Spain. Herrera was a prolific writer who produced some of the most important early histories of Spanish exploration and conquest of the New World. While he drew on numerous sources and made a genuine effort at objectivity, it is important to note that Herrera never actually visited the Americas. As a historian, he saw his task as comparing various firsthand accounts and synthesizing them into the most complete and accurate retelling of events possible. Thus, his emphasis was on description, not interpretation. Keep this in mind as you read Herrera's explanation of tlachtli. What did he include in his account? What did he leave out?

The game was called "Tlachtli," which is the same as "Trinquete" in Spanish. The ball was made of the gum from a tree which grows in the hot country. This tree, when tapped, exudes some large white drops, which soon congeal and when mixed and kneaded become as black as pitch: of this material the balls are made,

---

Alfred Percival Maudslay, *A Glimpse at Guatemala* (London: John Murray, 1899), 205–206.

and, although heavy and hard to the hand, they bound and rebound as lightly as footballs, and are indeed better, as there is no need to inflate them. They do not play for "chases" but to make a winning stroke—that is, to strike the ball against or to hit it over the wall which the opposite party defend. The ball may be struck with any part of the body, either such part as is most convenient or such as each player is most skillful in using. Sometimes it is arranged that it should count against any player who touches the ball otherwise than with his hip, for this is considered by them to show the greatest skill, and on this account they would wear a piece of stiff raw hide over the hips, so that the ball might better rebound. The ball might be struck as long as it bounded, and it made many bounds one after the other, as though it were alive.

They played in parties, so many on each side, and for such a stake as a parcel of cotton cloths, more or less, according to the wealth of the players. They also played for articles of gold and for feathers, and at times staked their own persons. The place where they played was a court on the level of the ground, long, narrow, and high, but wider above than below, and higher at the sides than at the ends. So that it should be better to play in, the court was well cemented, and the walls and floors made quite smooth. In the side walls were fixed two stones like millstones, with a hole pierced through the middle, through which there was just room for the ball to pass, and the player who hit the ball through the hole won the game; and as this was a rare victory, which few gained, by the ancient custom and law of the game, the victor had a right to the mantles of all the spectators. . . .

To those who saw the feat performed for the first time it seemed like a miracle, and they said that a player who had such good luck would become a thief or an adulterer, or would die soon. And the memory of such a victory lasted many days, until it was followed by another, which put it out of mind.

READING AND DISCUSSION QUESTIONS

1. What details did Herrera include to make the game intelligible to his European readers? What games might his readers have seen that were similar to tlachtli?

2. Describe the ball game court. What does the court suggest about the building capabilities of the Maya? Why might Herrera have thought it important to include details about the court's construction?

11-5 | The Gods Challenge Two Maya Heroes to a Game of Tlachtli

FATHER FRANCISCO XIMÉNEZ, From *Popol Vuh* (ca. 1701–1703)

As the Spanish were so successful at destroying the precontact cultural heritages of the indigenous Americans, it is often necessary to use much later sources to understand native societies. Some Spanish clergy, however, attempted to collect and preserve aspects of native culture, and because of the actions of a Dominican priest, Father Francisco Ximénez, a remarkable document known as the *Popol Vuh* has survived. It is thought to have originated with a native Maya text from the mid-sixteenth century. This passage describes how an invitation to a game of tlachtli by the gods led to the deaths of the twin heroes, Hun-Hunahpú and Vucub-Hunahpú. As you read it, consider what the passage reveals about the cultural implications of tlachtli. How does this passage enrich your understanding of the game as described by Herrera?

Having gone to play ball on the road to Xibalba,[2] they [Hun-Hunahpú and Vucub-Hunahpú] were overheard by Hun-Camé and Vucub-Camé, the lords of Xibalba.

"What are you doing on earth? Who are they who are making the earth shake, and making so much noise? Go and call them! Let them come here to play ball. Here we will overpower them! We are no longer respected by them. They no longer have consideration, or fear of our rank, and they even fight above our heads," said all the lords of Xibalba.

All of them held a council. Those called Hun-Camé and Vucub-Camé were the supreme judges. All the lords had been assigned their duties. Each one was given his own authority by Hun-Camé and Vucub-Camé.

They were, then, Xiquiripat and Cuchumaquic lords of these names. They were the two who caused the shedding of blood of the men.

Others were called Ahalpuh and Ahalganá, also lords. And their work was to make men swell and make pus gush forth from their legs and stain their faces yellow, what is called Chuganal. Such was the work of Ahalpuh and Ahalganá.

Others were Lord Chamiabac and Lord Chamiaholom, constables of Xibalba, whose staffs were of bone. Their work was to make men waste away until they were nothing but skin and bone and they died, and they carried them with their stomach and bones stretched out. This was the work of Chamiabac and Chamiaholom, as they were called.

Others were called Lord Ahalmez and Lord Ahaltocob; their work was to bring disaster upon men, as they were going home, or in front of it, and they

---

[2] **Xibalba:** The underworld, commonly translated as "the place of fear."

would be found wounded, stretched out, face up, on the ground, dead. This was the work of Ahalmez and Ahaltocob, as they were called.

Immediately after them were other lords named Xic and Patán whose work it was to cause men to die on the road, which is called sudden death, making blood to rush to their mouths until they died vomiting blood. The work of each one of these lords was to seize upon them, squeeze their throats and chests, so that the men died on the road, making the blood rush to their throats when they were walking. This was the work of Xic and Patán.

And having gathered in council, they discussed how to torment and wound Hun-Hunahpú and Vucub-Hunahpú. What the Lords of Xibalba coveted were the playing implements of Hun-Hunahpú and Vucub-Hunahpú—their leather pads and rings and gloves and crown and masks which were the playing gear of Hun-Hunahpú and Vucub-Hunahpú. . . .

The messengers of Hun-Camé and Vucub-Camé arrived immediately.

"Go, Ahpop Achih!" they were told. "Go and call Hun-Hunahpú and Vucub-Hunahpú. Say to them, 'Come with us. The lords say that you must come.' They must come here to play ball with us so that they shall make us happy, for really they amaze us. So, then, they must come," said the lords. "And have them bring their playing gear, their rings, their gloves, and have them bring their rubber balls, too," said the lords. "Tell them to come quickly," they told the messengers. . . .

Hun-Hunahpú and Vucub-Hunahpú went immediately and the messengers took them on the road. Thus they were descending the road to Xibalba, by some very steep stairs. . . .

Immediately they arrived at the House of Gloom. There was only darkness within the house. Meanwhile the Lords of Xibalba discussed what they should do.

"Let us sacrifice them tomorrow, let them die quickly, quickly, so that we can have their playing gear to use in play," said the Lords of Xibalba to each other.

Well, their fat-pine sticks were round and were called *zaquitoc*, which is the pine of Xibalba. Their fat-pine sticks were pointed and filed and were as bright as bone; the pine of Xibalba was very hard.

Hun-Hunahpú and Vucub-Hunahpú entered the House of Gloom. There they were given their fat-pine sticks, a single lighted stick which Hun-Camé and Vucub-Camé sent them, together with a lighted cigar for each of them which the lords had sent. They went to give them to Hun-Hunahpú and Vucub-Hunahpú.

They found them crouching in the darkness when the porters arrived with the fat-pine sticks and the cigars. As they entered, the pine sticks lighted the place brightly.

"Each of you light your pine sticks and your cigars; come and bring them back at dawn, you must not burn them up, but you must return them whole; this is what the lords told us to say." So they said. And so they were defeated. They burned up the pine sticks, and they also finished the cigars which had been given to them.

There were many punishments in Xibalba; the punishments were of many kinds.

The first was the House of Gloom, Quequma-ha, in which there was only darkness.

The second was Xuxulim-ha, the house where everybody shivered, in which it was very cold. A cold, unbearable wind blew within.

The third was the House of Jaguars, Balami-ha, it was called, in which there were nothing but jaguars which stalked about, jumped around, roared, and made fun. The jaguars were shut up in the house.

Zorzi-há, the House of Bats, the fourth place of punishment was called. Within this house there were nothing but bats which squeaked and cried and flew around and around. The bats were shut in and could not get out.

The fifth was called Chayim-há, the House of Knives, in which there were only sharp, pointed knives, silent or grating against each other in the house.

There were many places of torture in Xibalba, but Hun-Hunahpú and Vucub-Hunahpú did not enter them. We only mention the names of these houses of punishment.

When Hun-Hunahpú and Vucub-Hunahpú came before Hun-Camé and Vucub-Camé, they said: "Where are my cigars? Where are my sticks of fat pine which I gave you last night?"

"They are all gone, Sir."

"Well. Today shall be the end of your days. Now you shall die. You shall be destroyed, we will break you into pieces and here your faces will stay hidden. You shall be sacrificed," said Hun-Camé and Vucub-Camé.

They sacrificed them immediately and buried them in the Pucbal-Chah, as it was called. Before burying them, they cut off the head of Hun-Hunahpú, and buried the older brother together with the younger brother.

"Take the head and put it in that tree which is planted on the road," said Hun-Camé and Vucub-Camé. And having put the head in the tree, instantly the tree, which had never borne fruit before the head of Hun-Hunahpú was placed among its branches, was covered with fruit. And this calabash tree, it is said, is the one which we now call the head of Hun-Hunahpú.

Hun-Camé and Vucub-Camé looked in amazement at the fruit on the tree. The round fruit was every where; but they did not recognize the head of Hun-Hunahpú; it was exactly like the other fruit of the calabash tree. So it seemed to all of the people of Xibalba when they came to look at it.

According to their judgment, the tree was miraculous, because of what had instantly occurred when they put Hun-Hunahpú's head among its branches. And the Lords of Xibalba said:

"Let no one come to pick this fruit. Let no one come and sit under this tree!" they said, and so the Lords of Xibalba resolved to keep everybody away.

The head of Hun-Hunahpú did not appear again, because it had become one and the same as the fruit of the gourd tree. Nevertheless, a girl heard the wonderful story. Now we shall tell about her arrival.

READING AND DISCUSSION QUESTIONS

1. Describe the Maya gods as they appear in this passage. What does their discussion of tlachtli reveal about their attitudes and characteristics?

2. What is the moral of this story? What might a prospective player of tlachtli have been meant to take from it?

VIEWPOINTS COMPARATIVE QUESTIONS

1. Based on these two documents, how would you describe tlachtli and what it meant to the Maya?

2. In your opinion, should tlachtli be described as a Maya "game"? If so, why? If not, what term would you substitute for *game*?

▪ COMPARATIVE QUESTIONS ▪

1. Based on the documents in this chapter, what can you say about the similarities and differences in culture and religion in the Americas before contact with Europeans?

2. Taking into consideration the depictions of the Mexica marketplace and the Maya ball game, describe the benefits entertainment provided to the civilizations of the Americas.

3. What role did law play in Inca and Mexica society? According to Cieza de León and Durán, how successful were the rulers of these civilizations in enforcing laws?

4. Compare the sources in this chapter to those on Africa (Chapter 10). Most of the material from both chapters is written from the perspective of outsiders. Can it be trusted? Why or why not? How might the information in such sources be verified?

5. How do the gods and the underworld in the *Popol Vuh* compare to those in *The Epic of Gilgamesh* (Document 2-1)?

Cultural Exchange in Central and Southern Asia

300–1400

During the medieval period, the climate of Central and southern Asia was one of contact and transformation. While Indian merchants sailed throughout Southeast Asia introducing Buddhism and Hinduism, Muslim merchants and, later, Muslim armies brought their own religion into India. In Central Asia, nomadic groups of Turks and Mongols began to abandon their traditional transitory lifestyles as they came into contact with settled civilizations. The Mongols evolved into cultural brokers who facilitated the exchange of people and ideas throughout their far-reaching empire. The Mongols never conquered India, allowing Indian traditions to develop as a complex blend of Hindu and Islamic customs. The sources in this chapter examine the changes under way in Central and southern Asia from approximately the fourth to the fifteenth centuries, with a special emphasis on the Mongol experience and empire.

VIEWPOINTS

The Mongols and Their Conquests

When Chinggis Khan (ca. 1162–1227) was born, the Mongols were just another nomadic group roaming the Central Asian grasslands. A hundred years later, they ruled a vast empire that spanned the width of Asia, from China's Pacific coast to the Middle East. This accomplishment owed much to the Mongols' extraordinary military prowess. Under the leadership of Chinggis Khan and his successors, mounted Mongol armies struck at their enemies with astonishing speed and ferocity. Faced with such an opponent, many of their would-be foes chose to surrender without a fight. Skill in battle, however, was not the only explanation for the Mongols' achievement. Once the Mongols had conquered a territory, they proved adept at maintaining control of their new lands, allowing existing institutions and elites to stay in place as long as Mongol rule was not resisted and tribute was paid. Finally, the Mongols embraced diversity. They were interested in the beliefs and ideas of other peoples and did not seek to impose religious and cultural homogeneity on their empire. As you read the documents included in this feature, think about the foundations and nature of Mongol rule. How did the Mongols conquer and control their large and diverse empire?

12-1 | Observations on Mongol Rule in China
Epitaph for the Honorable Menggu (ca. 1272)

The Mongol conquest of China occurred in stages and was not complete until the 1270s. The Mongols chose to continue using the established system of administration in China, but they distrusted local Chinese officials and the bureaucrats themselves. To watch the activities of the Chinese officials, the Mongols placed outsiders in key positions. Many were Mongols, such as the official described here, but many were imported from Central Asia and the Middle East. It is not known who wrote this epitaph, but it is thought to have been a Chinese official.

Epitaph for the Honorable Menggu, Great General of Huaiyuan, Governor of Huaimeng Route, and Military Administrator of Several Armies

Emperor Taizu [Chinggis Khan] received the mandate of Heaven and subjugated all regions. When Emperor Taizong [Ogodei Khan] succeeded, he revitalized the bureaucratic system and made it more efficient and organized. At court, one minister supervised all the officials and helped the emperor rule. In the provinces, commanderies and counties received instructions from above and saw that they got carried out. Prefects and magistrates were as a rule appointed only after submitting [to the Mongols]. Still one Mongol, called the governor, was selected to supervise them. The prefects and magistrates all had to obey his orders. The fortune of the common people and the quality of the government both were entirely dependent on the wisdom of the governor.

Zhangde, one of the ten routes,[1] is crucial to communication between north and south. In the fourth month of 1236, the court deemed Menggu capable of handling Zhangde, so promoted him from the post of legal officer of the troops of Quduqu to be its governor. At the time, the Jin[2] had fallen only three years earlier. The common people were not yet free of the army, the injured had not yet recovered, those who had fled had not yet returned, and the residents were not yet contented. Because regulations were lax, the soldiers took advantage of their victory to plunder. Even in cities and marketplaces, some people kept their doors closed in the daytime. As soon as Menggu arrived, he took charge. Knowing the people's grievances, he issued an order, "Those who oppress the people will be dealt with according to the law. Craftsmen, merchants, and shopkeepers, you must each go about your work with your doors open, peaceably attending to your business without fear. Farmers, you must be content with your lands and exert yourselves diligently according to the seasons. I will instruct or punish those who mistreat you." After this order was issued, the violent became obedient and no one any longer dared violate the laws. Farmers in the fields and travelers on the roads felt safe, and people began to enjoy life.

In the second month of 1238, Wang Rong, prefect of Huaizhou, rebelled. The grand preceptor and prince ordered Menggu to put down this rebellion, telling him to slaughter everyone. Menggu responded, "When the royal army suppresses rebels, those who were coerced into joining them ought to be pardoned, not to mention those who are entirely innocent." The prince approved his advice and followed it. When Wang Rong surrendered, he was executed but the region was spared. The residents, with jugs of wine and burning incense, saw Menggu off tearfully, unable to bear his leaving. Forty years later when he was put in charge of Henei, the common people were delighted with the news, saying, "We will all survive—our parents and relatives through marriage all served him before."

In 1239 locusts destroyed all the vegetation in Xiang and Wei, so the people were short of food. Menggu reported this to the great minister Quduqu who issued five thousand piculs[3] of army rations to save the starving. As a consequence no one had to flee or starve.

During the four years from 1240 to 1243, the great southern campaigns took place. Wherever the armies passed, the local officials complained. Menggu, through loyal and diligent preparations, was able to supply the troops without hurting the people.

---

[1] **the ten routes:** The Mongols transformed the adminstration of China by basing it on population size. One route equaled 100,000 households. Ten routes equaled a province.

[2] **the Jin:** Dynasty that ruled northern China from 1115 to 1234. The Jin were originally from north of the Great Wall in modern-day Manchuria.

[3] **piculs:** Weight equal to how much a man could carry on his shoulder.

In 1247 some previously pacified cities in the Huai and Han areas rose in revolt. Refugees fled north and south. Border generals and local officials joined the fray, fighting and plundering. Menggu, by establishing trust, was able to gather together more than ten thousand households and settle them down as commoners. Even children were included.

At that time the harvest failed for several years in a row, yet taxes and labor services were still exacted. Consequently, three or four of every ten houses was vacant. Menggu ordered the officials to travel around announcing that those who returned to their property would be exempt from taxes and services for three years. That year seventeen thousand households returned in response to his summons.

In the first month of 1248 Zhu Ge, a bandit from Huizhou, organized a gang and rebelled. The military officers were planning to go overboard in their response to this, but Menggu declared, "The state has honored me, enriched me, delegated control of the troops to me, and entrusted the fate of the region to me. Does it want me to pacify the bandits or become a bandit myself? There is no need to act recklessly. If the bandits are not caught or the rebellion not suppressed, I will accept the responsibility." He then personally led the troops, capturing thirty-eight bandits at Heilu Mountain, and restoring peace to the local population. By fall there were no more rebels. When the bandit Xie Zhiquan rebelled in the third month of 1249, he pacified him the same way.

General Chagan recognized Menggu's honesty and humanity. Whenever the other circuits condemned prisoners to death, he had Menggu conduct the review investigation. Innumerable times, Menggu relied on the law to redress grievances and reduce penalties. Ten years before, a peasant in Anyang had offended a noble and been ordered to turn over six young girls. Menggu ordered the noble official Alachur to marry them all out to commoners. There was a drought in the summer of 1250. After Menggu prayed for rain, moisture became adequate.

In the spring of 1262, Li Tan revolted and sent his henchmen to faraway places disguised as mounted couriers. They traveled through many routes, east and west, the officials unable to recognize them. Menggu discovered them and got them to admit their treacherous conspiracy, thus defeating them. When there was a drought in 1263, Menggu prayed for rain and it rained. That year he was given the title Brilliant and August General and made governor of Zhongshan prefecture. In 1270 he was transferred and became governor of Hezhong prefecture. In the spring of 1274 he was allowed to wear the golden tiger tablet in recognition of his long and excellent service, his incorruptibility, and the repute in which he was held where he had served. He was advanced out of order to great general of Huaiyuan, governor of Huaimeng route, and military administrator of several armies. On the 29th of the second month he died of illness in the main room of his private residence at the age of seventy-one.

Menggu was a Mongol, and when young was called Mongol Baer. His father was Xibaer, his mother Lengla. He had six wives . . . , seven sons, . . . six daughters. . . . Seven years after he was buried, Naohai and his other sons recorded Menggu's virtuous government service for an epitaph and came to ask me to write the inscription.

Alas! When I think about all the government officials of the past and present, I come to the realization that the greedy ones are invariably oppressive and the honest ones are invariably incorrupt, the connection between their virtues and their administrative behavior as automatic as shape to shadow or sound to echo. Those who are greedy are not satisfied; not satisfied, they take by force, not caring how much they harm the world. Those who are honest do not take what is not theirs, no matter how slight it might be. How would they harm others to benefit themselves? The house where Menggu lived when he governed Zhangde nearly forty years ago, and the fields from which he obtained food then, were just adequate to keep out the wind and rain and supply enough to eat. When he died there were no estates or leftover wealth to leave his sons or grandsons. Therefore they had to model themselves on him and concentrate on governing in a way that would bring peace and safety, show love for the people, and benefit all. They have no need to be ashamed even if compared to the model officials of the Han and Tang dynasties.

READING AND DISCUSSION QUESTIONS

1. How is the governor Menggu described in this passage? What might this reveal about Chinese attitudes about Mongol rule?

2. What does this document reveal about how the Mongol system of government worked in China?

3. In your opinion, should we treat this document as a credible and objective description of Menggu's character and policies? Why or why not?

12-2 | The Role of a Mongol Leader in Battle

RASHID-AL-DIN, *Chinggis Khan Fighting the Tartars* (ca. 1300)

Mongol military success was the result of many factors. The Mongols were expert horsemen who took full advantage of the speed and mobility of a mounted army. Moreover, the nomadic Mongol lifestyle was ideally suited to the training of tough, highly skilled warriors. In effect, Mongol boys grew up in a military camp, learning from an early age how to ride, hunt, fight, and survive. The skills they practiced daily made them formidable foes in battle. Finally, the Mongols were fortunate to have a remarkable leader in Chinggis Khan. As this illustration from a Persian history of the Mongols makes clear, Chinggis led his forces by example, placing himself at the head of his troops and plunging directly into battle. As you examine the illustration, ask yourself what it tells you about Mongol military prowess. How does it help explain the devastating effectiveness of Mongol armies?

TOM GRAVES ARCHIVE/ Bibliothèque Nationale, Paris, France/ Bridgeman Images.

READING AND DISCUSSION QUESTIONS

1. What weapons are the Mongols shown using? How might their choice of weapons have multiplied the military impact of their skill as horsemen?

2. What might the artist have wanted to convey about Chinggis's qualities as a leader? What choices did the artist make in composition and subject matter to highlight these qualities?

12-3 | A European Merchant Travels the Silk Road

MARCO POLO, From *Travels: Description of the World* (ca. 1298)

Marco Polo (ca. 1253–1324) was an Italian merchant who traveled through Central Asia to China. He served as a government official for many years in the court of Khubilai Khan. Upon returning to Europe in 1295 — approximately twenty-five years after he began his journey — Polo wrote a popular book describing his adventures. Although historians have at times doubted the veracity of some of Polo's claims, his *Travels* nonetheless provides an important record of Central Asia during the time of the Mongols. In this excerpt, Polo describes his journey along the Asian trade routes known as the Silk Road, including his crossing of the challenging Taklimakan Desert.

Marco Polo, *The Travels of Marco Polo*, trans. Ronald Latham (London: Penguin Classics, 1958), 82–85, 87–88. Copyright © 1958 Ronald Latham. Reproduced by permission of Penguin Books Ltd.

Let us turn next to the province of Yarkand [on the southwestern border of the Taklimakan Desert], five days' journey in extent. The inhabitants follow the law of Mahomet,[4] and there are also some Nestorian Christians. They are subject to the Great Khan's nephew, of whom I have already spoken. It is amply stocked with the means of life, especially cotton. But, since there is nothing here worth mentioning in our book, we shall pass on to Khotan,[5] which lies towards the east-north-east.

Khotan is a province eight days' journey in extent, which is subject to the Great Khan. The inhabitants all worship Mahomet. It has cities and towns in plenty, of which the most splendid, and the capital of the kingdom, bears the same name as the province, Khotan. It is amply stocked with the means of life. Cotton grows here in plenty. It has vineyards, estates, and orchards in plenty. The people live by trade and industry; they are not at all warlike.

Passing on from here we come to the province of Pem, five days' journey in extent, towards the east-north-east. Here too the inhabitants worship Mahomet and are subject to the Great Khan. It has villages and towns in plenty. The most splendid city and the capital of the province is called Pem. There are rivers here in which are found stones called jasper and chalcedony [both are quartz] in plenty. There is no lack of the means of life. Cotton is plentiful. The inhabitants live by trade and industry.

The following custom is prevalent among them. When a woman's husband leaves her to go on a journey of more than twenty days, then, as soon as he has left, she takes another husband, and this she is fully entitled to do by local usage. And the men, wherever they go, take wives in the same way.

You should know that all the provinces I have described, from Kashgar to Pem and some way beyond, are provinces of Turkestan [i.e., the area of Central Asia inhabited by Turks].

I will tell you next of another province of Turkestan, lying east-north-east, which is called Charchan. It used to be a splendid and fruitful country, but it has been much devastated by the Tartars [Mongols]. The inhabitants worship Mahomet. There are villages and towns in plenty, and the chief city of the kingdom is Charchan.[6] There are rivers producing jasper and chalcedony, which are exported for sale in Cathay and bring in a good profit; for they are plentiful and of good quality.

All this province is a tract of sand; and so is the country from Khotan to Pem and from Pem to here. There are many springs of bad and bitter water, though in some places the water is good and sweet. When it happens that an army passes through the country, if it is a hostile one, the people take flight with their wives

---

[4] **Mahomet:** Western Europeans mistakenly believed that Muslims worshipped a god named Mahomet, or Muhammad, who is in fact the founder of the Islamic religion and believed to be a prophet of God.

[5] **Khotan:** A city along a Silk Road trading route located on the southern border of the Taklimakan Desert.

[6] **Charchan:** This was the next major city along the trade route.

and children and their beasts two or three days' journey into the sandy wastes to places where they know that there is water and they can live with their beasts. And I assure you that no one can tell which way they have gone, because the wind covers their tracks with sand, so that there is nothing to show where they have been, but the country looks as if it had never been traversed by man or beast. That is how they escape from their enemies. But, if it happens that a friendly army passes that way, they merely drive off their beasts, because they do not want to have them seized and eaten; for the armies never pay for what they take. And you should know that, when they harvest their grain, they store it far from any habitation, in certain caves among these wastes, for fear of the armies; and from these stores they bring home what they need month by month.

After leaving Charchan, the road runs for fully five days through sandy wastes, where the water is bad and bitter, except in a few places where it is good and sweet; and there is nothing worth noting in our book. At the end of the five days' journey towards the east-north-east, is a city which stands on the verge of the Great Desert. It is here that men take in provisions for crossing the desert. Let us move on accordingly and proceed with our narrative.

The city I have mentioned, which stands at the point where the traveler enters the Great Desert, is a big city called Lop, and the desert is called the Desert of Lop. The city is subject to the Great Khan, and the inhabitants worship Mahomet. I can tell you that travelers who intend to cross the desert rest in this town for a week to refresh themselves and their beasts. At the end of the week they stock up with a month's provisions for themselves and their beasts. Then they leave the town and enter the desert.

This desert is reported to be so long that it would take a year to go from end to end; and at the narrowest point it takes a month to cross it. It consists entirely of mountains and sand and valleys. There is nothing at all to eat. But I can tell you that after traveling a day and a night you find drinking water [at an oasis]—not enough water to supply a large company, but enough for fifty or a hundred men with their beasts. And all the way through the desert you must go for a day and a night before you find water. And I can tell you that in three or four places you find the water bitter and brackish; but at all the other watering-places, that is, twenty-eight in all, the water is good. Beasts and birds there are none, because they find nothing to eat. But I assure you that one thing is found here, and that a very strange one, which I will relate to you.

The truth is this. When a man is riding by night through this desert and something happens to make him loiter and lose touch with his companions, by dropping asleep or for some other reason, and afterwards he wants to rejoin them, then he hears spirits talking in such a way that they seem to be his companions. Sometimes, indeed, they even hail him by name. Often these voices make him stray from the path, so that he never finds it again. And in this way many travelers have been lost and have perished. And sometimes in the night they are conscious of a noise like the clatter of a great cavalcade of riders away from the road; and, believing that these are some of their own company, they go where they hear the noise and, when day breaks, find they are victims of an illusion and in an awkward plight. And there are some who, in crossing this desert, have seen a host of men coming towards them and, suspecting that they were robbers, have taken flight; so, having left the beaten track and not knowing how to return to it, they have gone hopelessly astray. Yes, and even by daylight men hear these spirit voices, and often you fancy you are listening to the strains of many instruments, especially drums, and the clash of arms. For this reason bands of travelers make a point of keeping very close together. Before they go to sleep they set up a sign pointing in the direction in which they have to travel. And round the necks of all their beasts they fasten little bells, so that by listening to the sound they may prevent them from straying off the path.

That is how they cross the desert, with all the discomfort of which you have heard. . . .

Now I will tell you of some other cities, which lie towards the north-west near the edge of this desert.

The province of Kamul, which used to be a kingdom, contains towns and villages in plenty, the chief town being also called Kamul.[7] The province lies between two deserts, the Great Desert and a small one three days' journey in extent. The inhabitants are all idolaters [Buddhists] and speak a language of their own. They live on the produce of the soil; for they have a superfluity of foodstuffs and beverages, which they sell to travelers who pass that way. They are a very gay folk, who give no thought to anything but making music, singing and dancing, and reading and writing according to their own usage, and taking great delight in the pleasures of the body. I give you my word that if a stranger comes to a house here to seek hospitality he receives a very warm welcome. The host bids his wife do everything that the guest wishes. Then he leaves the house and goes about his own business and stays away two or three days. Meanwhile the guest stays with his wife in the house and does what he will with her, lying with her in one bed just as if she were his own wife; and they lead a gay life together. All the men of this city and province are thus cuckolded by their wives; but they are not the least ashamed of it. And the women are beautiful and vivacious and always ready to oblige.

Now it happened during the reign of Mongu Khan,[8] lord of the Tartars, that he was informed of this custom that prevailed among the men of Kamul of giving their wives in adultery to outsiders. Mongu thereupon commanded them under heavy penalties to desist from this form of hospitality. When they received this command, they were greatly distressed; but for three years they reluctantly obeyed. Then they held a council and talked the matter over, and this is what they did. They took a rich gift and sent it to Mongu and entreated him to let them use their wives according to the traditions of their ancestors; for their ancestors had declared that by the pleasure they gave to guests with their

---

[7] **Kamul:** Known today as Hami, this city is located along the northern route, which Polo is apparently describing from secondhand accounts.

[8] **Mongu Khan:** Brother of Khubilai Khan, who was Great Khan from 1251 to 1259.

wives and goods they won the favor of their idols and multiplied the yield of their crops and their tillage. When Mongu Khan heard this he said: "Since you desire your own shame, you may have it." So he let them have their way. And I can assure you that since then they have always upheld this tradition and uphold it still.

READING AND DISCUSSION QUESTIONS

1. What were some of the dangers of traveling the Silk Road?

2. Describe the role of the Mongols in the areas that Polo visited. What impact did the Mongol presence have in these territories?

3. Consider the story Polo tells regarding the wives of Kamul. What does the response of the Great Khan say about the political strength of the Mongol leader in his empire? What does it tell you about Mongol attitudes toward cultural and religious diversity?

VIEWPOINTS COMPARATIVE QUESTIONS

1. Taken together, how do these three documents help explain the Mongols' success?

2. Compare and contrast the depictions of Mongol rule offered by the Chinese official and by Marco Polo. What does each tell you about Mongol rule? How would you explain the differences you note?

12-4 | A Hindu Description of the Ideal Wife

VATSYAYANA, From the *Kamasutra: About a Wife* (ca. 150–1200)

Most Westerners know of the *Kamasutra* as a manual of sexual positions, but the text actually examines all facets of love, including this selection on the duties of a wife. Most scholars have dated the original text to the second century c.e., but it was revised and expanded in subsequent centuries. Traditionally, the text was said to have been recited by the doorkeeper of the Hindu god Shiva after hearing Shiva making love to his consort, Parvati. Whatever its origin, the *Kamasutra* was an immensely popular text throughout medieval India.

The Kama Sutra of Vatsyayana (1883 for the Kama Shastra Society of London and Benares), 97–100.

On the Manner of Living of a Virtuous Woman, and of Her Behavior During the Absence of Her Husband

A virtuous woman, who has affection for her husband, should act in conformity with his wishes as if he were a divine being, and with his consent should take upon herself the whole care of his family. She should keep the whole house well cleaned, and arrange flowers of various kinds in different parts of it, and make the floor smooth and polished so as to give the whole a neat and becoming appearance. She should surround the house with a garden, and place ready in it all the materials required for the morning, noon and evening sacrifices. Moreover she should herself revere the sanctuary of the Household Gods, for says Gonardiya,[9] "nothing so much attracts the heart of a householder to his wife as a careful observance of the things mentioned above."

Towards the parents, relations, friends, sisters, and servants of her husband she should behave as they deserve. In the garden she should plant beds of green vegetables, bunches of the sugar cane, and clumps of the fig tree, the mustard plant, the parsley plant, the fennel plant. . . . She should also have seats and arbors made in the garden, in the middle of which a well, tank or pool should be dug.

The wife should always avoid the company of female beggars, female buddhist mendicants, unchaste and roguish women, female fortune tellers and witches. As regards meals she should always consider what her husband likes and dislikes, and what things are good for him, and what are injurious to him. When she hears the sounds of his footsteps coming home she should at once get up, and be ready to do whatever he may command her, and either order her female servant to wash his feet, or wash them herself. When going anywhere with her husband, she should put on her ornaments, and without his consent she should not either give or accept invitations, or attend marriages and sacrifices, or sit in the company of female friends, or visit the temples of the gods. And if she wants to engage in any kind of games or sports, she should not do it against his will. In the same way she should always sit down after him, and get up before him, and should never awaken him when he is asleep. The kitchen should be situated in a quiet and retired place, so as not to be accessible to strangers, and should always look clean.

In the event of any misconduct on the part of her husband, she should not blame him excessively, though she be a little displeased. She should not use abusive language towards him, but rebuke him with conciliatory words, whether he be in the company of friends or alone. Moreover, she should not be a scold, for says Conardiya [Gonardiya], "there is no cause of dislike on the part of a husband so great as this characteristic in a wife." Lastly she should avoid bad expressions, sulky looks, speaking aside, standing in the doorway, and looking at passers-by, conversing in the pleasure groves, and remaining in a lonely place

---

[9] **Gonardiya:** The author of a Sanskrit grammar.

for a long time; and finally she should always keep her body, her teeth, her hair and everything belonging to her tidy, sweet, and clean.

When the wife wants to approach her husband in private her dress should consist of many ornaments, various kinds of flowers, and a cloth decorated with different colors, and some sweet-smelling ointments or unguents. But her every-day dress should be composed of a thin, close-textured cloth, a few ornaments and flowers, and a little scent, not too much. She should also observe the fasts and vows of her husband, and when he tries to prevent her doing this, she should persuade him to let her do it.

At appropriate times of the year, and when they happen to be cheap, she should buy earth, bamboos, firewood, skins, and iron pots, as also salt and oil. Fragrant substances, vessels made of the fruit of the plant wrightea antidy senterica, or oval leaved wrightea, medicines, and other things which are always wanted, should be obtained when required and kept in a secret place of the house. The seeds of the radish, the potato, the common beet, the Indian wormwood, the mangoe, the cucumber, the egg plant, the kushmanda, the pumpkin gourd, the surana, [the] bignonia indica, the sandal wood, the premma spinosa, the garlic plant, the onion, and other vegetables, should be bought and sown at the proper seasons.

The wife, moreover, should not tell to strangers, the amount of her wealth, nor the secrets which her husband has confided to her. She should surpass all the women of her own rank in life in her cleverness, her appearance, her knowledge of cookery, her pride, and her manner of serving her husband. The expenditure of the year should be regulated by the profits. The milk that remains after the meals should be turned into ghee or clarified butter. Oil and sugar should be prepared at home; spinning and weaving should also be done there; and a store of ropes and cords, and barks of trees for twisting into ropes should be kept. She should also attend to the pounding and cleaning of rice, using its small grain and chaff in some way or other. She should pay the salaries of the servants, look after the tilling of the fields, and keeping of the flocks and herds, superintend the making of vehicles, and take care of the rams, cocks, quails, parrots, starlings, cuckoos, peacocks, monkeys, and deer; and finally adjust the income and expenditure of the day. The worn-out clothes should be given to those servants who have done good work, in order to show them that their services have been appreciated, or they may be applied to some other use. The vessels in which wine is prepared, as well as those in which it is kept, should be carefully looked after, and put away at the proper time. All sales and purchases should also be well attended to. The friends of her husband she should welcome by presenting them with flowers, ointment, incense, betel leaves, and betel nut. Her father-in-law and mother-in-law she should treat as they deserve, always remaining dependent on their will, never contradicting them, speaking to them in few and not harsh words, not laughing loudly in their presence, and acting with their friends and enemies as with her own. In addition to the above she should not be vain, or too much taken up with her enjoyments. She should be liberal towards her servants, and reward them on holidays and festivals; and not give away anything without first making it known to her husband.

Thus ends the manner of living of a virtuous woman.

During the absence of her husband on a journey the virtuous woman should wear only her auspicious ornaments, and observe the fasts in honor of the gods. While anxious to hear the news of her husband, she should look after her household affairs. She should sleep near the elder women of the house, and make herself agreeable to them. She should look after and keep in repair the things that are liked by her husband, and continue the works that have been begun by him. To the abode of her relations she should not go except on occasions of joy and sorrow, and then she should go in her usual traveling dress, accompanied by her husband's servants, and not remain there for a long time. The fasts and feasts should be observed with the consent of the elders of the house. The resources should be increased by making purchases and sales according to the practice of the merchants, and by means of honest servants, superintended by herself. The income should be increased, and the expenditure diminished as much as possible. And when her husband returns from his journey, she should receive him at first in her ordinary clothes, so that he may know in what way she has lived during his absence, and should bring to him some presents, as also materials for the worship of the Deity.

READING AND DISCUSSION QUESTIONS

1. According to the *Kamasutra*, how should a virtuous wife act?

2. What is the ideal relationship between a husband and a wife, according to this text?

3. What does the passage tell you about Indian gender norms at the time the *Kamasutra* was written? What does it suggest about the place of women in Indian society?

12-5 | A Muslim Scholar Offers Guidance to His Fellow Believers

MAULANA BURHĀN UD-DĪN MARGHĪNĀNĪ, From *Guidance: Alms, Marriage, and Testimony* (ca. 1197)

The Islamic religion spread via merchants in the seventh century c.e., and the later advance of Muslim armies into Pakistan and India between the eighth and twelfth centuries led to centuries of Islamic control over northern India. Many converted, but many others retained their traditional religion. The Muslims of India followed a school of Islamic law called Hanafī, which was codified by the author Maulana Burhān ud-dīn Marghīnānī, who was born in what is now Uzbekistan. His *Guidance* (*al-Hidāyah*) remains one of the most important reference guides to Islamic law.

The Alms Tax

Alms-giving is an ordinance of God, incumbent upon every person who is free, sane, adult, and a Muslim, provided he be possessed, in full property, of such estate or effects as are termed in the language of the law a minimum, and that he has been in possession of the same for the space of one complete year. . . . The reason of this obligation is found in the word of God, who has ordained it in the Qur'ān, saying, "Bestow alms." The same injunction occurs in the traditions, and it is moreover universally admitted. The reason for freedom being a requisite condition is that this is essential to the complete possession of property. The reason why sanity of intellect and maturity of age are requisite conditions shall be hereafter demonstrated. The reason why the Muslim faith is made a condition is that the rendering of alms is an act of piety, and such cannot proceed from an infidel.

Of the Disbursement of Alms, and of the Persons to Whose Use It Is to Be Applied

The objects of the disbursement of alms are of eight different descriptions: first, the needy; secondly, the destitute; thirdly, the collector of alms; . . . fourthly, slaves [upon whom alms are bestowed in order to enable them, by fulfilling their contract (i.e., by procuring their purchase price) to procure their freedom]; fifthly, debtors not possessed of property amounting to a legal minimum; sixthly, in the service of God; seventhly, travelers; and eighthly, the winning over of hearts. And those eight descriptions are the original objects of the expenditure of alms, being particularly specified as such in the Qur'ān; and there are, therefore, no other proper or legal objects of its application. With respect to the last, however, the law has ceased to operate, since the time of the Prophet, because he used to bestow alms upon them as a bribe or gratuity to prevent them from molesting the Muslims, and also to secure their occasional assistance; but when God gave strength to the faith, and to its followers, and rendered the Muslims independent of such assistance, the occasion of bestowing this gratuity upon them no longer remained; and all the doctors[10] unite in this opinion. . . .

Polygamy

It is lawful for a freeman to marry four wives, whether free or slaves; but it is not lawful for him to marry more than four, because God has commanded in the Qur'ān, saying: "Ye may marry whosoever women are agreeable to you, two, three, or four," and the numbers being thus expressly mentioned, any beyond what is there specified would be unlawful. Shāfi'ī[11] alleges a man cannot lawfully marry more than one woman of the description of slaves, from his tenet as above

---

[10] **all the doctors:** All the Muslim judges.
[11] **Shāfi'ī:** Founder of a ninth-century school of thought on Sunni Islamic jurisprudence.

recited, that "the marriage of freemen with slaves is allowable only from necessity"; the text already quoted is, however, in proof against him, since the term "women" applies equally to free women and to slaves.

Testimony

In all rights, whether of property or otherwise, the probity of the witness, and the use of the word *shahādat* [evidence] is requisite; even in the case of the evidence of women with respect to birth, and the like; and this is approved; because *shahādat* is testimony, since it possesses the property of being binding; whence it is that it is restricted to the place of jurisdiction; and also, that the witness is required to be free; and a Muslim. If, therefore, a witness should say: "I know," or "I know with certainty," without making use of the word *shahādat*, in that case his evidence cannot be admitted. With respect to the probity of the witness, it is indispensable, because of what is said in the Qur'ān: "Take the evidence of two just men."

The testimony of *zimmīs* [protected unbelievers] with respect to each other is admissible, notwithstanding they be of different religions. Mālik[12] and Shāfi'ī have said that their evidence is absolutely inadmissible, because, as infidels are unjust, it is requisite to be slow in believing anything they may advance, God having said [in the Qur'ān]: "When an unjust person tells you anything, be slow in believing him"; whence it is that the evidence of an infidel is not admitted concerning a Muslim; and consequently, that an infidel stands [in this particular] in the same predicament with an apostate. The arguments of our doctors upon this point are twofold. First, it is related of the Prophet, that he permitted and held lawful the testimony of some Christians concerning others of their sect. Secondly, an infidel having power over himself, and his minor children, is on that account qualified to be a witness with regard to his own sect; and the depravity which proceeds from his faith is not destructive of this qualification, because he is supposed to abstain from everything prohibited in his own religion, and falsehood is prohibited in every religion. It is otherwise with respect to an apostate, as he possesses no power, either over his own person, or over that of another; and it is also otherwise with respect to a *zimmī* in relation to a Muslim, because a *zimmī* has no power over the person of a Muslim. Besides, a *zimmī* may be suspected of inventing falsehoods against a Muslim from the hatred he bears to him on account of the superiority of the Muslims over him.

READING AND DISCUSSION QUESTIONS

1. Why must Muslims give alms? Who should receive the alms?
2. What are the Islamic laws regarding marriage?
3. Who is allowed to give testimony? What does this reveal about the relationship between Muslims and other "people of the book"?

---

[12] **Mālik:** Founder of an eighth-century school of thought on Sunni Islamic jurisprudence.

■ COMPARATIVE QUESTIONS ■

1. What do the documents in this chapter reveal about the values that the Mongols prized? Were the values they held as nomads different from the values they held as rulers?

2. Characterize Mongol rule over Central and East Asia. How effective was Mongol rule?

3. How do the duties of a wife in the *Kamasutra* compare to Ban Zhao's ideas about the duties of a Chinese wife (Document 7-2)?

13

States and Cultures in East Asia

800–1400

Throughout the medieval period, East Asia saw unprecedented economic growth, created sophisticated governments, and experienced a cultural boom. China drove this development and led in technological innovations such as mastering the printing press and perfecting the compass for overseas navigation. The Song Dynasty (960–1279) in particular advanced new forms of governance through the creation of an elite corps of educated civil servants and established thriving trade with its neighbors in Southeast Asia and beyond. China's vitality earned it tremendous influence over its neighbors, including Korea, Vietnam, and Japan. The sources in this chapter focus on the economic successes of China during the medieval period, as well as its cultural developments, and include accounts from Heian Japan (794–1185) and the Kamakura period (1185–1333), high points in the development of Japanese government and culture.

VIEWPOINTS

Elite Values in Feudal Japan

The Heian and Kamakura periods saw the development of a diverse and sophisticated literary tradition in Japan. Japanese authors addressed a wide variety of subjects, drawing inspiration from sources such as Buddhism, daily life, and older oral traditions. Largely written by and for the wealthy, the literature of this period reflected the values, experiences, and beliefs of the Japanese elite. This is not to say, however, that medieval Japanese literature presented a single perspective. Court aristocrats lived very different lives than provincial warrior elites, and elite women, although often powerful, did not share the same experiences and status as their fathers, husbands, brothers, and sons. The two excerpts included here exemplify this point. The first, from *The Tale of Genji*, offers an elite woman's perspective on marriage. The second, from *The Tale of the Heike*, sheds light on experiences and feelings of the male warrior elite. As you read the passages, pay particular attention to the values and beliefs that the characters espouse. What values and beliefs do the characters in both tales share? What might explain the most important differences you note?

13-1 | Marriage and Female Virtue
MURASAKI SHIKIBU, From *The Tale of Genji* (ca. 1021)

Heian Japan (794–1185) developed a culturally vibrant aristocratic society—one in which women played remarkably important roles, especially in literary endeavors. During this period, the Japanese developed a phonetic writing system that appealed to women, who often lacked the education needed to master the more complicated Chinese-based writing system. Court society soon benefited from the entertainments of significant female writers such as Murasaki Shikibu, the author of the narrative masterpiece *The Tale of Genji*. In the excerpts below, the characters of the story discuss how to pick a good wife and the role of women in marriage.

They talked on, of the varieties of women.

"A man sees women, all manner of them, who seem beyond reproach," said the guards officer, "but when it comes to picking the wife who must be everything, matters are not simple. The emperor has trouble, after all, finding the minister who has all the qualifications. A man may be very wise, but no man can govern by himself. Superior is helped by subordinate, subordinate defers to superior, and so affairs proceed by agreement and concession. But when it comes to choosing the woman who is to be in charge of your house, the qualifications are altogether too many. A merit is balanced by a defect, there is this good point and that bad point, and even women who though not perfect can be made to do are not easy to find. I would not like to have you think me a profligate who has to try them all. But it is a question of the woman who must be everything, and it seems best, other things being equal, to find someone who does not require shaping and training, someone who has most of the qualifications from the start. The man who begins his search with all this in mind must be reconciled to searching for a very long time."

"There are those who display a womanly reticence to the world, as if they had never heard of complaining. They seem utterly calm. And then when their thoughts are too much for them they leave behind the most horrendous notes, the most flamboyant poems, the sort of keepsakes certain to call up dreadful memories, and off they go into the mountains or to some remote seashore. When I was a child I would hear the women reading romantic stories, and I would join them in their sniffling and think it all very sad, all very profound and moving. Now I am afraid that it suggests certain pretenses.

"It is very stupid, really, to run off and leave a perfectly kind and sympathetic man. He may have been guilty of some minor dereliction, but to run off with no understanding at all of his true feelings, with no purpose other than to attract attention and hope to upset him — it is an unpleasant sort of memory to have to live with. She gets drunk with admiration for herself and there she is, a nun. When she enters her convent she is sure that she has found enlightenment and has no regrets for the vulgar world.

"Her women come to see her. 'How very touching,' they say. 'How brave of you.'

"But she no longer feels quite as pleased with herself. The man, who has not lost his affection for her, hears of what has happened and weeps, and certain of her old attendants pass this intelligence on to her. 'He is a man of great feeling, you see. What a pity that it should have come to this.' The woman can only brush aside her newly cropped hair[1] to reveal a face on the edge of tears. She tries to hold them back and cannot, such are her regrets for the life she has left behind; and the Buddha is not likely to think her one who has cleansed her heart of passion. Probably she is in more danger of brimstone now in this fragile vocation than if she had stayed with us in our sullied world.

"The bond between husband and wife is a strong one. Suppose the man had hunted her out and brought her back. The memory of her acts would still be there, and inevitably, sooner or later, it would be cause for rancor. When there are crises, incidents, a woman should try to overlook them, for better or for worse, and make the bond into something durable. The wounds will remain, with the woman and with the man, when there are crises such as I have described. It is very foolish for a woman to let a little dalliance upset her so much that she shows her resentment openly. He has his adventures — but if he has fond memories of their early days together, his and hers, she may be sure that she matters. A commotion means the end of everything. She should be quiet and generous, and when something comes up that quite properly arouses her resentment she should make it known by delicate hints. The man will feel guilty and with tactful guidance he will mend his ways. Too much lenience can make a woman seem charmingly docile and trusting, but it can also make her seem somewhat wanting in substance. We have had instances enough of boats abandoned to the winds and waves. Do you not agree?"

---

[1] **newly cropped hair:** Buddhist nuns were expected to cut off their hair upon entering the convent.

Tô no Chûjô nodded. "It may be difficult when someone you are especially fond of, someone beautiful and charming, has been guilty of an indiscretion, but magnanimity produces wonders. They may not always work, but generosity and reasonableness and patience do on the whole seem best."

READING AND DISCUSSION QUESTIONS

1. According to the characters, how is a man's selection of a wife similar to the emperor's selection of a minister? Why is picking a wife more difficult?

2. What do the characters believe is the proper reaction of a wife when she learns of a "little dalliance" by her husband? In what ways, if any, may she show her disapproval?

3. Can the characters' views regarding the proper role of women in Japanese society be taken at face value? In what ways does the knowledge that the author of *The Tale of Genji* was a woman change its meaning?

4. Given the lack of educational opportunities for Heian Japanese women, who do you suppose was Shikibu's audience?

13-2 | The Experience of War in Feudal Japan
From *The Tale of the Heike* (ca. 1250)

The Tale of the Heike narrates the battle for power at the end of the twelfth century between two rival families, the Taira (Heike) and the Minamoto (Genji), in which the Minamoto, from the east, win convincingly. There was no single author of this work; rather, as with the poems by Homer (see Chapter 5), it seems that countless bards and storytellers added and altered tales as they saw fit before the work was assembled into one document in the middle of the thirteenth century. The tales themselves tend to be episodic in nature, as in the passages excerpted here. First the hero, Atsumori, is defeated, and then the entire Tairan force is destroyed.

The Death of Atsumori

When the Heike were routed at Ichi no tani, and their nobles and courtiers were fleeing to the shore to escape in their ships, Kumagai Naozane came riding along a narrow path onto the beach, with the intention of intercepting one of their great captains. Just then his eye fell on a single horseman who was attempting to reach one of the ships in the offing. The horse he rode was dappled-gray, and its saddle

---

Donald Keene, ed., *Anthology of Japanese Literature from the Earliest Era to the Mid-Nineteenth Century* (New York: Grove Press, 1955), 179–184. Copyright © 1955 by Grove Press. Used by permission of Grove/Atlantic, Inc. Any third party use of this material, outside of this publication, is prohibited.

glittered with gold mounting. Not doubting that he was one of the chief captains, Kumagai beckoned to him with his war fan, crying out: "Shameful! to show an enemy your back. Return! Return!"

The warrior turned his horse and rode back to the beach, where Kumagai at once engaged him in mortal combat. Quickly hurling him to the ground, he sprang upon him and tore off his helmet to cut off his head, when he beheld the face of a youth of sixteen or seventeen, delicately powdered and with blackened teeth,[2] just about the age of his own son and with features of great beauty. "Who are you?" he asked. "Tell me your name, for I would spare your life."

"Nay, first say who you are," replied the young man.

"I am Kumagai Naozane of Musashi, a person of no particular importance."

"Then you have made a good capture," said the youth. "Take my head and show it to some of my side, and they will tell you who I am."

"Though he is one of their leaders," mused Kumagai, "if I slay him it will not turn victory into defeat, and if I spare him, it will not turn defeat into victory. When my son Kojiro- was but slightly wounded at Ichi no tani this morning, did it not pain me? How this young man's father would grieve to hear that he had been killed! I will spare him."

Just then, looking behind him, he saw Doi and Kajiwara coming up with fifty horsemen. "Alas! look there," he exclaimed, the tears running down his face, "though I would spare your life, the whole countryside swarms with our men, and you cannot escape them. If you must die, let it be by my hand, and I will see that prayers are said for your rebirth in Paradise."

"Indeed it must be so," said the young warrior. "Cut off my head at once."

Kumagai was so overcome by compassion that he could scarcely wield his blade. His eyes swam and he hardly knew what he did, but there was no help for it; weeping bitterly he cut off the boy's head. "Alas!" he cried, "what life is so hard as that of a soldier? Only because I was born of a warrior family must I suffer this affliction! How lamentable it is to do such cruel deeds!" He pressed his face to the sleeve of his armor and wept bitterly. Then, wrapping up the head, he was stripping off the young man's armor when he discovered a flute in a brocade bag. "Ah," he exclaimed, "it was this youth and his friends who were amusing themselves with music within the walls this morning. Among all our men of the Eastern Provinces I doubt if there is any one of them who has brought a flute with him. How gentle the ways of these courtiers!"

When he brought the flute to the Commander, all who saw it were moved to tears; he discovered then that the youth was Atsumori, the youngest son of Tsunemori, aged sixteen years. From this time the mind of Kumagai was turned toward the religious life.

---

[2] **delicately powdered and with blackened teeth:** It was believed impolite to show one's teeth, so courtiers would often color their teeth black. Pale faces were considered most beautiful, so the elite would also powder their faces.

The Fight at Dan No Ura

Yoshitsune [General of the Minamoto clan], after his victory at Yashima, crossed over to Suwo to join his brother. Just at this time the High Priest of Kumano, who was under great obligations to the Heike, suddenly had a change of heart and hesitated as to which side he should support. He went to the shrine of Imakumano at Tanabe and spent seven days in retirement there, having sacred dances performed and praying before the deity. He received as a result an oracle commanding him to adhere to the white [Genji] banner, but he was still doubtful. He then held a cockfight before the shrine, with seven white cocks and seven red ones; the red cocks were all beaten and ran away. He therefore made up his mind to join the Genji.

Assembling all his retainers, to the number of some two thousand men, and embarking them on two hundred ships of war, he put the emblem of the deity of the shrine on board his ship, and painted the name of the Guardian God on the top of his standard. When this vessel with its divine burden approached the ships of the Genji and Heike at Dan no ura both parties saluted it reverently, but when it was seen to direct its course toward the fleet of the Genji the Heike could not conceal their chagrin. To the further consternation of the Heike, Michinobu of the province of Iyo also came rowing up with a hundred and fifty large ships and went over to the fleet of their enemies.

Thus the forces of the Genji went on increasing, while those of the Heike grew less. The Genji had some three thousand ships, and the Heike one thousand, among which were some of Chinese build. Thus, on the twenty-fourth day of the third month of 1185, at Ta no ura in the province of Bungo and at Dan no ura in the province of Nagato, began the final battle of the Genji and the Heike.

Both sides set their faces against each other and fought grimly without a thought for their lives, neither giving an inch. But as the Heike had on their side an emperor endowed with the Ten Virtues and the Three Sacred Treasures of the Realm,[3] things went hard with the Genji and their hearts were beginning to fail them, when suddenly something that they at first took for a cloud but soon made out to be a white banner floating in the breeze came drifting over the two fleets from the upper air, and finally settled on the stern of one of the Genji ships, hanging on by the rope.

When he saw this, Yoshitsune, regarding it as a sign from the Great Bodhisattva Hachiman,[4] removed his helmet and after washing his hands did obeisance; his men all followed his example. Just then a shoal of thousands of dolphins appeared and made straight for the ships of the Heike. One of the Heike generals called a diviner and said, "There are always many dolphins about here, but I have never seen so many before; what may it portend?" "If they turn back,"

---

[3] **the Ten Virtues . . . Treasures of the Realm:** The emperor, therefore, had not committed the ten sins and held the sword, mirror, and jewels of the kingdom.

[4] **Hachiman:** Originally the Shinto god of war, but in this period considered a bodhisattva.

replied the diviner, "the Genji will be destroyed, but if they go on our own side will be in danger." No sooner had he finished speaking than the dolphins dived under the Heike ships and passed on.

As things had come to this pass, Shigeyoshi, who for three years had been a loyal supporter of the Heike, made up his mind that all was lost, and suddenly forsook his allegiance and deserted to the enemy.

The strategy of the Heike had been to put the stoutest warriors on board the ordinary fighting ships and the inferior soldiers on the big ships of Chinese build; the Genji would be induced to attack the big ships, thinking that the commanders were on board them, and the Heike could then surround and destroy them. But when Shigeyoshi went over and joined the Genji he revealed this plan to them, with the result that they left the big ships alone and concentrated their attacks on the smaller ones, which bore the Heike champions. Later on the men of Shikoku and Kyushu all left the Heike in a body and went over to the Genji. Those who had so far been their faithful retainers now turned their bows against their lords and drew their swords against their own masters. On one shore the heavy seas beat on the cliff so as to forbid any landing, while on the other stood the serried ranks of the enemy waiting with leveled arrows to receive them. And so on this day the struggle for supremacy between the Genji and the Heike was at last decided.

Meanwhile the Genji warriors sprang from one Heike vessel to the other, shooting and cutting down the sailors and helmsmen,—who left their posts and flung themselves in panic to the bottom of the ships. Tomomori rowed in a small boat to the Imperial vessel and cried out, "You see what affairs have come to! Clean up the ship, and throw everything unsightly into the sea!" He ran about the ship from bow to stern, sweeping and cleaning and gathering up the dust with his own hands. "How goes the battle, Tomomori?" asked the court ladies. "Oh, you'll soon see some rare gallants from the east," he replied, bursting into loud laughter. "What? Is this a time for joking?" they answered, and they lifted up their voices and wept aloud.

Then the Lady Nii, who had already resolved what she would do, donned a double outer dress of dark gray mourning and tucking up her long skirts put the Sacred Jewel under her arm and the Sacred Sword in her sash. She took the Emperor in her arms and said, "Though I am but a woman, I will not fall into the hands of the enemy. I will accompany our Sovereign Lord. Let those of you who will, follow me." She moved softly to the gunwale of the vessel.

The Emperor was seven years old that year but looked much older than his age. He was so lovely that he seemed to shed a brilliant radiance about him, and his long black hair hung loose far down his back. With a look of surprise and anxiety on his face he asked the Lady Nii, "Where are you going to take me?"

She turned to the youthful sovereign, with tears streaming down her cheeks, and answered, "Perhaps Your Majesty does not know that he was reborn to the Imperial throne in this world as a result of the merit of the Ten Virtues practiced in former lives. Now, however, some evil karma claims you.

Turn to the east and bid farewell to the deity of the Great Shrine of Ise and then to the west and say the *nembutsu*,[5] that Amida Buddha and the Holy Ones may come to welcome you to the Pure Western Land. Japan is small as a grain of millet, but now it is a vale of misery. There is a pure land of happiness beneath the waves, another capital where no sorrow is. It is there that I am taking my Sovereign."

   She comforted him, and bound up his long hair in his dove-colored robe. Blinded with tears, the child sovereign put his beautiful little hands together. He turned first to the east to say farewell of the deity of Ise and then to the west to repeat the *nembutsu*. The Lady Nii took him tightly in her arms and with the words, "In the depths of the ocean is our capital," sank with him at last beneath the waves.

READING AND DISCUSSION QUESTIONS

1. What values were prized among the Japanese warrior elite?

2. Why did the imperial family commit suicide?

3. The Heike were the losers in a civil war, and yet the victors allowed these tales to circulate. Why would they permit this? Why was *The Tale of the Heike* so popular?

4. How does this document demonstrate the importance of Buddhist philosophy in Japan?

VIEWPOINTS COMPARATIVE QUESTIONS

1. What role do emotions play in each tale? What emotions seem to have been associated with women? What about with men?

2. Taken together, what do these two documents tell you about family life and familial relationships in feudal Japan?

3. Based on these two documents, how would you characterize the values and beliefs of Japanese elites in the Heian and Kamakura periods?

---

   [5] *nembutsu*: Prayer to the Amida Buddha. It was thought that prayer to him would allow one to enter into the Pure Western Land.

13-3 | A Chinese Sculptor Envisions Enlightenment
Figure of a Lohan, Yuan Dynasty (1260–1368)

Despite the hardships and disruptions caused by Mongol rule, the sophisticated Chinese artistic culture that had flowered during the Song Dynasty continued to produce extraordinary works during the Yuan Dynasty. This sculpture of a Lohan is a case in point. In Theravada Buddhism, a Lohan is one who has traveled the Buddha's Eight-Fold Path, achieved enlightenment, and is therefore no longer subject to rebirth. Many believed that upon achieving enlightenment Lohans acquired supernatural powers. Sculptures and paintings of Lohans were common elements in Chinese Buddhist temples, and many of these works featured stereotypical poses and expressions. The sculpture pictured here, however, transcended the conventions of the genre, taking on the challenge of presenting a Lohan as a unique, fully human individual. As you examine the sculpture, ask yourself why the artist made the choices he did. What might he have wanted to say about the nature of enlightenment?

Private Collection/Bridgeman Images.

READING AND DISCUSSION QUESTIONS

1. In what ways, if any, does the sculpture hint at the Lohan's spiritual status?

2. How would you characterize the Lohan's expression? What do you imagine he is thinking and feeling?

13-4 | The Islamic World as Seen from a Chinese Perspective

CHAU JU-KUA, *On the Arab People of Quanzhou* (ca. 1250)

The commercial growth of Song China was not confined to its borders. China conducted extensive international trade through ongoing traffic along the Silk Road and the use of sea routes through Southeast Asia that connected China to the Islamic world. The following account describes China's trading partners through the eyes of Chau Ju-Kua (1170–1228), a customs inspector of the southern port city of Quanzhou. Although Chau's knowledge was probably not firsthand, his descriptions hint at the important role that Arab merchants played in facilitating international trade.

Ta-shï [Arabs]

The Ta-shï are to the west and north (or north-west) of Ts'üan-chóu [Quanzhou] at a very great distance from it, so that the foreign ships find it difficult to make the voyage there direct. After these ships have left Ts'üan-chóu they come in some forty days to Lan-li, where they trade. The following year they go to sea again, when with the aid of the regular wind they take some sixty days to make the journey.

The products of the country are for the most part brought to San-fo-ts'i [another port in Sumatra], where they are sold to merchants who forward them to China.

This country of the Ta-shï is powerful and warlike. Its extent is very great, and its inhabitants are pre-eminent among all foreigners for their distinguished bearing.

The climate throughout a large part of it is cold, snow falling to a depth of two or three feet; consequently rugs are much prized.

The capital of the country, called Mi-sü-li, is an important center for the trade of foreign peoples. . . .

The streets are more than fifty feet broad; in the middle is a roadway twenty feet broad and four feet high for the use of camels, horses, and oxen carrying

---

Chau Ju-Kua: His Work on the Chinese and Arab Trade in the Twelfth and Thirteenth Centuries, Entitled Chu-fan-chi, trans. Friedrich Hirth and W. W. Rockhill (St. Petersburg: Printing Office of the Imperial Academy of Sciences, 1911), 114–116, 124–125, 154–155.

goods about. On either side, for the convenience of pedestrians' business, there are sidewalks paved with green and black flagstones of surpassing beauty.

The dwellings of the people are like those of the Chinese, with this difference that here thin flagstones are used instead of tiles.

The food consists of rice and other cereals; mutton stewed with fine strips of dough is considered a delicacy. The poor live on fish, vegetables and fruits only; sweet dishes are preferred to sour. Wine is made out of the juice of grapes, and there is also the drink *ssï*, a decoction of sugar and spices. By mixing of honey and spices they make a drink *meï-ssï-ta-hu*, which is very healing.

Very rich persons use a measure instead of scales in business transactions in gold or silver. The markets are noisy and bustling, and are filled with great store of gold and silver damasks, brocades, and such like wares. The artisans have the true artistic spirit.

The king, the officials and the people all serve Heaven. They have also a Buddha by the name of Ma-hia-wu [Muhammad]. Every seven days they cut their hair and clip their finger nails. At the New Year for a whole month they fast and chant prayers. Daily they pray to Heaven five times.

The peasants work their fields without fear of inundations or droughts; a sufficiency of water for irrigation is supplied by a river whose source is not known. During the season when no cultivation is in progress, the level of the river remains even with the banks; with the beginning of cultivation it rises day by day. Then it is that an official is appointed to watch the river and to await the highest water level, when he summons the people, who then plough and sow their fields. When they have had enough water, the river returns to its former level.

There is a great harbor in this country, over two hundred feet deep, which opens to the south-east on the sea, and has branches connecting with all quarters of the country. On either bank of the harbor the people have their dwellings and here daily are held fairs, where crowd boats and wagons, all loaded with hemp, wheat, millet, beans, sugar, meal, oil, firewood, fowls, sheep, geese, ducks, fish, shrimps, date-cakes, grapes and other fruits.

The products of the country consist in pearls, ivory, rhinoceros horns, frank-incense, ambergris, putchuck, cloves, nutmegs, benzoin, aloes, myrrh, dragon's-blood, ... borax, opaque and transparent glass, ... shell, coral, cat's-eyes, gardenia flowers, rose-water, nut-galls, yellow wax, soft gold brocades, camel's-hair cloth, ... and foreign satins.

The foreign traders who deal in these merchandise, bring them to San-fo-ts'i and to Fo-lo-an to barter. ...

Ma-kia [Mecca]

The country of Ma-kia is reached if one travels from the country of Ma-lo-pa for eighty days westward by land.

This is the place where the Buddha Ma-hia-wu was born. In the House of the Buddha the walls are made of jade stone (or precious stones) of every color.

Every year, when the anniversary of the death of the Buddha comes round, the people from all countries of the Ta-shï assemble here, when they vie with each other in bringing presents of gold, silver, jewels and precious stones. Then also is the House adorned anew with silk brocade.

Farther off there is the tomb of the Buddha. Continually by day and night there is at this place such a brilliant refulgence that no one can approach it; he who does loses his sight.

Whosoever in the hour of his death rubs his breast with dirt taken from this tomb, will, they say, be restored to life again by the power of the Buddha. . . .

Mu-lan-p'i [Mulanpi, Southern Spain]

The country of Mu-lan-p'i is to the west of the Ta-shï country. There is a great sea, and to the west of this sea there are countless countries, but Mu-lan-p'i is the one country which is visited by the big ships of the Ta-shï. Putting to sea from T'o-pan-ti in the country of Ta-shï, after sailing due west for full a hundred days, one reaches this country. A single one of these (big) ships of theirs carries several thousand men, and on board they have stores of wine and provisions, as well as weaving looms. If one speaks of big ships, there are none so big as those of Mu-lan-p'i.

The products of this country are extraordinary; the grains of wheat are three inches long, the melons six feet round, enough for a meal for twenty or thirty men. The pomegranates weigh five catties, the peaches two catties, citrons over twenty catties, salads weigh over ten catties and have leaves three or four feet long. Rice and wheat are kept in silos for tens of years without spoiling. Among the native products are foreign sheep, which are several feet high and have tails as big as a fan. In the spring-time they slit open their bellies and take out some tens of catties of fat, after which they sew them up again, and the sheep live on; if the fat were not removed, (the animal) would swell up and die.

If one travels by land (from Mu-lan-p'i) two hundred days journey, the days are only six hours long. In autumn if the west wind arises, men and beasts must at once drink to keep alive, and if they are not quick enough about it they die of thirst.

READING AND DISCUSSION QUESTIONS

1. What Islamic religious practices does Chau describe? In what ways does his experience with Buddhism influence his understanding of Islam?

2. What are some of the goods traded along the routes that Chau describes? How is trade encouraged along these routes?

3. How would you characterize Chau's opinion of the Islamic world? What does his account tell you about Chinese attitudes toward foreigners?

13-5 | Widowhood and Female Virtue in Medieval China
Widows Loyal unto Death (ca. 1754)

The ordained and practical roles of women in medieval China present several contradictions. Surviving records suggest that women were active members of society—serving as midwives, living as Buddhist nuns, and helping their families run businesses—yet several popular practices constrained the lives of women, such as the right of husbands to take concubines and the custom of binding the feet of elite women. One of the more destructive traditions, described in the stories below, was the idea that a widow should give up her life after the death of her husband in order to demonstrate her personal virtue.

Xu Sungjie, daughter of Xu Yuanyan, married Chen Boshan at the age of seventeen. When her husband was gravely ill, he told her to remarry because she had no son. At his death, she embraced him and cried bitterly. After the coffin was closed, she hanged herself to die with her husband. The official Bai Bi was impressed with her fidelity and so arranged for her burial and had a banner with the inscription "filial piety and propriety" displayed at her door.

Lin Shunde, the daughter of the prefect Lin Jin, was engaged to Sun Mengbi. When Mengbi died, she was with her father at his post. Once the announcement of her fiance's death reached her, she put on mourning dress and wept to tell her parents that she wished to go to his home. Her parents packed for her and told her to behave properly. On arriving there, she performed the rituals for her first meeting with her parents-in-law, then she made an offering at her fiance's coffin. After he was buried, she served her mother-in-law for the rest of her life. The local official inscribed a placard with "She hurried to the funeral of a husband she had never seen. Suffering cold and frost, she swore not to remarry." . . .

Fu Xiajie was the wife of Chen Banghuai. Her husband was taken hostage by some bandits. She supported herself by making hemp cloth. After a long time someone told her that her husband had died. She was spinning at the time. She then immediately entered her bedroom and hanged herself.

Wu Jinshun was the wife of Sun Zhen. On the first anniversary of her husband's death, she was so forlorn that she died of grief.

Zhang Zhongyu was engaged to Chen Shunwei, who died prematurely when Zhongyu was eighteen. When she learned of his death, she decided to hurry to the Chen family. Her parents tried to stop her, but she cried and said, "Once you betrothed me to the Chen family, I became a daughter-in-law of the Chen family." So, she hurried to attend her fiance's funeral and bow to her mother-in-law. Then, she cut her hair and removed her ornaments. She lived a secluded life. In the first month of the xinsi year [1461], there was a fire in her neighborhood. She leaned herself against her husband's coffin, wanting to be burned up with her husband. Suddenly a wind came and extinguished the fire. Only her house survived. On the sixth day of the sixth month of the wuzi year [1468], a large army approached. People in the county fled helter-skelter. Zhongyu remained to guard the coffin, keeping a knife with her. When the army arrived the next day, she showed the banner and the tablet from the previous official. The soldiers recognized her righteousness, and general Bai attached his order on the door so that no other soldiers would enter her house. One day she became severely ill and told her mother-in-law, "Don't let any men put their hands on me when I am shrouded after I die. Use the money in the small box that I earned by splicing and spinning to bury me with my husband." Then she died.

Sun Yinxiao was the daughter of Sun Keren and married Lin Zengqing at the age of seventeen. Lin, who made his living fishing, drowned after they had been married for only two months. Sun was determined to kill herself. After the mourning period was over, she made a sacrifice with utmost grief. That night, she dressed carefully and bound a wide girdle round the beam to hang herself. When the magistrate Xu Jiadi heard of this, he paid a visit to offer a sacrifice to her soul.

Wang Yingjie was the wife of Qiu Bianyu. She was widowed at nineteen before bearing any children. As a consequence she decided to die. Her family had long been rich and her dowry was particularly ample. She gave it all to her husband's younger brother so that in the future he could arrange for an heir to succeed to her husband. Then she ceased eating. Her mother forced her to stop, so she had no alternative but to pretend to eat and drink as usual. When her mother relaxed her vigilance, she hanged herself.

Wang Jingjie, whose family had moved to Nantai, married Fu Yan, a candidate for the examinations. Yan studied so hard that he got ill and died. When Wang learned of this, she emptied out her savings and gave it to her father-in-law to pay for her husband's funeral, asking him to do it properly. The evening after he was buried, her brother came to console her and she asked how her parents were doing. Her brother slept in another room. At dawn, when the members of the family got up, they kept shouting to her, but she did not answer. When they pried open her door, she was already dead, having hanged herself. She was solemnly facing the inside, standing up straight. She was twenty-one.

Zhang Xiujie married He Liangpeng when she was eighteen. Before a year had passed, he became critically ill. He asked her what she would do, and she pointed to Heaven and swore to follow her husband in death. Since she wished to commit suicide, the other family members had to prevent her. After several months, their only son died of measles. Zhang wept and said, "It is my fate. I had been living for him." That night she hanged herself.

Huang Yijie was engaged to Chen Rujing from Changle who lived in Lianjiang. Before they were married, he died. When she was fifteen, she heard of it and was saddened by it. As she slowly understood what it meant, streams of tears rolled down her cheeks. Without her knowledge a matchmaker arranged a new engagement. In the fifth month of the bingyin year [1506], her first fiance's mother came to call. Huang followed the courtesies appropriate to a daughter-in-law when she went out to meet her, and they both expressed their grief, not holding back. After a while she asked her mother-in-law why she had come, and she told her that she had heard of the new engagement and so had come to get the brideprice back. The girl was startled and thought, "Could this be true? Only in extremely unfortunate circumstances is a dead man's wife sold." She told her mother-in-law, "Fortunately not much has been done with it. Let me make a plan." Disoriented, for a long time she sat, not saying a word. Then she asked her mother-in-law to stay for the night and told her everything she wanted to say. She gave her the hairpins and earrings she had received as betrothal gifts, saying, "Keep these to remember your son by." At dusk, her mother-in-law took her leave, and the girl, weeping, saw her to the gate. She then took a bath, combed her hair, and changed into new clothes. Those things done, she took a knife and cut her throat. The first cut did not sever it, so she had to cut it again before she died. In the morning when her family found her body, there were traces of three cuts.

READING AND DISCUSSION QUESTIONS

1. How did a widow demonstrate her virtue and integrity after the death of her husband? To whom was she obligated after the death of her husband?

2. How did accounts like these perpetuate the practice of widows committing suicide?

■ COMPARATIVE QUESTIONS ■

1. Compare and contrast the reading "Widows Loyal unto Death" with *The Tale of Genji*. In what ways did Chinese and Japanese societies have similar expectations for wives? In what ways did those expectations differ?

2. Both Marco Polo (Document 12-3) and Chau Ju-Kua describe the Islamic world and its people from the perspective of outsiders. What are their impressions of Islam? What do their accounts suggest about the role of religion in the development of commercial relationships?

3. Compare the ideals that these sources indicate for men in Japan and China during this period. How were these ideals similar, and how were they different?

14

Europe and Western Asia in the Middle Ages
800–1450

After the division of Charlemagne's empire in 843, Europe entered a period known as the Middle Ages. Although later Renaissance scholars dismissively labeled this time the "Dark Ages" preceding their own cultural boom, in truth the Middle Ages witnessed a dynamic restructuring of Europe's political, social, and religious life. Europe's kings slowly consolidated their territories and their claim to power, while the introduction of feudalism and manorialism brought stability and order to European society. Although the medieval European experience was extremely diverse because of increased foreign encroachment, catastrophic outbreaks of disease, and civil and international warfare, the thriving Christian Church was a prominent and unifying element of society. Together, the church, territorial leaders, and scholars guided society toward the development of a distinct European way of life and identity.

VIEWPOINTS

The Crusades

When Pope Urban II called for a crusade in 1095, the vast majority of Europeans knew little or nothing about the Middle East. Italian merchants had well-established trading connections in the eastern Mediterranean, but their firsthand knowledge of the region and its peoples had not made its way into the popular consciousness. Thus, for most European participants in the First Crusade, the Muslim Turks were simply the "other," defined almost entirely by the fact that they were not Christian Europeans. While many Muslims held a similar view of Christians, the Islamic world was far more diverse and cosmopolitan than Christian Europe, and on the whole, Muslim views of Europeans tended to be more nuanced. As you read the documents included here, one written by a European knight and the other by a Muslim scholar, think about the connections between the Crusades and cross-cultural perceptions. How might the Crusades have reinforced Christian and Muslim stereotypes of one another? How might they have contradicted such stereotypes?

14-1 | The Pope Calls on Christians to Wage a Holy War

FULCHER OF CHARTRES, From *A History of the Expedition to Jerusalem: The Call for Crusade* (ca. 1100–1127)

The Frenchman (Frank) Fulcher of Chartres (ca. 1059–1127) was an eyewitness to the First Crusade and its aftermath. He traveled with the crusade across Asia Minor and participated in the siege of Edessa. When his lord, Baldwin I, became king of Jerusalem, Fulcher moved to Jerusalem and probably continued writing until his death. This passage describes Pope Urban II's call to Christians to go on crusade to the Holy Land, the place where Jesus lived. Fulcher may have been present at this event, but he does not explicitly say so.

The Council Held at Clermont. In the year 1095 after the Incarnation of Our Lord, while Henry the so-called emperor was reigning in Germany and King Philip in France, evils of all kinds multiplied throughout Europe because of vacillating faith. Pope Urban II then ruled in the city of Rome. He was a man admirable in life and habits who strove prudently and vigorously to raise the status of Holy Church ever higher and higher.

Moreover he saw the faith of Christendom excessively trampled upon by all, by the clergy as well as by the laity, and peace totally disregarded, for the princes of the lands were incessantly at war quarreling with someone or other. He saw that people stole worldly goods from one another, that many captives were taken unjustly and were most barbarously cast into foul prisons and ransomed for excessive prices, or tormented there by three evils, namely hunger, thirst, and cold, and secretly put to death, that holy places were violated, monasteries and villas consumed by fire, nothing mortal spared, and things human and divine held in derision.

When he heard that the interior part of Romania [modern Turkey] had been occupied by the Turks and the Christians subdued by a ferociously destructive invasion, Urban, greatly moved by compassionate piety and by the prompting of

---

Frances Rita Ryan, trans., Harold S. Fink, ed., *Fulcher of Chartres: A History of the Expedition to Jerusalem, 1095–1127*, 61–62, 65–67. Reprinted by permission of the publisher, University of Tennessee Press.

God's love, crossed the mountains and descended into Gaul and caused a council to be assembled in Auvergne at Clermont, as the city is called. This council, appropriately announced by messengers in all directions, consisted of 310 members, bishops as well as abbots carrying the crozier [staff of office].

On the appointed day Urban gathered them around himself and in an eloquent address carefully made known the purpose of the meeting. In the sorrowing voice of a suffering church he told of its great tribulation. He delivered an elaborate sermon concerning the many raging tempests of this world in which the faith had been degraded as was said above.

Then as a suppliant he exhorted all to resume the powers of their faith and arouse in themselves a fierce determination to overcome the machinations of the devil, and to try fully to restore Holy Church, cruelly weakened by the wicked, to its honorable status as of old. . . .

Urban's Exhortation Concerning a Pilgrimage to Jerusalem. When these and many other matters were satisfactorily settled, all those present, clergy and people alike, spontaneously gave thanks to God for the words of the Lord Pope Urban and promised him faithfully that his decrees would be well kept. But the pope added at once that another tribulation not less but greater than that already mentioned, even of the worst nature, was besetting Christianity from another part of the world.

He said, "Since, oh sons of God, you have promised Him to keep peace among yourselves and to faithfully sustain the rights of Holy Church more sincerely than before, there still remains for you, newly aroused by Godly correction, an urgent task which belongs to both you and God, in which you can show the strength of your good will. For you must hasten to carry aid to your brethren dwelling in the East, who need your help for which they have often entreated.

"For the Turks, a Persian people, have attacked them, as many of you already know, and have advanced as far into Roman territory as that part of the Mediterranean which is called the Arm of St. George. They have seized more and more of the lands of the Christians, have already defeated them in seven times as many battles, killed or captured many people, have destroyed churches, and have devastated the kingdom of God. If you allow them to continue much longer they will conquer God's faithful people much more extensively.

"Wherefore with earnest prayer I, not I, but God exhorts you as heralds of Christ to repeatedly urge men of all ranks whatsoever, knights as well as footsoldiers, rich and poor, to hasten to exterminate this vile race from our lands and to aid the Christian inhabitants in time.

"I address those present; I proclaim it to those absent; moreover Christ commands it. For all those going thither there will be remission of sins if they come to the end of this fettered life while either marching by land or crossing by sea, or in fighting the pagans. This I grant to all who go, through the power vested in me by God.

"Oh what a disgrace if a race so despicable, degenerate, and enslaved by demons should thus overcome a people endowed with faith in Almighty God and resplendent in the name of Christ! Oh what reproaches will be charged against you by the Lord Himself if you have not helped those who are counted like yourselves of the Christian faith!

"Let those," he said, "who are accustomed to wantonly wage private war against the faithful march upon the infidels in a war which should be begun now and be finished in victory. Let those who have long been robbers now be soldiers of Christ. Let those who once fought against brothers and relatives now rightfully fight against barbarians. Let those who have been hirelings for a few pieces of silver [Matt. 27:3] now attain an eternal reward. Let those who have been exhausting themselves to the detriment of body and soul now labor for a double glory. Yea on the one hand will be the sad and the poor, on the other the joyous and the wealthy; here the enemies of the Lord, there His friends.

"Let nothing delay those who are going to go. Let them settle their affairs, collect money, and when winter has ended and spring has come, zealously undertake the journey under the guidance of the Lord."

READING AND DISCUSSION QUESTIONS

1. According to Fulcher, what was the political situation in Europe and the Middle East in the years before 1095? What implicit explanation does he offer for the pope's decision to convene a council at Clermont?

2. How did the pope describe the Muslim Turks? What connection did he make between this characterization and the necessity of a crusade?

3. Given the fact that events in the Holy Land posed no direct threat to western Europe, what motives likely lay behind the pope's call for a crusade? Why did so many European elites heed his call?

14-2 | A Muslim View of the Franks

ZAKARIYA AL-QAZWINI, From *Monuments of the Lands: An Islamic View of the West* (1275–1276)

Zakariya al-Qazwini (1203–1283), born in Persia, served as a professor of Islamic law and culti-vated interests in astronomy and geography. A prolific writer, he is best known for two works: *Wonders of the Created Things* and *Monuments of the Lands* (*Athar al-bilad*). *Monuments* is a geographic text compiled from other sources, which suggests that al-Qazwini did not actually visit many of the peoples and places that he writes about. In this passage, he describes "Frank-land," as the Muslims called western Europe, in the aftermath of the Crusades.

Zakariya al-Qazwini, *Islam from the Prophet Muhammed to the Capture of Constantinople*, ed. and trans. Bernard Lewis, vol. 2: *Religion and Society* (New York: Walker, 1987), 123. Used by permission of Oxford University Press, Inc.

Frank-land, a mighty land and a broad kingdom in the realms of the Christians. Its cold is very great, and its air is thick because of the extreme cold. It is full of good things and fruits and crops, rich in rivers, plentiful of produce, possessing tillage and cattle, trees and honey. There is a wide variety of game there and also silver mines. They forge very sharp swords there, and the swords of Frank-land are keener than the swords of India.

Its people are Christians, and they have a king possessing courage, great numbers, and power to rule. He has two or three cities on the shore of the sea on this side,[1] in the midst of the lands of Islam, and he protects them from his side. Whenever the Muslims send forces to them to capture them, he sends forces from his side to defend them. His soldiers are of mighty courage and in the hour of combat do not even think of flight, rather preferring death. But you shall see none more filthy than they. They are a people of perfidy and mean character. They do not cleanse or bathe themselves more than once or twice a year, and then in cold water, and they do not wash their garments from the time they put them on until they fall to pieces. They shave their beards, and after shaving they sprout only a revolting stubble. One of them was asked as to the shaving of the beard, and he said, "Hair is a superfluity. You remove it from your private parts, so why should we leave it on our faces?"

READING AND DISCUSSION QUESTIONS

1. How does al-Qazwini describe the Frankish lands? How does he describe the Frankish people?

2. What light does al-Qazwini's description of the Franks shed on Muslim views of the Crusades? How might al-Qazwini have characterized the Crusades? As a mighty clash of cultures? As a footnote to the larger history of the Islamic world?

VIEWPOINTS COMPARATIVE QUESTIONS

1. How did medieval European Christians view Muslims? How did Muslims view European Christians? What was the basis for each side's view of the other?

2. How might a twelfth-century European have characterized the First Crusade? What about a twelfth-century Muslim Turk? How would you explain the differences you note?

---

[1] **He has two or three . . . on this side:** Lands in the Middle East captured during the Crusades.

14-3 | The Virgin Mary in Popular Religion

JACQUES DE VITRY, *The Virgin Mary Saves a Monk and His Lover* (ca. 1200)

Ordinary medieval people were not passive participants in their religion. Their engagement with Christianity was not limited to kneeling mute and uncomprehending in church as a priest intoned the prescribed Latin words and phrases. Rather, medieval Christianity was an integral part of daily experience—something that ordinary people helped shape, even as it influenced almost every aspect of their lives. This story of the Virgin Mary's intercession on behalf of a monk and his lover, as told by the priest and scholar Jacques de Vitry (ca. 1160/70–1240), provides a sense of medieval popular religion. As you read it, think about the moral of the story. What attitudes and beliefs might de Vitry have hoped to inspire in his audience?

A certain very religious man told me that this happened in a place where he had been staying. A virtuous and pious matron came frequently to the church and served God most devoutly, day and night. Also a certain monk, the guardian and treasurer of the monastery, had a great reputation for piety, and truly he was devout. When, however, the two frequently conversed together in the church concerning religious matters, the devil, envying their virtue and reputation, tempted them very sorely, so that the spiritual love was changed to carnal. Accordingly they made an agreement and fixed upon a night in which the monk was to leave his monastery, taking the treasures of the church, and the matron was to leave her home, with a sum of money which she should secretly steal from her husband.

After they had fled, the monks on rising in the morning, saw that the receptacles were broken and the treasures of the church stolen; and not finding the monk, they quickly pursued him. Likewise the husband of the said woman, seeing his chest open and the money gone, pursued his wife. Overtaking the monk and the woman with the treasure and money, they brought them back and threw them into prison. Moreover so great was the scandal throughout the whole country and so much were all religious persons reviled that the damage from the infamy and scandal was far greater than from the sin itself.

Then the monk restored to his sense, began with many tears to pray to the blessed Virgin, whom from infancy he had always served, and never before had any such misfortune happened to him. Likewise the said matron began urgently to implore the aid of the blessed Virgin whom, constantly, day and night, she was accustomed to salute and to kneel in prayer before her image. At length, the blessed Virgin very irate, appeared and after she had upbraided them severely, she said, "I am able to obtain the remission of your sins from my son, but what can I do about such an awful scandal? For you have so befouled the name of religious persons before all the people that in the future no one will trust them. This is an almost irremediable damage."

From Dana Carleton Munro, ed., *Translations and Reprints from the Original Sources of European History*, vol. 2, series 4 (Philadelphia: History Department of the University of Pennsylvania, 1897), 2–4.

Nevertheless the pious Virgin, overcome by their prayers, summoned the demons, who had caused the deed, and enjoined upon them that, as they had caused the scandal to religion, they must bring the infamy to an end. Since, indeed, they were not able to resist her commands, after much anxiety and various conferences they found a way to remove the infamy. In the night they placed the monk in his church and repairing the broken receptacle as it was before, they placed the treasure in it. Also they closed and locked the chest which the matron had opened and replaced the money in it. And they set the woman in her room and in the place where she was accustomed to pray by night.

When, moreover, the monks found the treasure of their house and the monk, who was praying to God just as he had been accustomed to do; and the husband saw his wife and the treasure; and they found the money just as it had been before, they became stupefied and wondered. Rushing to the prison they saw the monk and the woman in fetters just as they had left them. For one of the demons was seen by them transformed into the likeness of a monk and another into the likeness of a woman. When all in the whole city had come together to see the miracle, the demons said in the hearing of all, "Let us go, for sufficiently have we deluded these people and caused them to think evil of religious persons." And, saying this, they suddenly disappeared. Moreover all threw themselves at the feet of the monk and of the woman and demanded pardon.

Behold how great infamy and scandal and how inestimable damage the devil would have wrought against religious persons, if the blessed Virgin had not aided them.

READING AND DISCUSSION QUESTIONS

1. What role does the Devil play in this story? What does this depiction suggest about medieval ideas concerning sin and the Devil?

2. How did the Virgin Mary respond to the monk's and the matron's prayers for help? What powers did she employ to resolve the situation?

3. How did the Virgin Mary's actions reinforce the piety of the community at large? What do you think is the intended moral of the story?

14-4 | Royal Power and the Rule of Law

KING JOHN OF ENGLAND, From *Magna Carta: The Great Charter of Liberties* (1215)

In many ways, the Magna Carta is a traditional feudal document. A contract between King John of England (r. 1199–1216) and his barons, the Magna Carta represents an effort by England's rebellious nobility to ensure that the king could not make unfair demands of his vassals. However, the importance of the contract exceeds its feudal origins. It became the founding document for the development of justice and law in England and helped give rise to ideas such as the rule of law and due process.

John, by the grace of God, king of England, lord of Ireland, duke of Normandy and Aquitaine, and count of Anjou, to the archbishops, bishops, abbots, earls, barons . . . and faithful subjects, greeting. . . .

We have . . . granted to all free men of our kingdom, for ourselves and our heirs, for ever, all the liberties written below, to be had and held by them and their heirs of us and our heirs. . . .

No widow shall be forced to marry so long as she wishes to live without a husband, provided that she gives security not to marry without our consent if she holds [a fief] of us, or without the consent of her lord of whom she holds, if she holds of another.

No scutage [payment in lieu of performing military service] or aid shall be imposed in our kingdom unless by common counsel of our kingdom, except for ransoming our person, for making our eldest son a knight, and for once marrying our eldest daughter; and for these only a reasonable aid shall be levied. . . .

Neither we nor our bailiffs will take, for castles or other works of ours, timber which is not ours, except with the agreement of him whose timber it is.

We will not hold for more than a year and a day the lands of those convicted of felony, and then the lands shall be handed over to the lords of the fiefs.

No free man shall be arrested or imprisoned or disseised [dispossessed] or outlawed or exiled or in any way victimized, neither will we attack him or send anyone to attack him, except by the lawful judgment of his peers or by the law of the land.

To no one will we sell, to no one will we refuse or delay right or justice.

We will not make justices, constables, sheriffs, or bailiffs save of such as know the law of the kingdom and mean to observe it well. . . .

Moreover all the subjects of our realm, clergy as well as laity, shall, as far as pertains to them, observe, with regard to their vassals, all these aforesaid customs and liberties which we have decreed shall, as far as pertains to us, be observed in our realm with regard to our own.

Inasmuch as, for the sake of God, and for the bettering of our realm, and for the more ready healing of the discord which has arisen between us and our barons, we have made all these aforesaid concessions,—wishing them to enjoy for ever entire and firm stability, we make and grant to them the following security: that the barons, namely, may elect at their pleasure twenty five barons from the realm, who ought, with all their strength, to observe, maintain and cause to be observed, the peace and privileges which we have granted to them and confirmed by this our present charter. In such wise, namely, that if we, or our justice, or our bailiffs, or any one of our servants shall have transgressed against any one in any respect, or shall have broken some one of the articles of peace or security,

David C. Douglas and Harry Rothwell, eds., *English Historical Documents*, vol. 3 (London: Eyre and Spottiswoode, 1975), 316–321; Ernest F. Henderson, trans. and ed., *Select Historical Documents of the Middle Ages* (London: George Bell and Sons, 1892), 146–148. Reprinted by AMS Press, New York, 1968.

and our transgression shall have been shown to four barons of the aforesaid twenty five: those four barons shall come to us, or, if we are abroad, to our justice, showing to us our error; and they shall ask us to cause that error to be amended without delay. And if we do not amend that error, or, we being abroad, if our justice do not amend it within a term of forty days from the time when it was shown to us or, we being abroad, to our justice: the aforesaid four barons shall refer the matter to the remainder of the twenty five barons, and those twenty five barons, with the whole land in common, shall distrain and oppress us in every way in their power,—namely, by taking our castles, lands and possessions, and in every other way that they can, until amends shall have been made according to their judgment. Saving the persons of ourselves, our queen and our children. And when amends shall have been made they shall be in accord with us as they had been previously. And whoever of the land wishes to do so, shall swear that in carrying out all the aforesaid measures he will obey the mandates of the aforesaid twenty five barons, and that, with them, he will oppress us to the extent of his power. And, to any one who wishes to do so, we publicly and freely give permission to swear; and we will never prevent any one from swearing. Moreover, all those in the land who shall be unwilling, themselves and of their own accord, to swear to the twenty five barons as to distraining and oppressing us with them: such ones we shall make to swear by our mandate, as has been said. And if any one of the twenty five barons shall die, or leave the country, or in any other way be prevented from carrying out the aforesaid measures,—the remainder of the aforesaid twenty five barons shall choose another in his place, according to their judgment, who shall be sworn in the same way as the others. Moreover, in all things entrusted to those twenty five barons to be carried out, if those twenty five shall be present and chance to disagree among themselves with regard to some matter, or if some of them, having been summoned, shall be unwilling or unable to be present: that which the majority of those present shall decide or decree shall be considered binding and valid, just as if all the twenty five had consented to it. And the aforesaid twenty five shall swear that they will faithfully observe all the foregoing, and will cause them to be observed to the extent of their power. And we shall obtain nothing from any one, either through ourselves or through another, by which any of those concessions and liberties may be revoked or diminished. And if any such thing shall have been obtained, it shall be vain and invalid, and we shall never make use of it either through ourselves or through another.

And we have fully remitted to all, and pardoned, all the ill-will, anger and rancor which have arisen between us and our subjects, clergy and laity, from the time of the struggle. Moreover we have fully remitted to all, clergy and laity, and—as far as pertains to us—have pardoned fully all the transgressions committed, on the occasion of that same struggle, from Easter of the sixteenth year of our reign until the re-establishment of peace. In witness of which, moreover, we have caused to be drawn up for them letters patent of lord Stephen, archbishop of Canterbury, lord Henry, archbishop of Dublin, and the aforesaid bishops and master Pandulf, regarding that surety and the aforesaid concessions.

Wherefore we win and firmly decree that the English church shall be free, and that the subjects of our realm shall have and hold all the aforesaid liberties, rights and concessions, duly and in peace, freely and quietly, fully and entirely, for themselves and their heirs, from us and our heirs, in all matters and in all places, forever, as has been said. Moreover it has been sworn, on our part as well as on the part of the barons, that all these above mentioned provisions shall be observed with good faith and without evil intent. The witnesses being the above mentioned and many others. Given through our hand, in the plain called Runnimede between Windsor and Stanes, on the fifteenth day of June, in the seventeenth year of our reign.

READING AND DISCUSSION QUESTIONS

1. What practices of the king did the Magna Carta specifically prohibit? Under what conditions could the king engage in these practices?

2. What are some of the legal rights that the Magna Carta guarantees for individuals?

3. What redress did nobles have if the king failed to live up to this agreement?

4. In your opinion, what are the most important provisions of the Magna Carta? Why?

14-5 | A Scholastic Places Logic in the Service of Theology

THOMAS AQUINAS, From *Summa Theologica: Can It Be Demonstrated That God Exists?* (1268)

The development of the university was one of the most significant changes that occurred during the Middle Ages in Europe. Universities allowed for a flowering of European scholarship. Thomas Aquinas (ca. 1225–1274) was a Dominican priest and professor at the University of Paris. Aquinas practiced Scholasticism, using logic and reason to provide explanations for beliefs usually accepted on faith. In his massive *Summa Theologica*, Aquinas assembled a compendium for all knowledge regarding theology. The excerpt below is a perfect example of the Scholastic method. In it, Aquinas asks if it can be proven that God exists and then cites authorities, such as biblical passages, in order to provide a reasoned solution to the query.

We proceed thus to the Second Article: —

Objection 1. It seems that the existence of God cannot be demonstrated. For it is an article of faith that God exists. But what is of faith cannot be demonstrated, because a demonstration produces scientific knowledge; whereas faith is of the unseen (Heb. xi. 1). Therefore it cannot be demonstrated that God exists.

Thomas Aquinas, *Summa Theologica*, q. 2, art. 2, pt. 1, trans. Fathers of the English Dominican Province (London: Burns, Oates & Washbourne, 1912, reprinted in 1981 by Christian Classics, Westminster, Md.).

Obj. 2. Further, the essence is the middle term of demonstration. But we cannot know in what God's essence consists, but solely in what it does not consist; as Damascene[2] says (*De Fid. Orth.* i. 4). Therefore we cannot demonstrate that God exists.

Obj. 3. Further, if the existence of God were demonstrated, this could only be from His effects. But His effects are not proportionate to Him, since He is infinite and His effects are finite; and between the finite and infinite there is no proportion. Therefore, since a cause cannot be demonstrated by an effect not proportionate to it, it seems that the existence of God cannot be demonstrated.

On the contrary, The Apostle says: *The invisible things of Him are clearly seen, being understood by the things that are made* (Rom. i. 20). But this would not be unless the existence of God could be demonstrated through the things that are made; for the first thing we must know of anything is, whether it exists.

I answer that, Demonstration can be made in two ways: One is through the cause, and is called *a priori*, and this is to argue from what is prior absolutely. The other is through the effect, and is called a demonstration *a posteriori*; this is to argue from what is prior relatively only to us. When an effect is better known to us than its cause, from the effect we proceed to the knowledge of the cause. And from every effect the existence of its proper cause can be demonstrated, so long as its effects are better known to us; because since every effect depends upon its cause, if the effect exists, the cause must pre-exist. Hence the existence of God, in so far as it is not self-evident to us, can be demonstrated from those of His effects which are known to us.

Reply Obj. 1. The existence of God and other like truths about God, which can be known by natural reason, are not articles of faith, but are preambles to the articles; for faith presupposes natural knowledge, even as grace presupposes nature, and perfection supposes something that can be perfected. Nevertheless, there is nothing to prevent a man, who cannot grasp a proof, accepting, as a matter of faith, something which in itself is capable of being scientifically known and demonstrated.

Reply Obj. 2. When the existence of a cause is demonstrated from an effect, this effect takes the place of the definition of the cause in proof of the cause's existence. This is especially the case in regard to God, because, in order to prove the existence of anything, it is necessary to accept as a middle term the meaning of the word, and not its essence, for the question of its essence follows on the question of its existence. Now the names given to God are derived from His effects; consequently, in demonstrating the existence of God from His effects, we may take for the middle term the meaning of the word "God."

Reply Obj. 3. From effects not proportionate to the cause no perfect knowledge of that cause can be obtained. Yet from every effect the existence of the cause can be clearly demonstrated, and so we can demonstrate the existence of

---

[2] **Damascene:** Saint John, bishop of Damascus after the Muslim conquest of the Near East.

God from His effects; though from them we cannot perfectly know God as He is in His essence.

READING AND DISCUSSION QUESTIONS

1. Does Aquinas believe it can be shown that God exists? What is his argument?

2. In what ways does the *Summa Theologica* represent the medieval synthesis of Christian theology and classical philosophy?

■ COMPARATIVE QUESTIONS ■

1. Taken together, what do the following tell you about the nature of medieval Christianity: Pope Urban II's call for a crusade; the story of the Virgin Mary, the monk, and his lover; and Thomas Aquinas's proof of the existence of God?

2. Compare and contrast the Magna Carta with the law of the Twelve Tables (Document 6-1). How did each use the regulation of legal procedures to help define the relationship between individuals and government authorities?

3. How might Thomas Aquinas have responded to the story of the Virgin Mary, the monk, and his lover? Would he have viewed it as a harmless and amusing tale or as evidence of popular misunderstanding and distortion of Christian theology?

15

Europe in the Renaissance and Reformation

1350–1600

The devastation of plague and warfare that marked the late Middle Ages stimulated Europe's economy by condensing wealth in the cities and creating an impetus for diversifying and revolutionizing business practices to adjust to a drastic labor shortage. Europeans were hopeful for a new beginning, a wish that came to fruition with the Renaissance, French for "rebirth." Originating in the commercial centers of Italy in the fourteenth century, the Renaissance was a cultural movement that spread throughout Europe. Renaissance writers and artists struck out in new directions and declared a definitive break from their medieval heritage. They looked to the classical past for inspiration and praised the abilities and achievements of human beings. In the sixteenth century, a second break came in the form of the Protestant Reformation (ca. 1517–1648), which splintered the Christian church in the West. The following documents reveal the vibrant cultures of the Renaissance and Reformation and address the new attitudes and ideas articulated by their leading thinkers.

VIEWPOINTS

The Intellectual Foundations of the Renaissance

The school of humanism provided a major intellectual foundation for the Renaissance. Humanism was not so much a defined philosophy as it was a program of study. Humanists believed that by looking to writers and thinkers of the classical past for models, students could acquire the necessary tools to improve both themselves and society. In reaching back before the life of Christ for inspiration, the humanists were not rejecting Christianity. Humanists stressed the synthesis of human knowledge. Thus, while many found the methods of medieval Scholastics objectionable, they shared the Scholastics' conviction that there was no essential conflict between faith and reason. As you read the documents included in this feature, pay particular attention to how the authors deal with the relationship between Christian and classical works. What distinctions, if any, do they make between them?

15-1 | Petrarch Expresses His Admiration for Classical Works

PETRARCH, *Letters* (ca. 1354, 1360)

Around 1350, the Italian scholar and poet Francesco Petrarca, or Petrarch (1304–1374), pro-posed a new kind of education that centered on the study and emulation of the works of ancient Roman authors. In his view, the implementation of this program would produce a generation of young men capable of achievements unmatched in Europe for a thousand years. Petrarch and his followers came to be known as humanists, and their intellectual agenda had a profound influence on the art and ideas of their age.

Thanks for a Manuscript of Homer in Greek

[To Nicholas Sygeros]
I rejoice in possessing such a friend as you, wherever you may be. But your living voice, which could both rouse and sate my burning thirst for learning, no longer sounds in my ears. Without it your Homer is dumb to me, or rather I am deaf to him. Nevertheless I rejoice at his mere physical presence; often I clasp him to my bosom and say with a sigh: "O great man, how gladly would I hear you speak! But death has stopped one of my ears, and hateful remoteness has blocked the other."[1] Nevertheless I am very grateful to you for your magnificent gift.

I have long had a copy of Plato; it came to me from the west, rather remark-ably. He was the prince of philosophers, as you know. I am not afraid that you, with your intelligence, will object, like certain scholastics, to this statement. Cicero himself would not object, nor Seneca nor Apuleius nor Plotinus, that great Platonist, nor in later times our Ambrose and Augustine.[2] Now by your bounty the prince of Greek poets joins the prince of philosophers. Who would not rejoice and glory in housing such guests? I have indeed of both of them all that has been

---

David Thompson, ed., *Petrarch: A Humanist Among Princes* (New York: Harper & Row, 1971), 132–133, 179–181. Copyright © 1971 by David Thompson. Reprinted by permission of HarperCollins Publishers.

[1] **death has stopped . . . blocked the other:** This refers to two of Petrarch's Greek tutors.
[2] **Seneca . . . Augustine:** Petrarch refers to three other Roman philosophers, then to two early Christian thinkers. Cato was also a Roman.

translated into Latin from their own tongue. But it is certainly a pleasure, though no advantage, to regard the Greeks in their own dress. Nor have the years robbed me of all hope of making progress in your language; after all, we see that Cato made great strides in Greek at a very advanced age.

If you want anything that I can provide, feel free to call upon me without hesitation. You will see that I call freely upon you. And since the success of prayer begets still bolder prayers, I ask you to send me, if available, a Hesiod; and send me, I beg, Euripides.

So farewell, worthiest of men. And since my name is well known in the west, not for my merits but by the favor of men or of fortune, may you be pleased to mention it among the illustrious men of the Oriental palace. Thus may the Emperor of Constantinople not disdain one whom the Roman Caesar[3] cherishes.

He Turns from Profane to Religious Literature

[To Francesco Nelli]

I noticed in a letter of yours that you were pleased at my mixture of sacred and secular themes, and that you thought Saint Jerome would have been likewise pleased. You mention the charm of variety, the beauty of structure, the force of association. What can I reply? You must make your own judgments, and certainly you are not easily or commonly deceived, except that well-wishers readily err, and often are eager to do so.

But putting all this to one side, let me speak of myself and of my new but serious enthusiasm, which turns my thoughts and my writings to sacred literature. Let the supercilious laugh, who are revolted by the austerity of holy words, as the modest garb of a chaste matron repels those who are used to the flaunting colors of light women. I think that the Muses and Apollo will not merely grant me permission, they will applaud, that after giving my youth to studies proper to that age, I should devote my riper years to more important matters. Nor am I to be criticized, if I, who so often used to rouse by night to work for empty fame and celebrate the futile lauds of men, should now arise at midnight to recite the lauds of my creator, and devote the hours proper to quiet and repose to him who shall neither slumber nor sleep while he keepeth Israel; nor is he content with universal custodianship, but he watches over me personally and is solicitous for my welfare. I am clearly conscious of this, and all men capable of gratitude must feel the same. He cares for each individual as if he were forgetful of mankind *en masse*; and so he rules the mass as if he were careless of each individual. Thus I have it firmly in mind that if it be heaven's will I shall spend the rest of my life in these studies and occupations. In what state could I better die than in loving, remembering, and praising him, without whose constant love I should be nothing, or damned, which is less than nothing? And if his love for me should cease, my damnation would have no end.

---

[3] **Roman Caesar:** Petrarch indicates he is better at Latin than at Greek.

I loved Cicero, I admit, and I loved Virgil. I delighted in their thought and expression so far that I thought nothing could surpass them. I loved many others also of the troop of great writers, but I loved Cicero as if he were my father, Virgil as my brother. My admiration, my familiarity with their genius, contracted in long study, inspired in me such love for their persons that you may think it hardly possible to feel a like affection for living men. Similarly I loved, of the Greeks, Plato and Homer. When I compared their genius with that of our own masters I was often in despair of sound judgment.

But now I must think of more serious matters. My care is more for my salvation than for noble language. I used to read what gave me pleasure, now I read what may be profitable. This is my state of mind, and it has been so for some time. I am not just beginning this practice, and my white hair warns me that I began none too soon. Now my orators shall be Ambrose, Augustine, Jerome, Gregory;[4] my philosopher shall be Paul, my poet David.[5] You remember that years ago, in the first eclogue of my *Bucolicum carmen*[6] I contrasted him with Homer and Virgil, and I left the victory among them undecided. But now, in spite of my old deep-rooted habit, experience and the shining revelation of truth leave me in no doubt as to the victor. But although I put the Christian writers first, I do not reject the others. (Jerome said that he did so, but it seems to me from the imitative style of his writing that he actually approved them.) I seem able to love both groups at once, provided that I consciously distinguish between those I prefer for style and those I prefer for substance. Why should I not act the prudent householder, who assigns part of his furniture for use and another for ornament, who appoints some of his slaves to guard his son, and others to provide the son with sport? Both gold and silver are kinds of money, and you must know their value and not confound them. Especially since those ancient writers demand nothing of me except that I do not let them fall into oblivion. Happy that I have spent upon them my early studies, they now let me give all my time to more important matters.

Since I had already come of myself to this conclusion, I shall now so act the more confidently thanks to your encouragement. If circumstances require, I shall practice, for style, Virgil and Cicero, and I shall not hesitate to draw from Greece whatever Rome may seem to lack. But for the direction of life, though I know much that is useful in the classics, I shall still use those counselors and guides to salvation, in whose faith and doctrine there can be no suspicion of error. First among them in point of merit will David always be to me, the more beautiful for his naivety, the more profound, the more vigorous, for his purity. I want to have his Psalter always at hand during my waking hours where I may steal a glance at it; and I want to have it beneath my pillow when I sleep and when I come to die. I

---

[4] **Jerome, Gregory:** Jerome translated the Bible into Latin and was the author of numerous works; Gregory was a famous pope.

[5] **my poet David:** David, king of Jerusalem, thought to have written the Psalms.

[6] *Bucolicum carmen:* A series of twelve poems written in Latin.

think that such an outcome will be no less glorious for me than was the act of Plato, greatest of philosophers, in keeping the *Mimes* of Sophron[7] under his pillow.

Farewell, and remember me.

READING AND DISCUSSION QUESTIONS

1. How do these letters demonstrate the importance of Greek and Latin texts to the development of the Renaissance? Why would Petrarch want to read Homer in the original Greek?

2. What were Petrarch's thoughts on the value of Christianity to the humanists?

3. What were the advantages of studying the Greek and Latin classics? What about Christian literature?

4. What kind of person would Petrarch consider ideal? How would this person act and think?

15-2 | Pico della Mirandola Argues for the Importance of Philosophical Debate

PICO DELLA MIRANDOLA, From *On the Dignity of Man* (1486)

As the Renaissance progressed, Renaissance thinkers developed a broader knowledge of classical literature, branching out from Latin works to explore writings in Greek, Arabic, and Hebrew. As their knowledge and skills grew, so did their confidence in the capacity of living individuals to match, or even exceed, the accomplishments of their classical counterparts. The Florentine philosopher Pico della Mirandola sought, in his *900 Questions*, to synthesize all of human knowledge, religious and secular, through the lens of Plato's philosophy. His most famous work, *On the Dignity of Man*, written when Pico was just twenty-three years old, argued that humans have the capacity to rationally understand the world. In this excerpt, he defends the vocation of philosophy and his right to discuss his *900 Questions* publicly.

These are the reasons, most reverend fathers, that have not merely inspired me but compelled me to the study of philosophy. I was certainly not going to state them, except as a reply to those accustomed to condemning the study of philosophy in princes especially, or more generally, in men of ordinary fortune. Already (and this is the misfortune of our age) all this philosophizing makes for contempt and contumely [insulting treatment] rather than for honor and glory. This destructive and monstrous opinion that no one, or few, should philosophize, has much invaded the minds of almost everybody. As if it were absolutely nothing to have the causes of things, the ways of nature, the reason of the universe, the counsels of

Charles Glenn Wallis, trans., *Pico della Mirandola: On the Dignity of Man* (Indianapolis: Bobbs-Merrill, 1965), 17–19.

[7] *Mimes* **of Sophron:** Sophron was the first writer of mimes, crude comedic performances.

God, the mysteries of heaven and earth very certain before our eyes and hands, unless someone could derive some benefit from it or acquire profit for himself. It has already reached the point that now (what sorrow!) those only are considered wise who pursue the study of wisdom for the sake of money; so that one may see chaste Pallas,[8] who stays among men by a gift of the gods, chased out, hooted, hissed; who loves and befriends her does not have her unless she, as it were prostituting herself and receiving a pittance for her deflowered virginity, bring back the ill-bought money to her lover's money-box. I say all these things not without great grief and indignation, not against the princes, but against the philosophers of this age, who believe and preach that there should be no philosophizing because there is no money for philosophers, no prizes awarded them; as if they did not show by this one word that they are not philosophers. Since their whole life is set on money-making or ambition, they do not embrace the knowledge of truth for itself. I shall give myself this credit and shall not blush to praise myself in this respect, that I have never philosophized for any reason other than for the sake of philosophizing, that I have neither hoped nor sought from my studies, from my lucubrations [studies], any other gain or profit than cultivation of soul and knowledge of truth, always so greatly desired by me. I have always been so desirous of this truth and so much in love with it that, abandoning all care of public and private affairs, I gave my whole self over to the leisure of contemplating, from which no disparaging of the envious, no curses from the enemies of wisdom, have been able so far or will be able later to frighten me away. Philosophy herself has taught me to weigh things rather by my own conscience than by the judgments of others, and to consider not so much whether I should be badly spoken of as whether I myself should say or do anything bad. In fact, I was not ignorant, most reverend fathers, that this disputation of mine will be as pleasant and enjoyable to all you who delight in good arts and have wished to honor it with your most august presence, as it will be heavy and burdensome to many others; and I know that there are some who have condemned my undertaking before this, and who condemn it now under many names. Thus there are usually no fewer, not to say more, growlers who carry on well and in a holy way against virtue, than there are who do so wickedly and wrongly against vice.

There are some who do not approve of this whole class of disputes and this practice of debating in public about letters, asserting that it makes rather for the display of talent and learning than for acquiring knowledge. There are some who do not disapprove of this type of exercise, but who do not approve of it at all in my case, because I at my age, in only my twenty-fourth year, have dared, in the most famous city, in the largest assembly of the most learned men, in the apostolic senate,[9] to propose a disputation on the sublime mysteries of Christian theology, on the loftiest questions of philosophy, on unknown teachings. Others who give me leave to dispute are unwilling to give me leave to dispute about

---

[8] **Pallas:** Athena, the goddess of wisdom.
[9] **apostolic senate:** A body made up of the most famous Christian saints and theologians.

nine hundred questions, saying in slander that the proposal was made as needlessly and ambitiously as it was beyond my powers. I should have immediately surrendered to their objections if the philosophy which I profess had so taught me; and now, at her teaching me, I would not answer if I believed this disputation among us were set up for brawling and quarreling. Consequently, let every intent of detraction and irritation depart, and let malice, which, Plato writes, is always absent from the divine chorus, also depart from our minds. And let us learn in friendly fashion whether I ought to dispute, and on so many questions.

First, to those who slander this practice of disputing publicly, I am not going to say much, except that this crime, if they judge it a crime, is the joint work not only of all you very excellent doctors—who have often discharged this office not without very great praise and glory—but also of Plato and Aristotle and the most upright philosophers of every age, together with me. To them it was most certain that they had nothing better for reaching the knowledge of the truth which they sought than that they be very often in the exercise of disputing. As through gymnastics the forces of the body are strengthened, so doubtless in this, as it were, literary gymnasium, the forces of the soul become much stronger and more vigorous. I would not believe that the poets signified anything else to us by the celebrated arms of Pallas, or the Hebrews when they say *barzel*, iron, is the symbol of wise men, than that this sort of contest is very honorable, exceedingly necessary for gaining wisdom. Perhaps that is why the Chaldaeans,[10] too, desire that at the birth of him who is to become a philosopher, Mars should behold Mercury with triangular aspect, as if to say that if you take away these encounters, these wars, then all philosophy will become drowsy and sleepy.

READING AND DISCUSSION QUESTIONS

1. What does Pico say about the study of philosophy? Why might he argue that one should not be paid for being a philosopher?

2. How does he defend his right to instigate public debate on all the most important philosophical questions?

VIEWPOINTS COMPARATIVE QUESTIONS

1. How did Petrarch view the relationship between classical and Christian works? How did Pico view it? How can you explain the differences you note?

2. How might Petrarch have responded to Pico's ambitious philosophical project? Would he have supported Pico's plan to publicly debate his *900 Questions*?

3. What marks each of these men as humanists? What marks them as Renaissance, and not medieval, thinkers?

[10] **Chaldaeans:** The Greeks and Romans called astronomers from Mesopotamia *Chaldaeans* and associated them with magic. They were most famous for the development of astrology.

15-3 | A Female Renaissance Painter Examines Gender and Power

ARTEMISIA GENTILESCHI, *Susannah and the Elders* (1610)

Renaissance and early modern artists drew heavily for their inspiration on Christianity and the classical past, but this does not mean that they were uninterested in the present. *Susannah and the Elders* by the female Roman painter Artemisia Gentileschi (1593–ca. 1656) is a case in point. Taken from the Book of Daniel, the story of Susannah centers on a false accusation of adultery. As Susannah, a young wife, bathes in her garden, two elders of her community watch secretly. Filled with lust, the two men threaten to denounce her as an adulterer if she refuses to have sex with them. When she resists their attempts at blackmail, they follow through on their threat. Only the intervention of Daniel, who exposes inconsistencies in their story, saves Susannah from execution. As you examine the painting, pay particular attention to the way Gentileschi composed it. How does the placement of the three figures help amplify its message?

Fine Art Images/Superstock.

READING AND DISCUSSION QUESTIONS

1. How would you describe Gentileschi's Susannah? How does the position of her arms and head help convey her reaction to the unwanted advances of the elders?

2. How would you characterize the two elders? How does their placement in the painting reflect their power? What might explain Gentileschi's decision to depict them whispering to one another at the very moment they accost Susannah?

3. What does the painting tell us about the connections that Gentileschi made between gender, power, and violence?

15-4 | Luther Calls on the German Nobility to Break with the Catholic Church

MARTIN LUTHER, From *Address to the Christian Nobility of the German Nation* (1520)

Martin Luther (1483–1546) was an Augustinian monk from eastern Germany whose translation of the Bible contributed to the development of the modern German language. In penning
his *Ninety-Five Theses* (1517) criticizing the Catholic Church's sale of indulgences, which
allowed for the remission of sins without penance, Luther became the father of the Protestant
Reformation. Some scholars argue that the theses, which Luther enclosed in a letter to a
German archbishop, were posed in a format traditionally used as an invitation to debate and
that their author could not have foreseen the consequences of his dissension, which led to his
excommunication from the Catholic Church in 1521. In the following reading, Luther attacks
the extravagance and corruption of the Catholic hierarchy.

Of the Matters to Be Considered in the Councils

Let us now consider the matters which should be treated in the councils, and with which popes, cardinals, bishops, and all learned men should occupy themselves day and night, if they love Christ and His Church. But if they do not do so, the people at large and the temporal powers must do so, without considering the thunders of their excommunications. For an unjust excommunication is better than ten just absolutions, and an unjust absolution is worse than ten just excommunications. Therefore let us rouse ourselves, fellow-Germans, and fear God more than man, that we be not answerable for all the poor souls that are so miserably lost through the wicked, devilish government of the Romanists, and that the dominion of the devil should not grow day by day, if indeed this hellish government can grow any worse, which, for my part, I can neither conceive nor believe.

    1. It is a distressing and terrible thing to see that the head of Christendom, who boasts of being the vicar of Christ and the successor of St. Peter, lives in a

Harry Emerson Fosdick, ed., *Great Voices of the Reformation: An Anthology* (New York: Modern Library, 1952), 109–111, 114–115.

worldly pomp that no king or emperor can equal, so that in him that calls himself most holy and most spiritual there is more worldliness than in the world itself. He wears a triple crown, whereas the mightiest kings only wear one crown. If this resembles the poverty of Christ and St. Peter, it is a new sort of resemblance. They prate of its being heretical to object to this; nay, they will not even hear how unchristian and ungodly it is. But I think that if he should have to pray to God with tears, he would have to lay down his crowns; for God will not endure any arrogance. His office should be nothing else than to weep and pray constantly for Christendom and to be an example of all humility.

However this may be, this pomp is a stumbling-block, and the pope, for the very salvation of his soul, ought to put it off, for St. Paul says, "Abstain from all appearance of evil" (I Thess. v. 21), and again, "Provide things honest in the sight of all men" (II Cor. viii. 21). A simple miter would be enough for the pope: wisdom and sanctity should raise him above the rest; the crown of pride he should leave to antichrist, as his predecessors did some hundreds of years ago. They say, He is the ruler of the world. This is false; for Christ, whose viceregent and vicar he claims to be, said to Pilate, "My kingdom is not of this world" (John xviii. 36). But no viceregent can have a wider dominion than his Lord, nor is he a viceregent of Christ in His glory, but of Christ crucified, as St. Paul says, "For I determined not to know anything among you save Jesus Christ, and Him crucified" (II Cor. ii. 2), and "Let this mind be in you, which was also in Christ Jesus, who made Himself of no reputation, and took upon Himself the form of a servant" (Phil. ii. 5, 7). Again, "We preach Christ crucified" (I Cor. i.). Now they make the pope a viceregent of Christ exalted in heaven, and some have let the devil rule them so thoroughly that they have maintained that the pope is above the angels in heaven and has power over them, which is precisely the true work of the true antichrist.

2. What is the use in Christendom of the people called "cardinals"? I will tell you. In Italy and Germany there are many rich convents, endowments, fiefs, and benefices, and as the best way of getting these into the hands of Rome, they created cardinals, and gave them the sees, convents, and prelacies, and thus destroyed the service of God. That is why Italy is almost a desert now: the convents are destroyed, the sees consumed, the revenues of the prelacies and of all the churches drawn to Rome; towns are decayed, the country and the people ruined, because there is no more any worship of God or preaching; why? Because the cardinals must have all the wealth. No Turk could have thus desolated Italy and overthrown the worship of God.

Now that Italy is sucked dry, they come to Germany and begin very quietly; but if we look on quietly Germany will soon be brought into the same state as Italy. We have a few cardinals already. What the Romanists mean thereby the drunken Germans are not to see until they have lost everything—bishoprics, convents, benefices, fiefs, even to their last farthing. Antichrist must take the riches of the earth, as it is written (Dan. xi. 8, 39, 43). They begin by taking off the cream of the bishoprics, convents, and fiefs; and as they do not dare to destroy everything as they have done in Italy, they employ such holy cunning to join together ten or twenty prelacies, and take such a portion of each annually that the total amounts to a considerable sum. The priory of Würzburg gives one thousand guilders; those of Bamberg, Mayence, Treves, and others also contribute. In this way they collect one thousand or ten thousand guilders, in order that a cardinal may live at Rome in a state like that of a wealthy monarch. . . .

This precious roman avarice has also invented the practice of selling and lending prebends[11] and benefices on condition that the seller or lender has the reversion, so that if the incumbent dies, the benefice falls to him that has sold it, lent it, or abandoned it; in this way they have made benefices heritable property, so that none can come to hold them unless the seller sells them to him, or leaves them to him at his death. Then there are many that give a benefice to another in name only, and on condition that he shall not receive a farthing. It is now, too, an old practice for a man to give another a benefice and to receive a certain annual sum, which proceeding was formerly called simony. And there are many other such little things which I cannot recount; and so they deal worse with the benefices than the heathens by the cross dealt with Christ's clothes.

But all this that I have spoken of is old and common at Rome. Their avarice has invented another device, which I hope will be the last and choke it. The pope has made a noble discovery, called *Pectoralis Reservatio*, that is, "mental reservation"—*et propius motus*, that is, "and his own will and power." The matter is managed in this way: Suppose a man obtains a benefice at Rome, which is confirmed to him in due form; then comes another, who brings money, or who has done some other service of which the less said the better, and requests the pope to give him the same benefice: then the pope will take it from the first and give it him. If you say, that is wrong, the Most Holy Father must then excuse himself, that he may not be openly blamed for having violated justice; and he says "that in his heart and mind he reserved his authority over the said benefice," whilst he never had heard of or thought of the same in all his life. Thus he has devised a *gloss* which allows him in his proper person to lie and cheat and fool us all, and all this impudently and in open daylight, and nevertheless he claims to be the head of Christendom, letting the evil spirit rule him with manifest lies.

This wantonness and lying reservation of the popes has brought about an unutterable state of things at Rome. There is a buying and a selling, a changing, blustering and bargaining, cheating and lying, robbing and stealing, debauchery and villainy, and all kinds of contempt of God, that antichrist himself could not rule worse. Venice, Antwerp, Cairo, are nothing to this fair and market at Rome, except that there things are done with some reason and justice, whilst here things are done as the devil himself could wish. And out of this ocean a like virtue overflows all the world. Is it not natural that such people should dread a reformation and a free council, and should rather embroil all kings and princes than that their unity should bring about a council? Who would like his villainy to be exposed?

---

[11] **prebends:** A stipend paid by the Catholic Church to the clergy.

READING AND DISCUSSION QUESTIONS

1. How does Luther describe the papal court? Why does it anger him so?

2. What problems does Luther say were caused by the expansion of the Catholic hierarchy through the appointment of cardinals?

3. Why does Luther attack the selling and lending of prebends and benefices by the Catholic Church?

4. Why was it important for Luther to convince the German nobility to join his side?

15-5 | John Calvin Explains His Views on Faith and the Clergy

JOHN CALVIN, From *Instruction in Faith* (1537)

John Calvin (1509–1564) received a Catholic education but came to reject the authority of the Catholic Church around 1529, while studying at the University of Bourges. He went on to publish a number of texts about Christian theology during the Reformation and is seen as the principal thinker of Calvinism, which stresses predestination and God's role as ultimate authority. This selection comes from his *Instruction in Faith*, which is a condensation of his more famous *Institutes*. The *Instruction in Faith* was intended to be read by the common person. It therefore describes how individuals should understand his theology in their daily lives.

We Apprehend Christ Through Faith

Just as the merciful Father offers us the Son through the word of the Gospel, so we embrace him through faith and acknowledge him as given to us. It is true that the word of the Gospel calls all to participate in Christ, but a number, blinded and hardened by unbelief, despise such a unique grace. Hence, only believers enjoy Christ; they receive him as sent to them; they do not reject him when he is given, but follow him when he calls them.

Election and Predestination

Beyond this contrast of attitudes of believers and unbelievers, the great secret of God's counsel must necessarily be considered. For, the seed of the word of God takes root and brings forth fruit only in those whom the Lord, by his eternal election, has predestined to be children and heirs of the heavenly kingdom. To all the others (who by the same counsel of God are rejected before the foundation of the world) the clear and evident preaching of truth can be nothing but an odor of death unto death. Now, why does the Lord use his mercy toward some and exercise the rigor of his judgment on the others? We have to leave the reason of this to be known by him alone. For, he, with a certainly excellent intention, has willed to keep it hidden from us all. The crudity of our mind could not indeed bear such a great clarity, nor our smallness comprehend such a great wisdom. And in fact all those who will attempt to rise to such a height and will not repress the temerity of their spirit, shall experience the truth of Solomon's saying (Prov. 25:27) that he who will investigate the majesty shall be oppressed by the glory. Only let us have this resolved in ourselves that the dispensation of the Lord, although hidden from us, is nevertheless holy and just. For, if he willed to ruin all mankind, he has the right to do it, and in those whom he rescues from perdition one can contemplate nothing but his sovereign goodness. We acknowledge, therefore, the elect to be recipients of his mercy (as truly they are) and the rejected to be recipients of his wrath, a wrath, however, which is nothing but just.

Let us take from the lot of both the elect and the others, reasons for extolling his glory. On the other hand, let us not seek (as many do), in order to confirm the certainty of our salvation, to penetrate the very interior of heaven and to investigate what God from his eternity has decided to do with us. That can only worry us with a miserable distress and perturbation. Let us be content, then, with the testimony by which he has sufficiently and amply confirmed to us this certainty. For, as in Christ are elected all those who have been preordained to life before the foundations of the world were laid, so also he is he in whom the pledge of our election is presented to us if we receive him and embrace him through faith. For what do we seek in election except that we be participants in the life eternal? And we have it in Christ, who was the life since the beginning and who is offered as life to us in order that all those who believe in him may not perish but enjoy the life eternal. If, therefore, in possessing Christ through faith we possess in him likewise life, we need not further inquire beyond the eternal counsel of God. For Christ is not only a mirror by which the will of God is presented to us, but he is a pledge by which life is as sealed and confirmed to us.

What True Faith Is

One must not imagine that the Christian faith is a bare and mere knowledge of God or an understanding of the Scripture which flutters in the brain without touching the heart, as is usually the case with the opinion about things which are confirmed by some probable reason. But faith is a firm and solid confidence of the heart, by means of which we rest surely in the mercy of God which is promised to us through the Gospel. For thus the definition of faith must be taken from the substance of the promise. Faith rests so much on this foundation that, if the latter be taken away, faith would collapse at once, or, rather, vanish away. Hence, when the Lord presents to us his mercy through the promise of the Gospel, if we certainly and without hesitation trust him who made the promise, we are said to apprehend his word through faith. And this definition is not different from that of the apostle (Heb. 11:1) in which he teaches that faith is the certainty of the things to be hoped for and the demonstration of the things not apparent; for he means a sure and secure possession of the things that God promises, and an evidence of the things that are not apparent, that is to say, the life eternal. And this we conceive through confidence in the divine goodness which is offered to us through the Gospel. Now, since all the promises of God are gathered together and confirmed in Christ, and are, so to speak, kept and accomplished in him, it appears without doubt that Christ is the perpetual object of faith. And in that object, faith contemplates all the riches of the divine mercy.

Faith Is a Gift of God

If we honestly consider within ourselves how much our thought is blind to the heavenly secrets of God and how greatly our heart distrusts all things, we shall not doubt that faith greatly surpasses all the power of our nature and that faith is a unique and precious gift of God. For, as St. Paul maintains (I Cor. 2:11), if no one can witness the human will, except the spirit of man which is in man, how will man be certain of the divine will? And if the truth of God in us wavers even in things that we see by the eye, how will it be firm and stable where the Lord promises the things that the eye does not see and man's understanding does not comprehend?

Hence there is no doubt that faith is a light of the Holy Spirit through which our understandings are enlightened and our hearts are confirmed in a sure persuasion which is assured that the truth of God is so certain that he can but accomplish that which he has promised through his holy word that he will do. Hence (II Cor. 1:22; Eph. 1:13), the Holy Spirit is called like a guarantee which confirms in our hearts the certainty of the divine truth, and a seal by which our hearts are sealed in the expectation of the day of the Lord. For it is the Spirit indeed who witnesses to our spirit that God is our Father and that similarly we are his children (Rom. 8:16). . . .

The Pastors of the Church and Their Power

Since the Lord has willed that both his word and his sacraments be dispensed through the ministry of men, it is necessary that there be pastors ordained to the churches, pastors who teach the people both in public and in private the pure doctrine, administer the sacraments, and by their good example instruct and form all to holiness and purity of life. Those who despise this discipline and this order do injury not only to men, but to God, and even, as heretics, withdraw from the society of the church, which in no way can stand together without such a ministry. For what the Lord has once (Matt. 10:40) testified is of no little importance: It is that when the pastors whom he sends are welcomed, he himself is welcomed, and likewise he is rejected when they are rejected. And in order that their ministry be not contemptible, pastors are furnished with a notable mandate: to bind and to loose, having the added promise that whatever things they shall have bound or loosed on earth, are bound or loosed in heaven (Matt. 16:19). And Christ himself in another passage (John 20:23) explains that to bind means to retain sins, and to loose means to remit them. Now, the apostle declares what is the mode of loosing when (Rom. 1:16) he teaches the Gospel to be the power of God unto salvation for each believer. And he tells also the way of binding when he declares (II Cor. 10:4–6) the apostles to have retribution ready against any disobedience. For, the sum of the Gospel is that we are slaves of sin and death, and that we are loosed and freed by the redemption which is in Christ Jesus, while those who do not receive him as redeemer are bound as by new bonds of a graver condemnation.

But let us remember that this power (which in the Scripture is attributed to pastors) is wholly contained in and limited to the ministry of the word. For Christ has not given this power properly to these men but to his word, of which he has made these men ministers. Hence, let pastors boldly dare all things by the word of God, of which they have been constituted dispensators; let them constrain all the power, glory, and haughtiness of the world to make room for and to obey the majesty of that word; let them by means of that word command all from the greatest to the smallest; let them edify the house of Christ; let them demolish the reign of Satan; let them feed the sheep, kill the wolves, instruct and exhort the docile; let them rebuke, reprove, reproach, and convince the rebel—but all through and within the word of God. But if pastors turn away from the word to their dreams and to the inventions of their own minds, already they are no longer to be received as pastors, but being seen to be rather pernicious wolves, they are to be chased away. For Christ has commanded us to listen only to those who teach us that which they have taken from his word.

READING AND DISCUSSION QUESTIONS

1. What is Calvin's understanding of predestination and salvation?
2. According to Calvin, what is faith?
3. What is the role of pastors in Calvin's ideal church?

▪ COMPARATIVE QUESTIONS ▪

1. In what ways were the Renaissance and the Reformation a break from what had come before in European society? In what ways were they a continuation?
2. How did humanists contribute to the Reformation?
3. How similar are the ideas of Martin Luther and John Calvin? Support your answer with evidence from the sources.
4. How did Renaissance thinkers and artists use the past to illuminate the present?

16

The Acceleration
of Global Contact
1450–1600

Although long-standing trade routes meant that many of the world's civilizations were in contact with one another before 1500, this interaction accelerated drastically in the sixteenth century when Europe became a much larger player in world trade. Europe began establishing trade routes to the newly discovered Americas and sent Christian missionaries to all corners of the globe. The sources in this chapter examine the impact of Europe's entrance into the global community and address the continued importance of the civilizations that had established earlier trade routes in the Indian Ocean.

16-1 | The World as Europeans Knew It in 1502
World Map (1502)

Created in 1502, this map shows the world as Europeans knew it ten years after the voyages of Christopher Columbus. The African coastline is rendered in extraordinarily accurate detail. Trading destinations in India and Southeast Asia are also clearly indicated. The Americas, however, remain a rough sketch, a largely imagined place, not a known one. Nonetheless, the map offers a glimpse of the future. In 1494, Spain and Portugal signed the Treaty of Tordesillas, which established a line of demarcation running north-south (the blue line on the left side of the map running through modern-day Brazil). All non-European territories to the west of the line were to be Spanish. All those to the east were to be Portuguese. As you examine the map, think about what it reveals about the European age of expansion. How does it tell the story of the previous century of exploration? What does it suggest about the course of conquests yet to come?

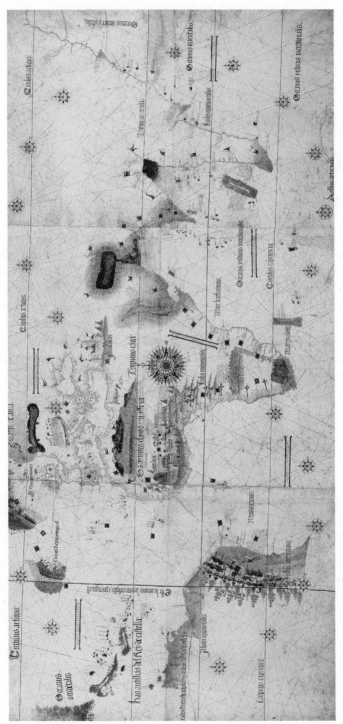

READING AND DISCUSSION QUESTIONS

1. How would you explain the prominence of Africa on the map? How did Europeans develop such an accurate sense of its coastline?

2. What were the larger implications of the Treaty of Tordesillas? What does it tell you about the importance the Spanish and Portuguese attached to the discoveries and achievements of the fifteenth century?

VIEWPOINTS

The Motives of Columbus and His Patrons

The year 1492 was a momentous one in Spanish history. With the fall of the Muslim state of Granada, Ferdinand of Aragon and Isabella of Castile completed the Christian *reconquista* (reconquest) of the Iberian Peninsula. Having driven the "infidels" from their last Iberian stronghold, they turned to the "enemy within," issuing a proclamation expelling all Jews from their lands. It was at this moment, fired with a crusading spirit and eager to gain access to the wealth of Asia, that Ferdinand and Isabella chose to sponsor the exploratory westward voyage of Christopher Columbus. Keep this larger context in mind as you read the documents included in this feature. How does this history help explain the motives and expectations of Columbus and his patrons?

16-2 | Columbus Defends His Accomplishments

CHRISTOPHER COLUMBUS, *Letter from the Third Voyage* (1493)

When King Ferdinand and Queen Isabella decided to fund Columbus's expeditions, they were not engaging in an act of charity. They were making an investment. This is not to say that their motives were strictly material. Both were devout Catholics and were committed to spreading the faith. Nonetheless, Columbus claimed that he knew a faster route to Asia, and to late-fifteenth-century Europeans, Asia meant, first and foremost, a highly profitable trade in luxury goods. Thus when Columbus failed to deliver on his implied promise to deliver fabulous wealth, he knew he would have to explain himself. As you read the letter, think about Columbus's intended audience. How did he seek to refute his critics? Why did he feel he had to?

Cecil Jane, ed. and trans., *Select Documents Illustrating the Four Voyages of Columbus*. Published by Haklut Society, 1967.

Most serene and most high and most powerful princes, the king and queen, our sovereigns: The Holy Trinity moved Your Highnesses to this enterprise of the Indies, and of His infinite goodness, He made me the messenger thereof, so that, being moved thereunto, I came with the mission to your royal presence, as being the most exalted of Christian princes and so ardently devoted to the Faith and to its increase. The persons who should have occupied themselves with the matter held it to be impossible, for they made of gifts of chance their riches and on them placed their trust.

On this matter I spent six or seven years of deep anxiety, expounding, as well as I could, how great service might in this be rendered to the Lord, by proclaiming abroad His holy name and His faith to so many peoples, which was all a thing of so great excellence and for the fair fame of great princes and for a notable memorial for them. It was needful also to speak of the temporal gain therein, foreshadowed in the writings of so many wise men, worthy of credence, who wrote histories and related how in these parts there are great riches. And it was likewise necessary to bring forward in this matter that which had been said and thought by those who have written of the world and who have described it. Finally, Your Highnesses determined that this enterprise should be undertaken.

Here you displayed that lofty spirit which you have always shown in every great affair, for all those who had been engaged on the matter and who had heard the proposal, one and all laughed it to scorn, save two friars who were ever constant.

I, although I suffered weariness, was very sure that this would not come to nothing, and I am still, for it is true that all will pass away, save the Word of God, and all that He has said will be fulfilled. And He spake so clearly of these lands by the mouth of Isaiah, in many places of his Book, affirming that from Spain His holy name should be proclaimed to them.

And I set forth in the name of the Holy Trinity, and I returned very speedily, with evidence of all, as much as I had said, in my hand. Your highnesses undertook to send me again, and in a little while I say that, . . . by the grace of God, I discovered three hundred and thirty-three leagues of Tierra Firme,[1] the end of the East, and seven hundred islands of importance, over and above that which I discovered on the first voyage, and I circumnavigated the island of Española, which in circumference is greater than all Spain, wherein are people innumerable, all of whom should pay tribute.

Then was born the defaming and disparagement of the undertaking which had been begun there, because I had not immediately sent caravels laden with gold, no thought being taken of the brevity of the time and the other many obstacles which I mentioned. And on this account, for my sins or, as I believe that it will be, for my salvation, I was held in abhorrence and was opposed in whatever I said and asked.

---

[1] **Tierra Firme:** The mainland.

For this cause, I decided to come to Your Highnesses, and to cause you to wonder at everything, and to show you the reason that I had for all. And I told you of the peoples whom I had seen, among whom or from whom many souls may be saved. And I brought to you the service of the people of the island of Española, how they were bound to pay tribute and how they held you as their sovereigns and lords. And I brought to you abundant evidence of gold, and that there are mines and very great nuggets, and likewise of copper. And I brought to you many kinds of spices, of which it would be wearisome to write, and I told you of the great amount of brazil[2] and of other things, innumerable.

READING AND DISCUSSION QUESTIONS

1. What religious implications did Columbus attach to his voyages? Why do you think he chose to highlight the opportunity his discoveries created for the spread of Catholicism?

2. What material advantages did Columbus claim would result from his discoveries? How might his readers have responded to his claims?

16-3 | Spanish Ambitions in the New World
THEODORE DE BRY, *Columbus at Hispaniola* (ca. 1590)

In his letters to King Ferdinand and Queen Isabella, Columbus told his side of the story, describing his voyages in ways that were meant both to please his patrons and to emphasize his personal accomplishments. His was not the last word, however. In the decades following Columbus's death, the motives behind his expeditions and the subsequent Spanish colonization of the Americas became matters of considerable debate. For example, this late-sixteenth-century engraving by the Protestant artist and engraver Theodore de Bry contains all of the motives mentioned by Columbus (see Document 16-2) but presents them in a way that *offers* an implicit rebuke to the Genoese explorer. As you examine it, think about its intended message. What did the artist see as the primary motives behind Spanish exploration and colonization? How did he want his viewers to feel about the scenes he included in this engraving?

---

[2] **brazil:** Brazilwood, a very expensive wood that was much sought after in Europe.

Private Collection/Bridgeman Images.

READING AND DISCUSSION QUESTIONS

1. Which motive did de Bry portray as most important? How did he indicate this?

2. What importance should we attach to the fact that the cross on the left is being erected by a small group of soldiers? What does the scene tell us about de Bry's views on Spanish missionary work in the Americas?

3. What should we make of the Native Americans fleeing the Spanish ships on the right side of the engraving? What are they afraid of? Did de Bry believe their fears were justified?

VIEWPOINTS COMPARATIVE QUESTIONS

1. What common elements are included in both Columbus's letter and de Bry's engraving? How do those elements combine in each document to tell the story of Columbus's voyages?

2. Why might Europeans have seen Columbus's voyages differently at the beginning of the sixteenth century than they did at the end? What intervening events, both in the Americas and in Europe, might have reshaped European perspectives?

16-4 | Cross-Cultural Communications and Conquest
BERNAL DÍAZ DEL CASTILLO, From *The True History of the Conquest of New Spain* (1568)

Initial Spanish occupation of the New World focused on exploiting native labor in the Caribbean. When the natives began to die off in large numbers because of disease and harsh treatment, some Spanish explorers (known as conquistadors) sought the conquest of new lands. One, Hernán Cortés, left his settlement at Cuba and landed in Central America in 1518. By 1519, he had collected a number of native tribes as allies and marched on the largest city in Mexico, Tenochtitlan, taking control of the entire area by 1521. This expedition is described by Bernal Díaz del Castillo, an eyewitness to the invasion. He wrote fifty years after participating in the conquest and named his work *The True History* to distinguish it from earlier accounts that were not written by eyewitnesses.

As Xicotenga was bad tempered and obstinate and proud, he decided to send forty Indians with food, poultry, bread and fruit and four miserable looking old Indian women, and much copal and many parrots' feathers. From their appearance we thought that the Indians who brought this present came with peaceful intentions, and when they reached our camp they fumigated Cortés with incense without doing him reverence, as was usually their custom. They said: "The Captain Xicotenga sends you all this so that you can eat. If you are savage Teules,[3] as the Cempoalans[4] say you are, and if you wish for a sacrifice, take these four women and sacrifice them and you can eat their flesh and hearts, but as we do not know your manner of doing it, we have not sacrificed them now before you; but if you are men, eat the poultry and the bread and fruit, and if you are tame

---

Bernal Díaz del Castillo, *The True History of the Conquest of New Spain*, trans. Alfred Percival Maudslay (London: Bedford Press, 1908), 257–263.

[3] **Teules:** A series of divinities from Central America. Occasionally they are considered wicked. Later, "Teules" virtually became a synonym for the Spanish.

[4] **Cempoalans:** A tribe in Central America.

Teules we have brought you copal (which I have already said is a sort of incense) and parrots' feathers; make your sacrifice with that."

Cortés answered through our interpreters that he had already sent to them to say that he desired peace and had not come to make war, but had come to entreat them and make clear to them on behalf of our Lord Jesus Christ, whom we believe in and worship, and of the Emperor Don Carlos, whose vassals we are, that they should not kill or sacrifice anyone as was their custom to do. That we were all men of bone and flesh just as they were, and not Teules but Christians, and that it was not our custom to kill anyone; that had we wished to kill people, many opportunities of perpetrating cruelties had occurred during the frequent attacks they had made on us, both by day and night. That for the food they had brought he gave them thanks, and that they were not to be as foolish as they had been, but should now make peace.

It seems that these Indians whom Xicotenga had sent with the food were spies sent to examine our huts and ranchos, and horses and artillery and [to report] how many of us there were in each hut, our comings and goings, and everything else that could be seen in the camp. They remained there that day and the following night, and some of them went with messages to Xicotenga and others arrived. Our friends whom we had brought with us from Cempoala looked on and bethought them that it was not a customary thing for our enemies to stay in the camp day and night without any purpose, and it was clear to them that they were spies, and they were the more suspicious of them in that when we went on the expedition to the little town of Tzumpantzingo, two old men of that town had told the Cempoalans that Xicotenga was all ready with a large number of warriors to attack our camp by night, in such a way that their approach would not be detected, and the Cempoalans at that time took it for a joke or bravado, and not believing it they had said nothing to Cortés; but Doña Marina[5] heard of it at once and she repeated it to Cortés.

So as to learn the truth, Cortés had two of the most honest looking of the Tlaxcalans taken apart from the others, and they confessed that they were spies; then two others were taken and they also confessed that they were spies from Xicotenga and the reason why they had come. Cortés ordered them to be released, and we took two more of them and they confessed that they were neither more nor less than spies, but added that their Captain Xicotenga was awaiting their report to attack us that night with all his companies. When Cortés heard this he let it be known throughout the camp that we were to keep on the alert, believing that they would attack as had been arranged. Then he had seventeen of those spies captured and cut off the hands of some and the thumbs of others and sent them to the Captain Xicotenga to tell him that he had had them thus punished for daring to come in such a way, and to tell him that he might come when he chose by day or by night, for we should await him here two days, and that if

---

[5] **Doña Marina:** A native woman who learned Spanish. She served as a translator for Cortés and became his lover, giving birth to a son.

he did not come within those two days that we would go and look for him in his camp, and that we would already have gone to attack them and kill them, were it not for the liking we had for them, and that now they should quit their foolishness and make peace.

They say that it was at the very moment that those Indians set out with their hands and thumbs cut off, that Xicotenga wished to set out from his camp with all his forces to attack us by night as had been arranged; but when he saw his spies returning in this manner he wondered greatly and asked the reason of it, and they told him all that had happened, and from this time forward he lost his courage and pride, and in addition to this one of his commanders with whom he had wrangles and disagreements during the battles which had been fought, had left the camp with all his men.

Let us get on with our story. . . .

* * *

While we were in camp not knowing that they would come in peace, as we had so greatly desired, and were busy polishing our arms and making arrows, each one of us doing what was necessary to prepare for battle, at that moment one of our scouts came hurrying in to say that many Indian men and women with loads were coming along the high road from Tlaxcala, and without leaving the road were making for our camp. . . . Cortés and all of us were delighted at this news, for we believed that it meant peace, as in fact it did, and Cortés ordered us to make no display of alarm and not to show any concern, but to stay hidden in our huts. Then, from out of all those people who came bearing loads, the four chieftains advanced who were charged to treat for peace, according to the instructions given by the old Caciques.[6] Making signs of peace by bowing the head, they came straight to the hut where Cortés was lodging and placed one hand on the ground and kissed the earth and three times made obeisance and burnt copal, and said that all the Caciques of Tlaxcala and their allies and vassals, friends and confederates, were come to place themselves under the friendship and peace of Cortés and of his brethren the Teules who accompanied him. They asked his pardon for not having met us peacefully, and for the war which they had waged on us, for they had believed and held for certain that we were friends of Montezuma and his Mexicans, who have been their mortal enemies from times long past, for they saw that many of his vassals who paid him tribute had come in our company, and they believed that they were endeavoring to gain an entry into their country by guile and treachery, as was their custom to do, so as to rob them of their women and children; and this was the reason why they did not believe the messengers whom we had sent to them. In addition to this they said that the Indians who had first gone forth to make war on us as we entered their country had done it without their orders or advice, but by that of the Chuntales Estomies [barbarous Otomís], who were wild people and very stupid, and that when they saw that we were so few in number, they

---

[6] **Caciques:** Leaders.

thought to capture us and carry us off as prisoners to their lords and gain thanks for so doing; that now they came to beg pardon for their audacity, and had brought us food, and that every day they would bring more and trusted that we would receive it with the friendly feeling with which it was sent; that within two days the captain Xicotenga would come with other Caciques and give a further account of the sincere wish of all Tlaxcala to enjoy our friendship.

As soon as they had finished their discourse they bowed their heads and placed their hands on the ground and kissed the earth. Then Cortés spoke to them through our interpreters very seriously, pretending he was angry, and said that there were reasons why we should not listen to them and should reject their friendship, for as soon as we had entered their country we sent to them offering peace and had told them that we wished to assist them against their enemies, the Mexicans, and they would not believe it and wished to kill our ambassadors; and not content with that, they had attacked us three times both by day and by night, and had spied on us and held us under observation; and in the attacks which they made on us we might have killed many of their vassals, but he would not, and he grieved for those who were killed; but it was their own fault and he had made up his mind to go to the place where the old chiefs were living and to attack them; but as they had now sought peace in the name of that province, he would receive them in the name of our lord the King and thank them for the food they had brought. He told them to go at once to their chieftains and tell them to come or send to treat for peace with fuller powers, and that if they did not come we would go to their town and attack them.

He ordered them to be given some blue beads to be handed to their Caciques as a sign of peace, and he warned them that when they came to our camp it should be by day and not by night, lest we should kill them.

Then those four messengers departed, and left in some Indian houses a little apart from our camp, the Indian women whom they had brought to make bread, some poultry, and all the necessaries for service, and twenty Indians to bring wood and water. From now on they brought us plenty to eat, and when we saw this and believed that peace was a reality, we gave great thanks to God for it. It had come in the nick of time, for we were already lean and worn out and discontented with the war, not knowing or being able to forecast what would be the end of it. . . .

I will leave off here and will go on to tell what took place later, about some messengers sent by the great Montezuma.

READING AND DISCUSSION QUESTIONS

1. How does this source describe the various Mexican tribes? What does Castillo's description of these people reveal about how Europeans viewed the natives of Central America?

2. How are the Europeans, especially Cortés, able to converse with the Mexica?

3. Describe the meeting between Cortés and the native tribes. What kind of agreement is struck between them? How do the natives interact with Cortés?

16-5 | Scenes from the Spanish Conquest of the Mexica

From *The Florentine Codex* (ca. 1577–1580)

A member of the Franciscan order, the Spaniard Bernardino de Sahagún (1499–1590) was one of the earliest missionaries to arrive in Mexico. Although committed to converting the native population of Mexico to Christianity, Sahagún learned the Aztec language of Nahuatl and helped compile an extensive study of Aztec culture and religious beliefs. This work raised concern among Sahagún's superiors for its sympathetic portrayal of the Aztec people. For this reason, his works were lost for more than two hundred years until their eventual discovery in a library in Florence. The manuscript contains writing in Nahuatl, occasionally with a Spanish translation, in addition to numerous illustrations made by native artists. Even though the text was influenced by European ideas—for example, the Mexica gods are called devils—it is one of the few sources written in a native language about the conquest. The illustration here shows the beginning of the conflict between the Spanish and the Mexica, when King Moctezuma was captured and put in chains.

DE AGOSTINI EDITORE/Bridgeman Images.

READING AND DISCUSSION QUESTIONS

1. How are the natives and the Spanish portrayed in this image, and does it suggest any bias? Explain your answer.

2. Judging from the drawings, why might the Spanish have had a military advantage over the natives?

▪ COMPARATIVE QUESTIONS ▪

1. Compare and contrast the descriptions of Native Americans offered by Columbus and by Castillo. How would you explain the differences you note?

2. Taken together, what do the documents included in this chapter tell you about the motives and goals behind Spanish exploration and colonization in the New World?

3. Compare and contrast de Bry's engraving of Columbus at Hispaniola and the images from *The Florentine Codex*. How did each deal with the issue of violence between Europeans and Native Americans?